YOUNG MOTHERS?

Family Life Series

Edited by Martin Richards, Ann Oakley, Christina Hardyment
and the late Jacqueline Burgoyne.

Published

David Clark and Douglas Haldane, *Wedlocked?*
Janet Finch, *Family Obligations and Social Change*
Lydia Morris, *The Workings of the Household*
Philip Pacey, *Family Art*
Jean La Fontaine, *Child Sexual Abuse*
Ann Phoenix, *Young Mothers?*

Forthcoming

Miriam David, *Mum's the Word: Relations between Families and Schools*

Young Mothers?

Ann Phoenix

Polity Press

Copyright © text: Ann Phoenix; data: The Crown

First published 1991 by Polity Press
in association with Basil Blackwell

Editorial office:
Polity Press, 65 Bridge Street,
Cambridge CB2 1UR, UK

Marketing and production:
Basil Blackwell Ltd
108 Cowley Road, Oxford OX4 1JF, UK

Basil Blackwell Inc.
3 Cambridge Center
Cambridge MA 02142, USA

ISBN 0 7456 0540 0
ISBN 0 7456 0854 X (pbk)

British Library Cataloguing in Publication Data
A CIP catalogue record for this book is available from
the British Library.

Library of Congress Cataloging in Publication Data
A CIP catalogue record for this book is available from the Library
of Congress.

Typeset in 10 on 12 pt Palatino
by Photo·graphics, Honiton, Devon
Printed in Great Britain by Billings & Sons Ltd, Worcester.

Contents

For Aisha

Acknowledgements

This book could not have been written without the involvement of a number of people. Peter Moss obtained the funding for the study on which this book is based. Thanks to him for making the whole project possible and to the Department of Health who provided the funding. Gratitude is also due to the other members of the research team who met consistently over the five years of the project to discuss both theoretical and practical issues. They were essential to every stage of the project from design to completion of the book. They were Peter Moss, Julia Brannen and Ted Melhuish.

The project advisory group of black women sociologists and psychologists was particularly helpful in debating issues and ideas with the project team. Thanks to Bebb Burchell (whose idea it was), Yaa Asare, Kum-Kum Bhavnani, Reena Bhavnani, Ronny Flynn and Irma La Rose.

The data collection for the project was sometimes onerous. The task was considerably lightened by the assistance of other interviewers. They were Liz Gould, Mary Baginsky, Gill Bolland and Ruth Foxman.

Martin Richards commissioned the book for the *Family Life* series. His comments on the proposal were very helpful. So too were Ann Oakley's editorial comments on drafts of the book. I particularly valued the time that Chris Griffin and Angela McRobbie gave to reading drafts. Their comments were both supportive and useful. Other people read parts of the book and made helpful comments. They were Barbara Tizard, Charlie Owen, Ian Plewis and Pat Petrie. Grateful thanks to them all, particularly to Charlie Owen for his assistance with my word processing crises. Thanks too to Sarah Ware who copy-edited this book.

Ann Phoenix

Introduction

Since the early 1980s there has been a kind of subdued moral panic simmering under the surface about young, unemployed girls becoming pregnant, staying single, and taking themselves out of the labour market by opting for full time motherhood. These girls become dependent on welfare benefits rather than on a male breadwinner and it is this which has caused stories to surface in the tabloids about girls jumping the housing queues by getting pregnant, or by using pregnancy to get extra 'handouts'.

Angela McRobbie, *The Guardian*, 5 September 1989

This book is concerned with women who give birth in their teenage years and with their children. While we were doing the research which informs discussion in the chapters which follow, I was asked hundreds of times what my research was about (as researchers usually are). Almost invariably the response to my explanation was in the nature of 'How awful!' 'Poor/Silly girls!' Or 'I bet you find some problems there!' As the research neared its end I began to reply that actually the women and their children were mostly doing fine, that lack of money was their major problem and that given their educational and family background it did not appear that their financial circumstances would necessarily have improved if they had deferred motherhood beyond their teenage years. Many people either simply did not believe me or added 'Yes, but . . .' caveats to my account. Other people were astonished that the stories 'young mothers' might have to tell would not simply be full of doom and gloom although some remembered that Princess Diana had not been much more than 20 when she had her first child.

The notion that 'teenage motherhood' is a social problem is so deeply ingrained in public consciousness that evidence to the contrary is hard for many people to believe. Disbelief is hardly surprising since certain sections of the media, government ministers, health and welfare professionals and researchers have all contributed to the view that teenage women make unsatisfactory mothers, and become pregnant for the wrong reasons. Professional health and welfare workers, for example, give some priority to mothers aged under 20 and to their children because they perceive them to be at higher risk than mothers over 20 and their children. The unquestioning way in which it is taken for granted that the children born to teenage mothers are 'at risk' is aptly illustrated by an incidental statement included in a recent *Guardian* book review.

> Still, in his horrible way, Hitler was pointing to a problem that is constant and, in today's 'underclass', very serious. How do you stop single teenage mothers from breeding up tomorrow's football hooligans? (Stone, 1989)

In both the USA and in Britain women who become mothers before they are 20 years of age have been the subjects of a great deal of research. Teenage pregnancy has been associated with a variety of antenatal and perinatal ills, and with disadvantages for mothers and their children.

Yet researchers are increasingly finding that the reported adverse consequences of early motherhood are not as widespread or as devastating as has been assumed. To some extent methodological problems with many studies (such as inappropriate choice of comparison groups, failure to control for socio-economic status and parity as well as lack of recognition of intra-group differences) were responsible for the exaggeration of differences between younger and older mothers. In any case the evidence for negative outcomes for teenage mothers is not as conclusive as might be expected from the volume of literature on the subject.

'Moral panics' about young women who give birth in their teenage years focus on their reasons for having children and on the effects of early childbearing on women and their children. Concerns on which moral panics are based are generally underpinned by three related, but usually implicit, assumptions. Firstly that 'teenage mothers' constitute a unitary group so that it makes sense to lump them all together when discussing cause and effect in teenage motherhood. Secondly that mothers aged under 20 are necessarily different from those over 20, and thirdly that deferring childbearing beyond the teenage years would necessarily be better for women and children.

An obvious difference between women who become mothers in their teenage years is that some (nearly a third) are legally married (although this is a decreasing percentage) and some cohabiting while others are single. The fact that mothers under 20 are more likely to be single than married when they give birth has generated its own moral panic. For while the stigma of illegitimacy as a legal status has been removed from children (in the Family Law Reform Act, 1987) stigma still attaches to women who are single when they give birth. Single (never-married) mothers are variously portrayed in the media as irresponsible in having children in circumstances in which they are likely to be dependent on State provision of income support and housing, and as morally suspect in wilfully depriving their children of fathers. Never-married mothers are clearly a group the current British government aims to diminish by reducing the benefits they are eligible to receive. Yet although discussions of 'teenage motherhood' are usually only of single teenage women, some teenage mothers do live with their children's fathers.

There are also similarities between mothers who give birth before they are 20 and those who give birth later. Poverty, for example, is not confined to the under 20s, and an increasing percentage (a third of 20–24 year olds for example) of women over 20 now have their children while they are single.

So although young chronological age is often discussed as if it signifies poor outcome for mothers and children and automatic difference from older mothers, this is too simplistic an analysis. If the factors which lead to good or poor outcome in mothering are to be understood, the social context in which teenage women have children needs to be a central consideration. Marriage, education, housing, (un)employment and social support are all essential features of the context in which mothers under 20 have and rear their children. In practice the evidence for negative outcomes for teenage mothers is not conclusive.

Age is, of course, often a feature in decisions about which people will make good parents. One has only to think of criteria for adoption, where in order to be given able bodied, healthy babies, prospective adoptive parents must neither be too young nor too old. Similarly the 1989 decision by the Court of Appeal in London that, even with a supportive family willing to help with childcare, a 17 year old father could not bring up his baby son centred on age. The Appeal Court judges based their judgement on the age of the father, deciding that at 17 he was 'too young' to bring up his son without its mother.

Most people would agree that at 14 years or less, young women in industrialized societies are not socially prepared for motherhood. They are not legally allowed to leave full time education, to have sexual intercourse, to marry or enter into certain financial arrangements. Some 14 year olds may also not be sufficiently biologically mature for unproblematic childbearing. But very few mothers under 20 give birth before they are 16 years old. The vast majority are, in fact, 18 or 19 years old when they give birth. A central argument developed in this book is that while mothers who are in their teenage years are clearly young people, most are not 'young mothers'. That is to say, they are not too young to be adequate mothers. The title of the book 'Young Mothers?' indicates that the taken for granted assumption that mothers under 20 are automatically *too* young needs to be questioned.

It may be argued that in questioning taken for granted assumptions about motherhood under 20 this book is underplaying the problems associated with teenage motherhood. This is, however, not the case. To say that young women's age does not constitute a problem with regard to most women who become mothers in their teenage years is not the same as saying that mothers under 20 have no problems. By the end of this book it will be apparent that most of the young women studied faced major problems. Those problems were essentially financial. Many young women lived in poverty with their children and poverty necessarily affected their lifestyles. Their parents and male partners were frequently equally poor. Through their own resilience and resourcefulness and with support from their parents, however, almost all coped well. It was evident that children were loved and valued additions to family networks.

The fact that poverty was common among the women interviewed underlined the multiple, contradictory positions women with children often occupy. Mothers are simultaneously dependent and responsible. Having a child gives a woman responsibility for protecting another vulnerable person, but increases her dependence on others to help with childcare and often to provide her with money. This vulnerability and powerlessness is often hidden if the woman has female relatives able and willing to help with childcare, and is married to a financially solvent man. When, however, women are dependent on provision of State benefits their dependence becomes obvious. In the case of mothers who give birth in their teenage years, 'welfare dependence' is often attributed to their age rather than to their socio-economic circumstances (which are shared by many older women). They are thus further contradictorily positioned as devalued mothers in a status (motherhood) which is popularly romanticised as valued (although in practice it is often devalued). Such contradictory positioning is likely to be heightened in Britain by changes in welfare legislation which (in real terms) reduce the benefits that parents can obtain from the State.

The story told in these pages is not one of pathology or unalloyed sadness. The young women whose accounts are analysed were not pathetic creatures requiring compassion. Nor were they irresponsible or foolish young women deserving censure. They had not become pregnant because they were ignorant of how conception occurs, or of the existence of contraception. Neither had they 'planned' to become pregnant in order to get 'handouts'. They were caring, thoughtful mothers struggling to give their children 'the best' in circumstances often made difficult by poverty. Women's own parents emerge from their accounts as similarly caring, often easing women's and children's lives by providing crucial financial and childcare assistance. Thus, although this book addresses issues generally considered problematic about motherhood in the teenage years, it comes to rather different conclusions from most work in this area. It also provides insights into issues common to all age groups of mothers.

It must, however, be remembered that the women whose accounts appear here gave birth in 1984 and 1985. Most of those who were dependent on supplementary benefits and council housing (the majority) had their children before government legislation removed special-needs payments for baby equipment, furniture and fittings. They have, however, been caught up in the 1988 changes in social security provision (laid down by the Social Security Act, 1986). The replacement of supplementary benefit by income support, changes in housing benefit, the replacement of special-needs payments by discretionary payments (often loans) from the Social Fund together with the replacement of family income supplement with family credit and lower payments for mothers under 18 seem likely to make the positions of already impoverished young women who become mothers (*and* those of their parents) worse, particularly if they do not earn well or live with men who have adequate levels of income. It is clear from most women's accounts that they and their children's fathers have experienced a great deal of difficulty in finding such work. They did not become dependent on State benefits because they are feckless, but because jobs which provide an adequate salary are not readily available to unqualified and unskilled young people.

Terminology

The choice of terminology in research reports often reflects the ways in which values about early motherhood intersect with apparently objective scientific methods. For example King and Fullard (1982) concluded from their study of teenage mothers that, 'The most important conclusion for the present study is that sweeping condemnations of teenage mothers are no longer appropriate.' Yet throughout their article King and Fullard compare 'young', 'adolescent', 'teenage' mothers with 'normal mothers'. Using 'normal' (instead of 'comparison' or 'control') to mean no more than 'older' demonstrates the tendency to view mothers under 20 as abnormal.

'Teenage/young/adolescent pregnancy/mother' are apparently simply precise descriptive terms. Women who become pregnant before they are twenty *are* in their teenage years, *are* young and *are* having children early in their reproductive careers. Although adolescence is hard to define, the teenage years overlap to some extent with the period of adolescence. Yet the juxtaposition of a term signifying youthfulness with the word 'mother' implies that women who are 'teenage mothers' or 'adolescent mothers' are immature. Since motherhood requires maturity, the implication is that 'young mothers' are really *too* young to be mothers. The terms 'teenage/young/adolescent' in conjunction with the word 'mother' thus have negative connotations about the ability of those who become mothers in their teenage years to provide good-enough mothering.

It can be argued that whatever terms are used to denote any devalued group will necessarily acquire pejorative connotations. The terms 'teenage mother', 'adolescent mother' and 'young mother' as used in this book are, however, in no way intended to convey negative comment on or add to the stigma attached to the groups under discussion. On most occasions longer winded descriptions of age are used instead. Sometimes women who gave birth under 20 and those who gave birth later are differentiated by the terms 'younger' and 'older mothers'. Women who have children when they have passed their teens will, hopefully, not mind being referred to as 'older'. The words 'early motherhood' are also used. Although this term is potentially confusing because it can refer to the first few years of being a mother, the context should make the usage clear.

In most studies of motherhood the word 'father' applies to mothers' husbands or male partners. In this study it can also apply to mothers' own fathers, who feature in their story because many women were living in their parental homes when they conceived. On the whole the term 'male partner' has been used to describe the men who fathered the children of the women in the study and 'father' has been used to refer to mothers' own fathers. The term 'putative father' which is frequently used in reports of single mothers under 20 has been avoided because it suggests that young, single women are likely to impute fatherhood to men who are not really the fathers of their children and hence suggests that women who become mothers in their teenage years are likely to be both 'promisuous' and dishonest.

For some purposes a distinction is made between married, cohabiting and single statuses since there were differences between the three groups. On some occasions, however, 'cohabiting' has been used to refer to all those women who lived with male partners, and thus includes married women as well as those living with, but not legally married to, male partners. The context hopefully makes the distinction clear. The ages given at the end of quotes from respondents refer to the ages when women gave birth since it is age at birth which is contentious for teenage mothers. Where names are given they are, of course, pseudonyms.

Comparisons between the USA and Britain

Much of the literature discussed in this book has been produced in the USA. This reflects the fact that most concern about early motherhood has been expressed in the USA and consequently most research in this area has been done there. There is a much higher birth rate to the under 20s in the USA than in Britain (see chapter 2).

There are other notable differences between the USA and Britain. For example sex education, access to birth control and abortion are all more restricted and more hotly contested in the USA than in Britain. School leaving ages also differ. Sixteen year olds can legitimately leave school with minimum qualifications in Britain, whereas young people in the USA do not obtain minimum qualifications if they do not complete high school at 18. Despite the changes wrought by the British Social Security Act of 1986, State benefits for single mothers are still more generous in Britain than they are in the USA.

It can be argued that research done in the USA is irrelevant to the British context. Yet although the old adage that when the USA sneezes Britain catches cold is overdramatic, British social trends do sometimes seem to follow trends in the USA. Thus while differences between the USA and Britain have to be borne in mind USA literature can, at the very least, illuminate how particular social contexts influence outcomes in early motherhood.

Structure of the book

The rest of this introductory section describes the research project which provides most of the accounts and the analyses for the book.

Chapter 1 uses literature on teenage mothers to illustrate why the social construction of mothers under 20 as pathological is unsatisfactory and inaccurate. Together with chapter 2, which considers demographic trends in early motherhood, it provides the context in which early motherhood occurs, and in which research on it is done.

Chapter 3 is the first in which data from the Thomas Coram study appears. It is concerned with women's reasons for becoming pregnant and deciding to keep their children, and considers women's stories from conception to late pregnancy. Chapter 4 examines teenage women's reasons for either marrying, cohabiting or remaining single when they have children.

Chapters 5 and 6 are concerned with the social support that women receive. Chapter 5 establishes the size and nature of women's social networks and then discusses which of the people potentially available to the women interviewed provided them with which kinds of social support. Chapter 6 considers the practical support women received. It focuses on childcare, housing and material support.

Chapters 7 and 8 provide overviews of how women and their children fared in the first two years after birth. Chapter 7 firstly discusses the evidence available in the literature on how children born to teenage mothers fare. It then discusses how women in the Thomas Coram study felt about their children, and the children's developmental status (assessed on a developmental test). Chapter 8 is concerned with how women felt about motherhood and with their experiences of employment and education in the first two years of their children's lives.

The endnote discusses the implications of the findings for future generations of mothers under 20.

The research

The analyses and women's accounts reported here come from a longitudinal study of women who have their first child between the ages of 16 and 19. It was decided not to include under 16s because in Britain they have not yet reached the legal age of consent or school leaving age (which are both 16 years) and cannot yet claim State benefits (but have to be dependent on their parents). In addition they are relatively rare since only a tiny percentage of women who give birth in their teenage years are under 16 years when they do so.

The study was done at the Thomas Coram Research Unit, Institute of Education, University of London. It was one of two studies in a programme of research on different types of family organisation, the first being the study of dual earner households in the first years of parenthood. Peter Moss obtained funding for the programme, and the programme was directed by Peter Moss and Edward Melhuish. Julia Brannen played an advisory role as a member of the research team and Ann Phoenix did interviews throughout the study while Liz Gould, Mary Baginsky, Gill Bolland and Ruth Foxman worked part time on different stages of the project.

The research team was greatly assisted in thinking through research issues by the project advisory group of black women sociologists and psychologists who met several times a year, carefully read everything they were sent and spent many hours in discussion with the researchers. Although their suggestions were not always taken up they were invaluable in the research process and the project was much improved as a result of their input. They were Yaa Asare, Bebb Burchell (who initially suggested that such an advisory group would prove helpful), Kum-Kum Bhavnani, Reena Bhavnani, Ronny Flynn and Irma la Rose.

The study aimed to document the women's life histories as well as their experiences and their children's experiences over the two years of the study. In particular, women's reproductive careers, the sources of social support available to them and their children and how the women and their children fared were investigated in the context of women's social and economic circumstances.

Women were interviewed on three occasions, in late pregnancy, roughly six months after birth and just before children were two years old. Children were given a developmental test at the last interview visit.

Women were recruited into the study from the antenatal clinics of two large London hospitals. If they were aged 16–19, spoke sufficient English to be comfortable in an interview and either had no previous live births or their previous children had died or been adopted, they were asked whether they would take part in the study. A total of 212 women were approached at antenatal clinics. Of these 25 did not fit the study criteria, mostly because they already had a child but occasionally because they were not in the correct age group. Relatively few women who fitted the study criteria actually refused to take part in the study when approached at antenatal clinics (N = 25). However, many more were not at home at the time they had suggested for initial interview appointments (N = 83).

A major problem in securing further appointments when women were out was that most women did not have telephones. Further appointments therefore had to be made in person and this proved immensely time consuming. Initially women were dropped from the study after two unsuccessful appointments. It was, however, soon obvious that it would not be possible to collect a sufficiently large sample unless more time was spent securing interviews. Subsequent women were visited on at least seven occasions if necessary. Fifty-eight women were unsuccessfully visited at least seven times. Seventy-nine women were eventually given tape recorded interviews which lasted between one-and-a-half and six-and-three-quarter hours and were fully transcribed. Many women who were successfully interviewed at home also required several visits before an interview could be done.

For the last four months of the 12 month period in which the sample was selected the design of the study was altered in order to take account of the difficulty of finding women at home. Members of the research team visited postnatal wards each week and while there interviewed women who fitted the sample criteria, but had not been given an in-depth interview. Altogether 102 women were interviewed in this way.

Short interviews covered basic socio-demographic data and served two functions. Firstly, because few women were missed, it enabled

Table 1.1 In-depth interviews arranged and done in late pregnancy

Women approached	212
Appointments made	162
Interviews done	79

an assessment of how the main sample compared with other 16–19 year olds using the two antenatal clinics from which women in the main interview sample came. Secondly, short interviews provided a 'pool' of women which could be used to replace women who proved difficult to interview at subsequent stages of the project.

In addition social workers at one hospital (who routinely saw pregnant women under 20) were asked to keep basic records on 16–19 year old mothers over the course of a year. The information they provided together with data from the short interviews served to reassure us that women in the main interview sample were not dissimilar from other women in the same age group who attended the same antenatal clincs.

Six months after birth, 87 women who had been interviewed in late pregnancy were given long interviews. Sixty-four of them had been part of the main sample interviewed in pregnancy. The remaining 15 women from the main sample could not be contacted, either because they were consistently not available or had moved without trace. Twenty-three mothers who were in the short interview sample in pregnancy were also interviewed at second contact. The third interview was done when children were about 21 months old. Since so many women were difficult to find at home they were interviewed at any time between 18 and 24 months that proved convenient to them. At the third contact 76 women were interviewed. Sixty-eight of them were given full, in-depth interviews and 62 children were given developmental assessments. In 14 cases children's developmental tests could not be done on the same day as the maternal interview and it proved difficult to find the women and children at home again. Altogether 50 women received full interviews at all three contacts. The remainder of the sample received a mixture of short and full interviews. In some ways, therefore, the study can be viewed as cross sectional, with some longitudinal elements.

On average it took more than three visits for each successful interview, and more than four visits for each unsuccessful interview.

Table 1.2 Numbers interviewed in pregnancy, 6 and 21 months after birth

	Pregnancy	*6 months*	*21 months*
Main interview	79	87	76
Short interview	102	–	–
Child developmental test	–	–	62

These figures mask the fact that some women interviewed needed to be visited only once, while others required more than ten visits (with a record of 18) to complete a successful interview. In a few cases interviews were never completed. This was because it was often necessary to snatch opportunites to start interviews, even if it was obvious that there would not be time to complete them. In some cases it was not possible to complete some sections of interviews at one sitting because the crowded households some women lived in made it difficult to ensure privacy for the interview. In late pregnancy more than a fifth of the women interviewed had at least one adult in the room for part of the interview. Since interviews required the disclosure of personal information, this could sometimes cause difficulties. In one instance, for example, a respondent's father demanded that the interviewer stop asking questions about himself and his wife. In other cases male partners were clearly annoyed at what women said about them and in other instances interviewers made further appointments in order to ask questions they felt should not be asked in front of other people.

In these circumstances it was easy to begin thinking of the sample as a 'difficult' one to study. Difficulties contacting women and finding them in for interviews which had been arranged were however, at least partially, reflections of the circumstances in which women lived. Many lived in accommodation which was cramped, sparsely furnished and expensive to heat. Many could not afford to spend much money on food. They often spent most of their days visiting relatives and friends and window shopping in order not to have to stay at home. In addition they mostly did not keep diaries. Interviewers' visits were not so important to them that they either remembered them accurately or felt any incentive to stay at home if they had something else to do. In retrospect, however, broken appointments did not necessarily indicate that women did not want to be in the study. Women who were successfully interviewed after more than ten visits generally reported that they had really enjoyed the interview.

Analysis

With the exception of the Bayley Scales of Infant Development, the material produced in the study is based on detailed, semi-structured and transcribed interviews. The emphasis in the study has been on qualitative analysis supplemented where appropriate by statistical analysis. The study aimed to provide an account of women's experiences of motherhood and reasons for becoming pregnant and having a child in their teenage years. It therefore required an analysis of women's accounts. Furthermore, while the sample is larger than those usually used in qualitative studies, it is too small to allow a great deal of statistical analysis.

In recent years many researchers studying motherhood, families or households have used life course perspectives to assist understanding of how different life 'careers' like marriage, education, employment and childrearing fit together in women's lives, and how social contexts and individual lives intersect. The trajectories followed by individual careers can be affected by intersections with other careers, and hence particular events can constitute turning points in particular careers.

In this study analyses were informed by a life course perspective which took account of the fact that careers can be salient when they are potential rather than real. Becoming a mother is thus a process which starts long before women conceive.

Some characteristics of the sample

Overall the women in the main interview sample came from large families of origin, were poorly educated and had experienced high rates of unemployment before they became pregnant. When they were employed, it was usually in poorly paid jobs requiring low levels of skill. Their male partners and parents were frequently in similar economic circumstances to the women themselves.

In line with national statistics most women (70%) were 18 and 19 when they gave birth and, again in line with national trends, most (67%) were single when they gave birth. The majority of women (86%) were born in Britain or the Republic of Ireland. The other 14% came from South-East Asia, Europe, Cyprus, the Caribbean and Australia. A half (51%) had parents who were born in Britain or Ireland, a quarter (26%) had one or both parents who came from six Caribbean islands. The other 23% had parents who came from Turkish Cyprus, Bangladesh, India, Sri Lanka, Nigeria, Malaysia, Europe and South Africa.

Just over half the women (55%) lived with one or both parents in late pregnancy. They came from larger than average families of origin; 65% having three or more siblings. Nearly half had left school with no qualifications whatsoever. Only a fifth had at least one 'O' level grade (equivalent to the top grades of the GCSEs that replaced 'O' levels). Four-fifths (83%) had experienced at least one

Table 1.3 Women in employment or education at conception

In education	17%	
On job training schemes	5%	
Part time jobs	4%	
Full time jobs	29%	
Unemployed	44%	(N=79)

Table 1.4 Comparisons of main, subsidiary and social worker samples on four factors

	Main sample (N=79)	Subsidiary sample (N=102)	Social worker sample (N=257)[a]
i Percentage of sample at each age			
Age			
16	11	3	15
17	19	21	22
18	29	32	35
19	41	44	28
ii Marital status			
Married	22	33	22
Cohabiting	11	13	14
Single	67	54	64
iii Educational qualifications: % with at least one 'O' level			
	22	24	10
iv Percentage living with own parents in late pregnancy			
	56	33	53

[a] Basic demographic details were collected over a 15 month period of the study by social workers in one of the two study hospitals.

period of unemployment and over a third (36%) had never been employed despite the fact that only 17% were still at school or at college doing 'O' levels when they became pregnant. Table 1.3 shows that at conception only 29% of the sample had proper, full time jobs (job training schemes were entered because women could not find permanent, adequately paid full time jobs). Such low rates of 'real employment' are not unusual for unqualified young working class women.

The women interviewed in the main interview sample seem to have been fairly representative of the population of mothers under 20 served by the two hospitals from which the samples were recruited. Table 1.4 shows that the characteristics of women who were given short interviews, as well as those interviewed by social workers in one of the study hospitals, were similar to those in the main interview sample in late pregnancy.

Comparisons of black mothers and white mothers

In the USA demographic data of all kinds is routinely broken down by colour and/or ethnic group. In the case of early motherhood it is clear that black women are more likely than white women to have children before they are 20 and also more likely to be single when they give birth. USA studies of motherhood in teenage women routinely compare black–white differences or concentrate on black young women. There has been a tendency to view 'the problem of teenage pregnancy' as a black issue.

It is now, however, well established that births to white mothers under 20 in the USA are higher than those of teenage women in other industrialized countries. Furthermore the proportion of births to white women under 20 which are to single women has undergone large increases in the last decades (from 7 per cent in 1960 to 42 per cent in 1984). This has led some researchers to question the view of early single motherhood as a 'black problem' and to view the dramatic increase in single motherhood in black teenage women as part of a general trend rather than as a consequence of black cultural patterns. Recognition of the pervasive association between early motherhood and poverty has influenced some researchers to consider the socio-economic correlates of early motherhood in young white women as well as young black women.

In Britain social statistics are not routinely broken down according to colour. There are thus no national figures for rates of early motherhood in young black women compared with rates for young white women. An indicator that there may be black–white differences in fertility early in reproductive life comes from a study done by Bruce Penhale. In his analysis of women who were 17–19 years of age at the 1981 census (using data from the British OPCS Longitudinal Study which derives indicators of ethnic origin from questions on

respondent's country of birth and their parents' country of origin)
Penhale (1989) found that employed and student women of Caribbean origin were much more likely than women from any other
countries to have children in the five years following the census.
The 1991 census is to include a direct question on ethnicity. A clearer
British picture of black–white differences in early childbearing may,
therefore, emerge if there is sufficient compliance with the 'ethnic
question'.

Some researchers in Britain have expressed the view that there
are particular cultural values among black 'West Indian' women
which predispose them to become mothers in their teenage years.
This ascription of marked cultural differences between young black
people (almost all of whom are now British born) and young white
people is not borne out by recent British research into friendship
patterns, language use and youth cultures (Hewitt, 1986; Jones, 1988).
It would indeed be surprising if young women of similar social class
who have grown up in the same areas and attended the same schools
were entirely distinct in their cultural practices.

It is not, however, being suggested that there are no differences
at all between black people and white people. In both Britain and
the USA there are a wealth of studies which show that racism serves
to maintain differentials in societal power and in access to resources
between black people and white people. As a consequence black
people and white people are, in general, likely to occupy different
socio-economic positions within society and this is likely to affect
the ways in which people live their lives.

Furstenberg (1987), for example, suggests that it is economically
less beneficial for young black women to marry than it is for young
white women. The reason for this is that black men are much less
likely than white men to be employed, and if employed to be earning
well. The indication is thus that not marrying may be a more sensible
strategy for many young black women than it is for young white
women. It also indicates that high rates of single motherhood are
more related to socio-economic factors than to cultural practices.

In the Thomas Coram Research Unit study of 16–19 year old, first
time mothers the original research proposal was for a comparison
of young black women and young white women. This would have
been consistent with the existing literature (most of which is from
the USA). Such comparisons, however, assume that there are clear
cultural similarities within groups of black women and groups of
white women and clear differences between them. These assumptions are not, however, well grounded. For example young black

people of Afro-Caribbean origin are predominantly British born and have parents who come from a range of countries. Cultural homogeneity within a black British group and difference from a white British group cannot, therefore, be assumed. Furthermore women of mixed parentage or with mixed parentage children (who constituted about 10 per cent of the sample) could not easily be dichotomised into one cultural group or another (although this can more easily be done if racism rather than culture is being studied).

It was decided that general comparisons of black women and white women would not illuminate the processes which lead some mothers under 20 to fare well while others fare badly and the data were analysed for the sample as a whole. In instances where it is well established that colour and/or ethnicity makes a difference to experiences and/or behaviour (for example related to racial discrimination) differences have been investigated and discussed. The issue of black–white comparisons with regard to early motherhood and reasons for not making such comparisons in this study are discussed more fully in Phoenix (1988b).

1

Setting the Scene

Since the beginning of the 1970s hundreds of academic articles and popular reports have been published on teenage mothers and their children. The sheer volume of published material suggests that 'teenage motherhood' is an important topic, and indeed much literature on early motherhood states that teenage motherhood is cause for concern.

> There can be little doubt that an association between teenage parenthood and a variety of social ills exists in the public as well as in the professional mind. Hardly a week has passed since this research project started without startling headlines in the papers about 'The-Perils-of-Young-Love' ... 'Teeny-Mums' and 'Adolescents-in-Trouble' also figure frequently. There have been several television programmes on the subject, and at least one national conference ... So whether or not teenage pregnancy and parenthood really do constitute problems, they are certainly treated as such by the media and widely believed to be so by the public. (Simms and Smith, 1986, pp. 4–5)

The research project referred to in this quotation is British, but relatively little material on motherhood in the under 20s is published in Britain. Most comes from the USA. This reflects the fact that more young women become pregnant before they are twenty in the USA than in most other industrialized countries.

Intervention projects (which are common in the USA) generally aim to ameliorate the perceived negative consequences of teenage motherhood. Often, however, they have the subsidiary aim of reducing the incidence of births to teenage women. The USA Children's Defense Fund Adolescent Pregnancy Prevention Clearinghouse publishes material on early motherhood with the express aim of furthering particular priorities:

CDF's first priority is to prevent a teen's first pregnancy. Our second priority is to ensure that teens who already have had one child do not have a second child. (Pittman, 1986)

Research attention on early pregnancy and motherhood has tended to mirror the focus of intervention projects. Studies of this issue have focused almost exclusively on attempts to understand why teenage pregnancies occur, with a view to preventing them.

The first half of this chapter discusses reasons for the widespread, mostly negative, interest in early motherhood. The second half considers issues related to research on early motherhood and argues that the social context within which research is done makes it likely that published accounts will emphasize negative findings.

Concerns underlying interest in teenage mothers

How can the pervasiveness of the association between teenage motherhood and poor outcomes be explained? The most obvious explanation is that the association is simply a reflection of reality. If motherhood in the teenage years is automatically damaging to young women and their children it would make sense for it to be negatively viewed. Concerns about outcomes are, however, only one possible type of explanation, and it is possible to identify three others:

- moral;
- to do with the ambiguity of adolescents' status;
- that it is perceived to be most common among groups which are seen to be problematic.

In practice, these three concerns, and concerns about outcomes for mothers and children are interlinked.

Moral concerns

The subject of teenage pregnancy seems to raise almost every politically explosive social issue facing the American public: the battle over abortion rights; contraceptives and the ticklish question of whether adolescents should have easy access to them ... Indeed, even the basic issue of adolescent sexuality is a subject that makes many Americans squirm. (Wallis, 1985, p. 30)

Teenage pregnancy provides clear evidence of sexual activity in the under 20s and as such raises moral issues that many people find uncomfortable. This is much more of a moral issue in the USA than it is in Britain. With the influence of the USA Moral Majority sexual activity among teenagers is considered unacceptable in some quarters.

Controversies about sexual activity in young people are not restricted to the USA. In Britain, for example, in 1985 the High Court ruled (on a case brought by Victoria Gillick and later overturned by the Law Lords) that under 16 year olds could not be prescribed contraception without parental consent. In addition, in 1988 the British government passed legislation designed to ensure that parents, not schools, are responsible for deciding what constitutes appropriate sex education for their children. Teenage sexuality is clearly considered an area for parental regulation by some members of British society.

Furthermore, a higher proportion of pregnancies in the under 20s (nearly a half in the USA and nearly a third in Britain) are medically terminated than in any other age group of mothers. Moral controversies about the easy availability of abortion are, therefore, particularly relevant to teenagers. The USA Supreme Court restrictions to the availability of abortion in July 1989 will, therefore, particularly affect pregnant under 20 year olds. A likely but unintended consequence will be an increase in the number of births to teenage mothers, and hence concerns about early motherhood.

Despite widespread alarm in the USA about rates of births to teenage mothers, motherhood was more common amongst the under 20s in 1957 than it is in the 1980s. Some of this decrease in teenage birth rate is accounted for by an increase in abortion rates following the legalization of abortion. The decrease in rates is thus partly for a morally controversial reason (see for example Ineichen, 1986). There has additionally, however, been a dramatic increase in the rate of births to *single* mothers under 20. The high incidence of single motherhood is considered immoral because it breaches accepted wisdom about the importance of children being reared within a stable marital relationship and makes heterosexual intercourse outside marriage obvious.

Arney and Bergen (1984) argue that pregnant teenagers used to be thought of as a moral problem, and as such were punished and excluded from society. In the 1970s they came to be seen as a 'technical problem' requiring continuous analysis and enquiry rather than exclusion and punishment. The power relations between young mothers and society did not, however, change. Pregnant teenagers were seen as social, rather than moral problems, but were still considered deviant and problematic. The solution to the problem of 'teenage motherhood' also changed. Punitive exclusion gave way to supportive rehabilitation with young women being encouraged to control their own sexual behaviour.

According to Arney and Bergen, the end of the 1960s marked a shift in the terminology used in the research literature. The concepts 'unwed mother' and 'illegitimate child' were much less used, and instead 'teenage pregnancy' came into popular usage.

> The change in terminology marks a shift in the kind of attention society shows the pregnant adolescent. Changes in terminology were accompanied by changes in patterns of care. We say care became more 'liberal' and 'humanized'. (Arney and Bergen, 1984, p. 11)

Arney and Bergen's account is a useful one, but they present the conceptual shift too starkly. In reality the terms 'unwed/single/unmarried mother', 'one-parent-family' and 'illegitimate child' have continued in widespread usage at the same time as the term 'teenage pregnancy' has gained currency. Indeed, 'teenage mother' is frequently used as if it were synonymous with 'single mother'. It is often not clear whether married mothers who are under 20 years of age are included within moral concerns to do with early motherhood.

In any event, in Britain and the USA, there has been a dramatic increase in the rates of births to single, rather than married women who are under 20 years of age. It is now more usual for mothers who are under 20 to be single than to be married when they give birth (see chapter 2). They therefore fail to conform to dominant reproductive ideologies which suggest that children should be reared by parents who are married to one another and that conception should follow marriage and a period of setting up home (Busfield, 1974).

Central to the notion of marriage preceding motherhood are the functions that society expects parents to fulfil. These functions are financial, social and developmental, and are expected to be divided between mothers and fathers. Fathers are expected to provide adequate financial support for their wives and children while mothers are expected to care for their children in such a way that their social, emotional and intellectual development are fostered. This model assumes that mothers will be dependent economically on their husbands, and that provision for all children's needs will be a private family affair, independent of State intervention.

For most women who give birth in their teenage years there are two problems with the model described above. Firstly, mothers who are under 20 years of age are much less likely than older mothers to be married when they give birth. But even married teenage women cannot guarantee that the fathers of their children will be able to provide economic support for them. The men who father children with women in this age group are more likely to experience unemployment than their age peers (Simms and Smith, 1986; Lamb and Elster, 1986). In addition they mainly come from larger than average, working class families which can provide few material resources to the children young men produce. Relatively few male partners of mothers who are under 20 years of age are therefore likely to be able to support women and children economically.

Secondly, since young women and their male partners are often unlikely to be able to make financial provision for their children they are likely to have to seek public financial support (income support or welfare). They therefore fail to fulfil the expectation that parents will make independent provision for their children. With increasing commercialization of childhood there are pressures on parents to provide expensive toys and clothes for their children, as if children were private luxury goods. Most mothers who are under 20 years of age are unlikely to be able to buy such toys and clothes. Mothers under 20 therefore come to public attention as deficient parents, whose inability to make material provision for children is seen in individualistic, rather than structural terms.

It is generally recognized that young women's and their male partners' material circumstances would not necessarily improve if they deferred motherhood (Bury, 1984; Pittman, 1986). Yet 'illegitimacy' and 'welfare dependence' are of major concern to those interested in early motherhood because they threaten the ideological framework in which children are to be reared, and are potentially costly to the State.

Evidence about how young mothers and their children actually fare is largely irrelevant to moral concerns about early motherhood. By their very existence, teenage mothers constitute a moral, and hence a social, problem. But what happens to women who become mothers before they are 20 years of age and to their children is, of course, also taken into account by those who feel that early motherhood is a worrying phenomenon. Moral and outcome concerns are often not clearly separable.

Concerns about outcomes

In comparison with older mothers and their children women who become mothers before they are 20 years of age and their children have been found to fare badly in a number of ways. For example, teenage motherhood has been associated with anaemia and toxaemia for pregnant women, as well as low birthweight and risks of peri-natal mortality for infants (Butler et al., 1981). The children of young mothers have been found to be at more risk of physical abuse and accidental injury than the children of older mothers, to do less well educationally than the children of older mothers (Alan Guttmacher Institute, 1981; Butler et al., 1981; Bury, 1984) and to be likely to start having children early in their life courses (Furstenberg et al., 1987).

Women who become mothers early in their life courses are believed (at least in the USA and in Canada) to have a greater than average number of children than those who start childbearing later (Furstenberg et al., 1987). Early motherhood has also been reported to damage young women's educational and employment prospects (Chilman, 1980; Phipps-Yonas, 1980; Wells, 1983; Simms and Smith, 1986; Furstenberg et al., 1987). The association between early mother-hood and larger than average completed family size is not estab-lished in Britain (Bury, 1984).

Wells (1983) referred to the catalogue of ills associated with early motherhood as a 'gloomy adumbration'. Yet many negative findings about early motherhood are now being questioned. An editorial in the American Journal of Public Health (1981) suggested that the late teenage years were biologically ideal for childbearing. Similarly it now seems that, even in Canada and the USA, women who start having children early in their life courses are not likely to have a large number of children (Balakrishnan et al., 1988; Furstenberg et al., 1987).

> Some researchers suggest that the evidence on which the worrying conclusions described above have been based is rather weak and that negative aspects of early motherhood have been overstated. (Furstenberg et al., 1987)

More recent studies which control for such factors as socio-economic status (SES), nutrition, maternal age, race (white/black), and prenatal care reveal good obstetric and paediatric outcomes among adolescent mothers. (Carlson et al., 1986)

Although this has become an increasingly popular area of research, our knowledge of adolescent parenting is still surprisingly limited. Among the problems accounting for this are methodological inadequacies. (Lamb and Elster, 1986)

Many of the negative consequences seem more likely to be the result of the poor socio-economic circumstances in which women who give birth before they are 20 years of age live, and of the fact that they are more likely than older mothers to be having their first child. If parity and various factors known to be correlated with social class are controlled for, the differences between younger and older mothers are greatly reduced (Butler et al., 1981).

Ambiguity of adolescence as a status

In many societies it is generally accepted that childhood and adulthood are qualitatively different. Adolescence is conceptualized as a developmental period of transition from childhood to adulthood (Coleman, 1976). The teenage years are considered to overlap with the period of adolescence, but adolescence is not well defined, and it is difficult to know when it can be said to have ended. There is, for instance, a disjunction between the age of biological maturity (the age of menarche for girls being about 13) and the age of social maturity which is not clearly defined, but is later than that of biological maturity.

As social and economic circumstances have changed over this century, the boundaries between adolescence and adulthood have become more blurred. Longer compulsory education and increasing participation in further education have kept teenagers in dependent status for longer and longer periods. The first pay packet used (at least for young men) to signal the start of financial independence. But with increasing unemployment (particularly for young, working class men) young men cannot guarantee that they will be able to signal their transition to adult status through gaining employment.

For young women, marriage was the equivalent status marker of adulthood. But women who are under 20 are less likely to marry than they were two decades ago. In Britain in 1971, 9 per cent of teenage women married for the first time, compared with 2 per cent in 1986. Almost a third (31 per cent) of all first marriages were to teenage women in 1971. But by 1986 this had reduced to just under a sixth (14 per cent). Relatively few teenage women therefore achieve adult status through marriage. So although teenagers are, in many ways, encouraged to see themselves as adult, the signifiers of adult status are harder to achieve than they once were. This ambiguity of status has been exacerbated by the 1988 changes in British social security legislation. People who are under 26 years of age now cannot be assured of financial independence from their parents if they are dependent on social security.

If the status of teenagers is ambiguous, the status of mothers who are in their teenage years is even more so, because they have taken on an adult role, without it being clear that they possess the maturity necessary to it. In addition there are concerns that early childbearing constitutes an insult to psychological development by preventing young women from coming to terms with the psychological tasks of adolescence. The status of British mothers who are under 18 years of age is particularly ambiguous since from 1988 they receive less income support than the over 18s and, as a consequence, are likely to be less financially independent than the over 18s.

Adolescence has often been conceptualized as a period of 'storm and stress' marked by conflicts with parents and other adults (Cohen, 1986) and as a time when identity development comes sharply into focus (Erikson, 1968). It is not, however, clear that adolescence is necessarily stormy or stressful (Coleman, 1976) and while many dramatic biological, emotional and social changes *may* occur in adolescence, little is known about whether the psychological development which occurs in adolescence is qualitatively different from development at other times in the life course. Thus, while some writers have expressed concern that motherhood in the teenage years may arrest young women's psychological development at a crucial point (Bucholz and Gol, 1986), there is currently insufficient research evidence to confirm or disconfirm this view.

While adolescence is perceived as a period of preparation for adulthood, adolescents are more likely to be thought of as children rather than adults (Murcott, 1980) because they are not generally expected to take part in many adult activities. As such they are conceptualized as needing to be in a state of innocence. Murcott argues that it is the conceptualization of adolescence as a period of childhood which makes the status of women who become pregnant in their teenage years ambiguous. Pregnancy is a clear indication of sexual activity, and as such, of loss of innocence. Giving birth is also considered to be an adult activity. Yet, because adult maturity is an ill defined social construct which is often described as if it is an inevitable correlate of maturity in years, it is not clear that women who give birth before they are 20 years of age are adult.

Who becomes a mother before she is 20?

The well established association between poverty and motherhood in the teenage years naturally raises important issues about the direction of causation. Does early motherhood *cause* or heighten poverty, or is poverty pre-existing in those who give birth in their teenage years? This question can partly be answered by considering the characteristics of women who become mothers while still teenagers.

Women who are working class by origin, who come from larger than average families of origin and have parents who have separated are more likely than other groups of young women to give birth early in their life course (Simms and Smith, 1986). On the whole women who become mothers in their teenage years have few material resources available to them, and many of their male partners are also poor. The relatively high 'welfare dependence', poor educational achievements and poor employment prospects of mothers who are under 20 has led some researchers to suggest that teenage women who can least afford to, are most likely to have children (Bolton, 1980; Pittman, 1986; Simms and Smith, 1986). The analyses provided by economic demographers supports the finding that women who are less affluent are likely to have children earlier than more affluent women. Joshi (1990), however, suggests that this happens because women who have relatively high earnings can least afford to lose the income they are likely to have to forego if they take time out of the employment market early in their adult lives. Women who do not have good earning potential have less reason to defer motherhood. Similarly Penhale (1989) found that 17–19 year old women who were unemployed at the 1981 census were much more likely than their peers to have a child within the ensuing five years.

It is increasingly recognized that simply deferring motherhood would not necessarily improve most women's socio-economic circumstances (Chilman, 1980; Bury, 1984; Pittman, 1986). It seems, therefore, that it is not age *per se* which is problematic for those who become mothers under 20, but their pre-existing socio-economic circumstances. Many nannies, for example, are under 20 years of age but are employed, often by older women, to provide childcare.

Further concern about which women become mothers has been generated in the USA (where statistics are routinely broken down by colour) by evidence that early motherhood is more common among young black than young white women (Jones et al., 1986). Greater rates of black than of white early motherhood together with the recognition that most black mothers who are under 20 years of age are single led researchers and practitioners in the USA to consider early motherhood a 'black problem'. Rates of early single motherhood among black women have not always been high, but have dramatically increased over the last 30 years (Benjamin, 1987; Furstenberg et al., 1987).

These dramatic changes helped create the belief that teenage childbearing is primarily a black issue. But recent trends suggest that blacks may simply have been pace setters for the population at large (Furstenberg et al., 1987, p. 5). White mothers of the same age group are now apparently following the same trends.

White USA teenage women are now recognized to have higher rates of births than women in most other industrialized countries, whether (like Britain) those countries have sizeable black populations or not (Jones et al., 1986). Early motherhood in the USA is not, therefore, simply a black issue. (Comparable information about black and white rates is not yet available in Britain although Penhale (1989) suggests that women of Caribbean origin are more likely to become mothers early in life than other young British women).

Research issues

The negative social construction of early motherhood provides the context within which early motherhood is discussed and studied. It is perhaps not surprising, therefore, that most research literature has assumed that early motherhood is problematic, and best prevented if possible. Research findings thus tend to reinforce popular beliefs that early motherhood is a social problem.

The intersection of social construction and research

Research on teenage mothers is considered to be scientifically objective. It therefore has the power to produce accounts of early motherhood which are widely accepted as valid (although accounts produced by other groups of professionals, such as medical practitioners, may also become accepted as 'common sense' knowledge).

In recent years there have been various challenges to the uncritical acceptance of social science research as scientifically objective and value free (Stanley and Wise, 1983; Henriques et al., 1984). These challenges have been partly based on demonstrations that social scientists 'have failed, on particular occasions, adequately to transcend the "folk knowledge" or "lay understandings" to which they as ordinary social participants are privy' (Kitzinger, 1987, p. 13).

As members of society researchers are necessarily influenced by dominant ideologies. In addition much social research aims to benefit society by attempting to contribute to the understanding and hence hopefully to solve particular social problems. In order to obtain research funding for the study of motherhood in the under 20s, and for research findings to have some impact, it is necessary to relate the research to early motherhood as a pre-identified social problem.

It is, therefore, difficult even for those researchers who do not endorse the view of early motherhood as a social problem to avoid using the negative social construction of 'teenage motherhood' as a starting point for research.

> The purpose of this study is to identify risks to mother and child associated with adolescent pregnancy . . . (Broman, 1980)

> The objective of this study was to assess the degree to which teenage parenting, a caretaking casualty risk factor, . . . might contribute to developmental delays of infants . . . (Field et al., 1980)

> This book describes a study that attempts to cast some light on the determinants of teenage pregnancy in the United States, and the means to prevent it . . . (Jones et al., 1986)

> This study, then, sought to investigate whether, . . . teenage pregnancy is as harmful a phenomenon as is widely believed, and if it is, what steps might be taken to mitigate it and to help other teenagers postpone or avoid it. (Simms and Smith, 1986)

Because the social construction of early motherhood is a negative one the very existence of teenage mothers is considered problematic. As the pattern of early motherhood changes, the focus of concern about it shifts, but concern remains. Thus researchers use increases in the numbers of teenage mothers to justify the importance of early motherhood as a study topic even when rates are decreasing. It is not uncommon for concern about a 'social problem' to be expressed when that phenomenon is becoming increasingly rare. For example, expressions of moral and professional concern with perinatal mortality in the 1970s coincided with a steady decline in rates of perinatal mortality (Oakley, personal communication). Similarly, David (1989, p. 22) points out 'that at the very moment when we [Americans] have become most concerned about black teenage pregnancy, it has started to decline.'

> Since early motherhood is now less common than it was in the 1970s, the importance of the topic is more frequently legitimated in terms of the increase in 'illegitimacy' than in birth rates *per se*. (Ineichen, 1986)

Like researchers, demographers are exposed to dominant views of teenage motherhood. Demographic trends in pregnancies and births to the under 20s are provided and attract attention because they are considered problematic.

> Demography is not a neutral enterprise; inevitably it is socially located. Issues are identified as worthy of focus prior to, and beyond demography. Teenage pregnancy . . . already has significance socially. (Murcott, 1980, p. 11)

Methodological issues

Various reviews of the literature on early motherhood in the 1980s have pointed out its many shortcomings (Chilman, 1980; Phipps-Yonas, 1980; Morrison, 1985).

> Methodological limitations are widespread. Control groups are often inadequate or unavailable and sample sizes are too small . . . Many of the study variables are highly correlated with teenage pregnancy, which makes it difficult to determine the extent to which each contributes to the problem . . . Heterogeneous groups . . . are all lumped together . . . Thus, it becomes virtually impossible to focus on antecedent variables or on outcomes or to generalize from one sample to others. (Bucholz and Gol, 1986)

COMPARISON GROUPS The methods commonly used in social scientific research often encourage negative interpretations of early motherhood. A good example of this is the use of control groups.

In an experiment a control group is assumed to be similar to the experimental group in every way except that it does not have the particular characteristic being investigated. In that way the effects of the factors being investigated can be unambiguously identified by reference to the comparison group. Social science research is usually conducted outside laboratories. Although traditional experimental designs are occasionally used, people (the subjects of social science research) do not fit neatly into categories constructed by researchers. It is thus very difficult to find control groups that meet the necessary criteria to be experimental control groups.

Research into early motherhood is often designed with a group of teenage mothers and a comparison group. While some research reports refer to non-teenage groups as 'control groups', the women in them tend to differ from those who become mothers before they are 20 in more ways than those generally considered to account for differences between them.

For instance mothers who are under 20 are frequently compared with mothers who are over 20. Age is not usually, however, the only factor which differentiates younger and older age groups of mothers. If the older group are having their first child they may well differ from the younger group on any of the following factors: class, education, employment histories, marital status, living accommodation and relationship with parents. If the older group are having a second or subsequent child, parity differentiates them since most mothers who are under 20 years of age are having their first child (Butler et al., 1981; Simms and Smith, 1986; Jones et al., 1986).

A comparison of young mothers with their age peers who do not have children is equally unsatisfactory since the two groups are likely to differ on social characteristics other than motherhood.

The use of comparison groups in early motherhood is therefore likely to confuse cause and effect. This is because the groups chosen for comparison differ in many unspecified ways other than early motherhood. It is therefore difficult to establish whether differences found between the groups are the result of early motherhood, or of pre-existing social differences.

The imperfect fit between the comparison group and the research group makes it difficult to draw firm conclusions from the data. Some researchers are clearly aware that the comparison group they use falls short of a control group, but continue to use the scientific term: 'For convenience, the comparison group in their twenties is referred to as a control group.' (Broman, 1980).

Comparisons can, in themselves, be problematic because they generally highlight and exaggerate differences between groups while ignoring similarities (Archer and Lloyd, 1982; Scott-Jones and Nelson-Le Gall, 1986). Such exaggeration of difference would not be important if the groups being compared were of equal status. But women who become mothers in their teenage years have a devalued status in comparison with women who give birth later in life. Comparisons between mothers who are under 20 with those who are over 20 are thus likely to construct older mothers as the 'norm' and younger ones as deviant. In reality there are many similarities between mothers who are under and those who are over 20 years of age when they give birth.

Just as the choice of comparison groups in early motherhood has frequently been unsatisfactory, so too has the choice of the target group. The use of the term 'teenage mother' to describe all women who give birth before they are 20 years of age allows researchers to study a disparate group of women without having to justify the choice of sample. Conversely it also means that researchers can generalize from particular subgroups of early mothers (for example, black, single, or under 18 year olds) to all teenage mothers.

The choice of subgroups of teenage mothers (like those mentioned in the last paragraph) for study is often underpinned by value laden assumptions. Such choices are motivated by views about which sorts of teenage mothers are most problematic, and hence will yield the most dramatically poor results.

Black teenage mothers, for instance, have been the focus of many studies of early motherhood in the USA. This would not be significant in itself if black mothers were routinely the subjects of research. However black mothers are usually excluded from studies which are concerned with the process of 'normal' mothering or 'normal' child development. In this context a devalued group of mothers (black mothers) are studied only as representatives of a devalued category of motherhood (teenage motherhood).

The explanations advanced for the existence of early motherhood in black women and in white women have usually been of different kinds. For black women they have been primarily socio-cultural, while for white women they have mainly been psychological, although there has been no evidence that young black women and young white women become pregnant for different reasons (Phipps-Yonas, 1980). Until the last few years (when the pattern of early motherhood for white women has moved closer to that of black women) many USA researchers and practitioners believed that early motherhood was really 'a black problem' (Jones et al, 1986; Pittman, 1986).

In Britain (where no studies of only-black teenage mothers have been done) there is also a tendency to search for 'cultural explanations' of pregnancy in young black women, but not in young white women (Phoenix, 1988b).

THE USE OF STANDARDIZED ASSESSMENTS Standardized assessments are a commonly used methodological tool in studies of the children of mothers who are under 20. Having been standardized and extensively presented, these assessments are often used as diagnostic and predictive tools. In particular the Caldwell and Bradley (1980) Home Observation for Measurement of the Environment (HOME) inventory and the Bayley Scales of Infant Development (Bayley, 1969) have often been used in assessments of children born to mothers who were under 20.

These instruments are, however, class biased. The HOME inventory, for example, has six subscales. Of these, four are widely used: 'avoidance of restriction and punishment' (subscale II); 'organization of the physical and temporal environment' (subscale III); 'provision of appropriate play materials' (subscale IV); and 'opportunities for variety in daily stimulation' (subscale VI).

A good score on many items in the HOME scales is dependent on parents having a good deal of physical space, relaxed time and material resources. Similarly infants are likely to do better on the 'mental scales' in the Bayley test if they have had the opportunity to practise the required skills on toys similar to those which form part of the Bayley kit. Middle class parents who have the money to provide such toys are more likely to have children who do well on the Bayley scale than are working class children.

Furthermore developmental assessments need to be presented in standarized situations. If assessments are conducted in infants' own homes, middle class children are likely to be privileged over working class ones because middle class children are more likely to live in environments in which they can be tested without distraction. In addition they are more likely than working class children to possess toys which are similar to test items. Given that women who give birth in their teenage years are predominantly from the working classes, it may well be that the numerous studies which report children of teenage mothers to fare badly on developmental tests are confounding age with class instead of obtaining a genuine age effect.

It is not, however, easy to control for social class effects. Butler et al. (1981) controlled statistically for various correlates of social class in their study of early motherhood. They found that controlling for socio-economic variables greatly reduced the differences between mothers who are under 20 years of age, and older mothers. But they could not be sure whether they had included all possible correlates of class in their statistical manipulation.

> The fact that the differences between teenage and other mothers were in general reduced by such attempts to control possibly confounding co-variables supports the view that there is little specific biological effect of maternal age that could not be explained by other intervening variables; we just haven't allowed for all the right ones. (Butler et al., 1981, p. 63)

The terms 'teenage pregnancy' and 'teenage motherhood' are often used in the literature as if they were synonyms for a range of social problems. Yet, even when researchers recognize that chronological age is not, of itself, problematic, they frequently do not explain how and why the factors identified as problematic are so.

These ill effects, however, may not be due mainly to the direct effects of low maternal age but to the frequently accompanying low socio-economic status, low educational attainment, lack of support and the inexperience of teenage mothers, together with illegitimacy and often poor housing and social environment (Butler et al., 1981). In the above example 'illegitimacy' is accorded the same status as the accompanying indices of low socio-economic status. It is, however, far from clear which disadvantages it is meant to signify, or indeed that 'illegitimacy' itself causes disadvantage. Yet the term 'illegitimate' is often used in a non-specific and therefore confusing way.

Some implications of research on early motherhood

One of the major concerns about early motherhood in the USA is the prevention of 'welfare dependence'. Young women who become mothers early in their life courses are frequently dependent on financial provision by the State. In recent years reported studies of early motherhood have more frequently than formerly noted the structural context in which mothers who are under 20 years of age live. Thus employment prospects, educational backgrounds and poverty are sometimes mentioned as factors which may influence young women to become mothers (Bury, 1984; Ineichen, 1986; Simms and Smith, 1986; Jones et al., 1986).

However relatively little account is taken of women's material backgrounds in analyses of their lives and behaviour, or deciding how best to deal with 'teenage motherhood'. Thus researchers from the Children's Defense Fund state, 'There is evidence . . . that the teens who find themselves unmarried, unemployed, dropout parents ' . . . would be unmarried, unemployed, and uncredentialed even if parenthood had not occurred' (Pittman, 1986). Yet the stated aim of preventing 'adolescent pregnancy' in order to 'ensure each child a *successful* adulthood' (my emphasis) takes no account of the fact that poverty may prevent some children from having 'successful' adulthoods.

The net result of failure to take full account of structural consider-ations in early motherhood is the individualizing of the problems associated with motherhood in the under 20s. Rather than being viewed as a phenomenon related to social factors, early motherhood has progressively come to be seen as the result of individual moral failing (Arney and Bergen, 1984). 'Blaming the victim' is not an uncommon phenomenon once a social problem has been identified. Early motherhood is merely one instance where a social problem is identified and it is then assumed that '. . . the individual is not only the culprit, but also the proper focus of social intervention . . .' (Seidman and Rappaport, 1986).

Summary

Those who express concern about the occurrence of motherhood in the teenage years usually do so for four interlinked sets of reasons. Firstly, the obvious relationship between early pregnancy and teen-age sexuality raises moral issues about early motherhood, as does the increasing tendency for women who become mothers before they are 20 to be single when they give birth.

Secondly, there are concerns about the consequences of early motherhood for young women and for their children. These outcome concerns have been widely reported, but many of the studies on which negative conclusions have been based are now reported to be methodologically flawed.

Thirdly, women who give birth in their teenage years are often referred to as 'adolescent'. Adolescence is a poorly defined period in the life course, but adolescents are more likely to be considered children than adults. In dominant ideologies, motherhood is there-fore proscribed to adolescents, and hence mothers who are in their teenage years have a more ambiguous status and arouse more public concern than adolescents in general.

Finally, women who become mothers in their teenage years are likely to come from groups which are socially devalued, and which often arouse public concern. Thus, for example, mothers under 20 are more likely than those who do not become mothers until after the teenage years to have few educational qualifications, poor employment experiences, and to come from larger than average families. In the USA a greater proportion of black women than of white women become mothers before they are 20 years of age. There are thus concerns about which women become mothers in their teenage years.

Research on early motherhood arises in a social context in which mothers who are under 20 are negatively socially constructed. It is therefore difficult for researchers, who are generally socially distant from mothers who are under 20, to avoid using the negative social construction as a starting point for their research. In consequence it is not surprising that most research on early motherhood concludes that it is problematic. Yet because of methodological limitations in many studies (of, for example, inadequate control groups) negative conclusions are recognized by many researchers to be more tentative than previously assumed.

2

Demographic Trends in Early Motherhood

This chapter will discuss demographic trends in births to the under 20s. It aims to provide a contextual background for discussion of early motherhood. The chapter concentrates particularly on trends in Britain and in the USA.

Interpreting trends

There is some variation in how demographic data on early motherhood is presented in published work. Some, for example, concentrate on the absolute numbers of those who become pregnant under 20, while others concentrate on rates. There are also differences in whether pregnancy rates or birth rates are presented. In addition, some published sources use different bases for calculation of trends, and so give different figures for the same year. This section discusses some of these variations.

In a climate of general social concern about early motherhood, the actual numbers (rather than just the rates) of pregnant teenage women become salient. For example, the numbers of young women who become pregnant in the USA sound more alarming than do the rates. At the beginning of the 1980s more than a million USA women under 20 were becoming pregnant each year (Ford Foundation Letter, 1 August 1983). Numbers in excess of a million permeate consciousness because they represent a vast number of people. They are consequently highlighted as alarming.

Absolute numbers are, of course, important to those who plan or deliver services to the under 20s or to mothers and children. They do, however, give a misleading picture of trends in birth rates. The numbers of women who are between 15 and 19 years of age (the age range in which most women under 20 give birth) fluctuates over time. As a result it is possible for the numbers of pregnant teenage women to increase from one year to another when early pregnancy has actually become less common within the age group. In order to get an accurate picture of how common early motherhood actually is, and of trends in its incidence, it is necessary to consider rates rather than numbers.

Pregnancy rates (sometimes called conception rates) are usually presented as the number of women who become pregnant per thousand women in the age group being considered. They are usually calculated as rates of abortions plus rates of births. This, in fact, is not totally accurate because 'many pregnancies end in miscarriage and these are not recorded' (Bury, 1984). It is probable, therefore, that conception rates for all age groups of mothers are to some extent inaccurate. Further inaccuracies arise when numbers and rates of conceptions are related to specific ages. The British Office of Population Censuses and Surveys (OPCS) says, 'The exact number of conceptions shown are subject to errors arising from the estimation of women's ages at conceptions' (OPCS, 1987). Jones et al. report similar problems when they say:

> The actual pregnancy rates are slightly understated since pregnancies are calculated here according to age at abortion or birth, not age at conception, which is younger and since miscarriages are excluded . . . Reported abortion rates for women aged 18 are generally higher than would be expected . . . This may be because some unmarried 17-year-olds report their age as 18 (the age of majority in most states) to keep their parents from knowing of the abortion . . . (Jones et al., 1986, p. 39)

Birth rates and abortion rates are more likely to be recorded accurately than are pregnancy rates, but (as Jones and her colleagues suggest) there may (at least in the USA) be some distortion in recorded age rates for abortion because some young women are frightened that their parents will be told that they have had abortions if they are known to be minors.

Since very few women who are under 15 give birth, pregnancy and birth rates are usually calculated using the number of women in the 15–19 age group rather than all teenage women. The few young women who give birth at 14 years or less are included in the rates for 15–19 year olds.

Further difficulties in establishing accurate trends arise because different sources yield different rates of early pregnancy and motherhood. Thus for the USA the Ford Foundation and the Alan

Guttmacher Institute provide different teenage pregnancy rates for the same years. See table 2.1.

Table 2.1 1981 reported teenage pregnancy rates per thousand teenage women

Ford Foundation	111
Alan Guttmacher Institute	96

Sources: Ford Foundation Letter, 1 August 1983; Jones et al., 1986.

It is not, therefore, always as straightforward as might be expected to determine rates of pregnancy in teenage women, or trends in its incidence from published articles.

Trends in the USA

Most studies of teenage pregnancy and motherhood reported in the literature have been done in the USA. The majority of North American researchers have considered early pregnancy and motherhood to be a major problem. In 1976 the Alan Guttmacher Institute (1976) claimed that the incidence of early pregnancy should be considered to be a national epidemic. Alarm about teenage pregnancy as a serious social problem helped to popularize the slogan 'epidemic of teenage pregnancy'.

The use of the term 'epidemic' is not only emotive, it is also inaccurate. Over the 1970s USA pregnancy rates in teenage women are estimated to have increased. It is, however, extremely difficult to make accurate assessments of pregnancy rates during the early 1970s in the USA. This is because abortion was not legalized for the USA as a whole until 1973. Before then (and for some years afterwards) there must have been a significant number of illegal, and hence unrecorded, abortions. As more pregnant women obtained legal abortions, offical pregnancy rates necessarily increased. The apparent rise in both teenage pregnancy and abortion rates in the early 1970s may therefore have been illusory. Abortion rates, however, continued to rise from the mid 1970s.

It is apparent from the figures in table 2.2 that, even if the rise in officially recorded pregnancy rates reflects a real increase in conception rates, the increase has been a gentle rather than a rapid one. Between 1973 and 1981 the rise in officially recorded pregnancy rates was less than 2%. In 1973 8% of 15–19 year olds were recorded as

Table 2.2 USA pregnancy, abortion and birth rates per thousand 15–19 year olds

Year	Pregnancy	Abortion	Birth
1971	Not known	Not known	64.5
1973	82.1	22.8	59.3
1976	87.1	34.3	52.8
1979	94.7	42.4	52.3
1981	96.0	43.3	52.7
1983			51.7
1984			50.9
1986			52.0

Sources: Jones et al. (1986); Furstenberg et al. (1987); Werner (1988).

having become pregnant, compared with less than 10% in 1981.

Teenage pregnancy rates had not therefore assumed 'epidemic' proportions in the USA of the mid 1970s, nor have they done so now. In fact *pregnancy* rates in the under 20s are now slightly lower than *birth* rates were in the post Second World War baby boom. In 1957 (the peak year for rates of births to the under 20s in the USA) nearly a tenth (9.73%) of women in the under 20 age group gave birth. A similar percentage of women under 20 years of age conceived in 1981, but only just over half of them actually gave birth (Jones et al., 1986). Nearly half the conceptions to the under 20s are now aborted in the USA, and only 5% of women in this age group now give birth. Throughout the 1970s births to the under 20s became progressively less common in the USA.

Trends in England and Wales

The scale on which British and American pregnancies and births occur is vastly different. A much larger percentage of USA than of British teenage women become pregnant and give birth each year. Since the USA is also much larger than Britain, the numbers of pregnant teenage women are also greater in the USA. In Britain government statistics are published separately for England and Wales and for Scotland. The figures presented here are mainly for England and Wales rather than for Britain as a whole. As a rule Scottish birth rates in the under 20s are roughly similar to those in

England and Wales. Abortion rates are, however, lower (partly because some Scottish women have abortions in England).

Abortion was legalized in Britain in 1967 (three years before it was legalized in the first USA State, New York, and six years before it became generally available in the USA). Before 1967 it was not possible to get good estimates of conception rates because illegal (and hence unrecorded) abortions occurred. In the decade 1970 to 1980 there was a doubling in the rate of abortions in the 15–19 age group in England and Wales from 9 per thousand to 18 per thousand (Bury, 1984). This increase in abortion rates was not, however, due to an increase in conception rates because conception rates actually declined over this period. In 1970 an estimated 58.5 teenage women in every thousand conceived. This compares with 48.5 per thousand in 1980 (Bury, 1984). It seems likely that the doubling in abortion rates between 1970 and 1980 reflects the time it took for the 1967 Abortion Act to be implemented in practice.

A clearer picture is provided by considering the decade 1974 to 1984. By 1974 the Abortion Act had already been in existence for seven years. In 1974 25% of pregnancies to women under 20 were legally terminated. By 1984 this had risen to 33%. In 1974 17.4 women in every thousand aged between 15 and 19 years had a legal abortion. In 1984 this legal abortion rate had gone up to 20 per thousand 15–19 year old women (OPCS, 1986b). The numbers also increased (from 29,600 to 39,500).

The provision of legal abortion has served to reduce birth rates to teenage women in England and Wales. Rates of legal abortion do not, however, entirely account for the lower birth rates in the under 20s. Pregnancy rates have themselves declined. Francome (1986) calculates that between 1971 and 1977 only one seventh of the fall in births to women under 20 can be attributed to an increase in abortions.

Figure 2.1 shows that birth rates to the under 20s have generally followed those for women of all ages and have undergone marked changes in the last four decades. In the late 1980s, however, rates of birth to women under 20 are not much higher than they were in the early 1950s. In 1951 there were 21.3 births per thousand 15–19 year old women in England and Wales. In the 1950s and 1960s there was a progressive increase in the rates of births to women under 20 years of age. This was followed by a continual decrease from the 1971 peak of 51 births per thousand to 26.8 per thousand in 1983. From 1984 there has been a slight upturn in birth rates to the under 20s (to 27.6 in 1984 and 31 per thousand in 1987). It is, however, too

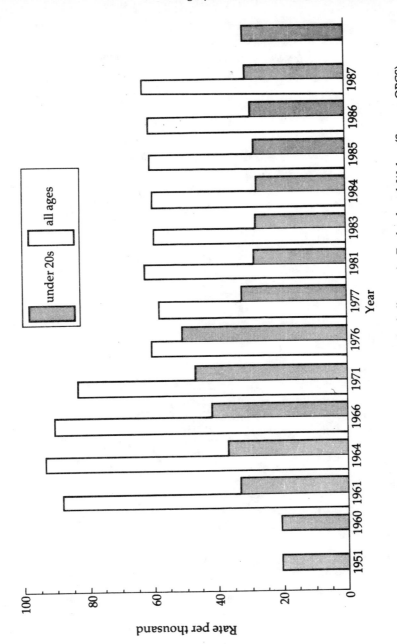

Figure 2.1 Rates of births to women under 20 and of all ages in England and Wales (Source: OPCS)

early to be sure whether this is the start of an upward trend or merely a minor fluctuation in birth rates.

If Scotland, England and Wales are aggregated there were 57,600 live births to 15–19 year olds in 1960 (a rate of 33 per thousand women in the age group). This rose to a peak of 96,100 in 1966 (a rate of 47 per thousand) then decreased to 63,500 in 1981 (a rate of 28 per thousand).

The numbers of births and the rates of births to the under 20s give slightly different pictures. In 1960, for example, there were 57, 600 births to the under 20s in England and Wales. In 1983 2,500 more teenage women gave birth than in 1960, yet early motherhood was less common for the 15–19 age group. The rate had fallen from 34 per thousand in 1960 to 27 per thousand 15–19 year olds in 1983. The numbers of births to the under 20s peaked in 1966, but early motherhood was most common in 1971.

Comparisons of trends in under 20s and over 20s

A focus on reproductive trends in teenage women necessarily decontextualizes them by making them seem exotic and worthy of special note. Yet trends in births and in abortions for the under 20s generally parallel those for the over 20s and hence for all women aged 15–44 (see figure 2.2). Thus, although there is a higher rate of abortions in the under than over 20s, trends in births and abortions are similar. The only trend in which under 20s are markedly different from over 20s (and where teenage women are in the vanguard) is the rate of births to single women. Figure 2.3 shows that women under 20 have become the first age group in Britain (as they are in the USA and Canada) in which it is normative for mothers to be single rather than married when they give birth.

Trends in other countries

In England and Wales and in the USA early motherhood is now less common than it has been for most of the last two decades. In the USA, however, conception rates in the under 20s have slightly increased since the introduction of legal abortion (1973), whereas in Britain they have declined. The USA has higher rates and higher numbers of teenage women who become pregnant and have infants than Britain.

In the USA in 1983 13.7% of all births were to women who were

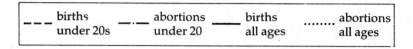

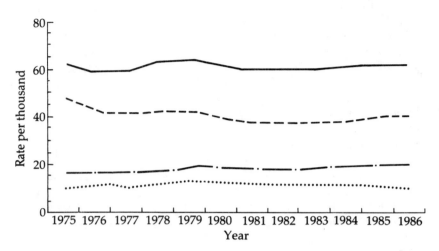

Figure 2.2 Rates of births and abortions to under 20s and all ages in England and Wales (Source: OPCS)

under 20 years of age. One USA teenage women in every ten was estimated to become pregnant (1.1 million teenage women). Half of these obtained legal abortions. Therefore one in 20 teenage women (499,038) gave birth (Pittman, 1986). In England and Wales, by comparison, births to teenage women accounted for 12% of all births in 1983. One woman in 18 was estimated to become pregnant (112,400 teenage women). One-third of them had abortions. Therefore one woman in 27 (75,000) went on to give birth (OPCS, 1985).

Figure 2.4 shows that USA rates of early pregnancy and motherhood are different from those in other industrialized countries. Jones et al. (1986) conducted a study of teenage pregnancy in 37 developed countries, paying particular attention to six of them. Their aim was to discover similarities and dissimilarities between the USA and other developed countries.

Basically Jones and her colleagues found that the USA birth rate is almost double that of England and Wales, of France and of Canada;

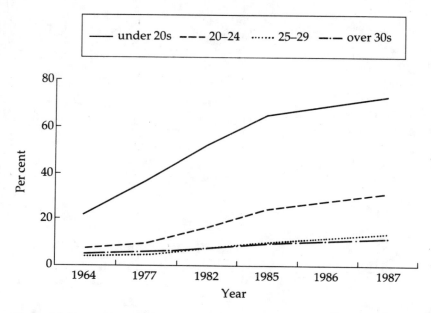

Figure 2.3 Proportion of births outside marriage to under and over 20s in England and Wales (Source: OPCS)

just under three times more than Sweden, nearly seven times that of the Netherlands and more than ten times that of Japan. Pregnancy rates were not available for many countries, but only Bulgaria, Chile, Cuba, Hungary, Puerto Rico and Romania had higher birth rates per thousand 15–19 year old women in 1980 than had the USA.

In general most of the 37 countries (including England and Wales and the USA) had declining birth rates. The exceptions were Ireland, Czechoslovakia, Greece, Hungary, Poland, Portugal, Romania and Spain (Jones et al., 1986). The most dramatic changes have been in Sweden and Denmark, where 5% of the age group gave birth in 1966, but only 1% did so in 1986 (Werner, 1988). The USA is thus very different from most other industrialized countries, while Britain occupies an intermediate position between the USA and other industrialized countries. In view of this it is perhaps not surprising that most published material on early motherhood comes from the USA.

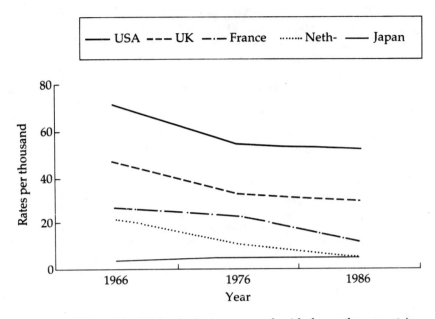

Figure 2.4 USA under 20s birth rates compared with four other countries (Source: Werner, 1988)

Differences between women who become mothers in their teenage years

So far trends in early pregnancy and motherhood have been discussed as if women who become pregnant before they are 20 years of age form a homogeneous group. Treating teenage women who become pregnant as if they are unvaried provides a general, overall picture of early fertility. A general picture, however, masks the heterogeneity of women in this group. The purpose of this section is to consider the ways in which young women who become pregnant tend to be similar, and the ways in which they differ.

The question of abortion

Research studies which compare young women who have abortions with those who continue with their pregnancies have identified some demographic differences between them. The main differences are to do with marital status, class and race.

Married women (in any age group) are less likely to have abortions than single women. In 1986 only 4% of married women under 20 who became pregnant terminated their pregnancies through legal abortions. This compares with 38% of single women under 20 who did so. The comparable abortion percentages for all age groups aggregated was 7% (of married women) compared with 36% (of single women).

In both Britain and the USA middle class women (of high socio-economic status) who are under 20 years of age are less likely to become pregnant than working class women. Those who do become pregnant are more likely to have abortions than to give birth. Working class teenage women (of low socio-economic status) are more likely than middle class teenagers to go on to give birth (Phipps-Yonas, 1980; Bury, 1984; Skinner, 1986). But although working class teenage women are more likely, once pregnant, to give birth than middle class teenagers, the fact that a greater proportion become pregnant means that they also have more abortions than do middle class women (Jones et al., 1986).

Sexual activity is now common among teenagers of all classes. By the time they are 20 years old the majority of women have had their first experience of sexual intercourse. In Britain more than 50% of women under 20 were estimated to be sexually active in the 1970s, (Farrell, 1978, Dunnell, 1979). In the USA just under 50% of teenage women are estimated to be sexually active, with 65% of 18–19 year old women being sexually active (Jones et al., 1986). It seems that middle class women do have sexual intercourse, but are more likely to use contraception than working class women (Skinner, 1986; Morrison, 1985). If they do become pregnant they are more likely to have abortions than are working class women.

In the USA this higher rate of abortion among relatively affluent American teenage women may in part be a reflection of ability to pay. Federal funding of abortions was banned in the USA in 1976 (Wallis, 1985), and in 1985 only 14 States provided federal funding (Jones et al., 1986). Similar factors may operate in Britain where in 1981 52% of abortions (to all age groups) were paid for privately (Jones et al., 1986) and where there is considerable regional variation in the availability of free abortions (Francome, 1986).

Black teenage women who become pregnant in the USA are slightly less likely to have an abortion than white teenage women (Jones et al., 1986). It is harder to establish whether this is the case in Britain because statistics are not routinely collected separately for black people and white people. In his survey of British abortion patients, Francome (1986) found that the relative proportion of black women and white women in his sample was what would be expected given the relative proportion of black people and white people in the population. Skinner (1986) in her study of one London health district found, however, that black teenage women were less likely than white teenage women to have abortions. Since there are few British studies of abortion, there is insufficient data to allow conclusions about relative abortion rates in black British and white British teenagers to be drawn.

Regional variations

It is difficult to get directly comparable information about regional variations in Britain and in the USA, but sufficient information is available to indicate that early motherhood is not evenly distributed within either Britain or the USA. The aim of this section is simply to signal some of these differences rather than to analyse them in detail.

In the USA Minnesota has the lowest percentage of births to the under 20s and Mississippi has the highest. In 1983 8% of Minnesota births were to teenage women, while births to the under 20s accounted for 22% of births in Mississippi.

In Britain in 1986 the rates of births to women between 15 and 19 years of age varied between 32 per thousand in the South West and 56 per thousand in Greater Manchester. The South West also had the lowest conception rate for 15–19 year olds (51 per thousand women in the age group) while the West Midlands had the highest (81 per thousand women in the age group). In 1986 the rate for abortions to teenage women was highest in the Greater London region (28 per thousand women in the age group) and lowest in the North region (17 per thousand women in the age group). The West Midlands had both relatively high rates of abortion (26 per thousand) and of births (55 per thousand) (OPCS series FMI 15, pers. comm.).

High rates of abortion may be expected in the Greater London area because, since the introduction of the 1967 Abortion Act, many women from outside England and Wales have come to Britain for abortions, and many of them have come to London, being the capital. In 1984 over 30,000 abortions on women (of all ages) not resident in England and Wales were performed in England and

Wales (Francome, 1986). It is also likely that some women resident outside London come to London for abortions.

The British rates of conceptions and births to single teenage women were also subject to these regional variations. In 1986 the proportion of all teenage conceptions which were to single teenage women was highest in Merseyside (93%) and lowest in East Anglia (76%) the West Midlands and West Yorkshire (at 83% each). In Greater London two-fifths of conceptions to single teenage women were terminated by legal abortion while only 7% resulted in a birth to a teenage woman who had married during pregnancy. The Northern region showed a rather different distribution, by outcome, of conceptions to teenage women. In the North less than a quarter of conceptions to the under 20s were terminated by legal abortion while 12% resulted in births to teenage women who married during pregnancy (OPCS series FM1 15, pers. comm.).

Different regions obviously have different characteristics as well as different patterns of early motherhood. In Britain, for instance, the 'north–south divide' is such that those who live in the south tend to be more affluent than those who live in the north, and people who live in inner city areas are more likely to be disadvantaged than those who do not. It may well be that the pattern of early motherhood differs between regions *because* early motherhood is related to structural differences.

Social class

In both Britain and the USA early motherhood is more common amongst working class women (those of low socio-economic status) than among middle class women (Simms and Smith, 1986; Skinner, 1986; Jones et al., 1986). In a nationally representative study of one in eight teenagers who gave birth in 1979, Simms and Smith (1986) found that women in their study were disproportionately from the working classes and had fewer years in full time education than the national average.

In Simms and Smith's sample 81% came from working class backgrounds whereas only 59% of the general population were estimated to be working class. On average Simms and Smith's sample came from families with an average of 4.4 children. This was more than double the national average at the time. Only 7% had stayed on at school past 16 years (the minimum school leaving age) compared with 30% nationally.

In the USA poor teenagers are more likely to become pregnant and to have babies than affluent teenagers (Jones et al., 1986). It has also been estimated that 'Disadvantaged young women, whether black, white, or Hispanic, are three to four times more likely to become unwed parents than are non-poor teens' (Pittman, 1986). Young USA women who become pregnant in their teenage years (like their British counterparts) tend to have fewer years of formal education than their peers (Jones et al., 1986).

Early motherhood is thus generally located within sections of the working classes which are not highly educated and not in employment which offers stepwise career progression. It is therefore important to take account of the structural position of women who become mothers early in their life course when considering the impact of early motherhood on women and their children.

'Race'

In the USA, where statistics are routinely collected by 'race', the conception rate among black teenage women is almost double that of whites. The circumstances in which black teenagers conceive and give birth is also different from that in which young white teenagers conceive and give birth.

In 1981 8% of white USA 15–19 year olds were married, compared with 4% of black 15–19 year olds. White teenage women who become pregnant are much more likely to be married than black teenagers who conceive. Single white teenagers are also more likely to marry during pregnancy than their black peers (Jones et al., 1986). This may well be because the structural differences between young black men and young white men in the USA are such that young white men are better able to make financial contributions to their households. Furstenberg (1987) suggests that marriage is economically more beneficial for white than for black mothers under 20.

Hispanic teenage women have conception and birth rates which fall between those of black teenage women and white teenage women. Hispanic women tend to be treated as one group within the USA despite their different places of origin and different patterns of fertility behaviour. Teenage Hispanic women from Mexico, for example, tend to be married when they have children, while teenage Hispanic women whose origins lie in Puerto Rico tend to be single when they have children (*Adolescent Pregnancy Prevention: Next Steps* conference, 20 February 1987).

Because most of the USA population is white, black teenage conception and birth rates make relatively little difference to the total conception and birth rates of women under 20 years of age. Thus black teenagers account for 17% of women aged 15–19 years in the USA and 28% of births to 15–19 year olds. The belief that rates of early pregnancy are higher in the USA than in Europe because of the higher rate of pregnancy in black teenage women is therefore unfounded (Jones et al., 1986).

Young black women in the USA do, however, influence USA rates of births to single teenage women. Black teenage women account for only one in ten births to married teenage women, but half the births to single teenage women (Jones et al., 1986). But white teenagers in the USA are increasingly likely to be single when they give birth.   -

> But recent trends suggest that blacks may simply have been pacesetters for the population at large. Marriage rates among whites have been declining rapidly, and both the rate and ratio of out-of-wedlock childbearing have risen sharply . . . U.S. whites have the highest rates of teenage pregnancy and childbearing of any Western nation. (Furstenberg et al., 1987, p. 5)

Similarly, white American teenagers who give birth have, in the last three decades, become more similar to black teenagers in being unlikely to give their children up for adoption (Phipps-Yonas, 1980).

Unlike the USA, Britain and other European countries do not routinely collect statistics by 'race'. There have, however, been suggestions that young black British women are more likely than young white women to become mothers early in their life course (Ineichen, 1984/5; Skinner, 1986). High rates of births to teenage women in the Caribbean has been cited to explain why there might be higher rates of black than of white pregnancies to women under 20 years of age. It is, however, unsatisfactory to presume that black British women, many of whom have never been to the Caribbean, are likely to be more influenced by their parents' place of origin than by their own experiences in Britain (see Phoenix, 1988a & b for further discussion of this).

In the absence of national statistics it is difficult to be sure that the pattern of African American and black British pregnancies in the teenage years are similar. The only national study of early motherhood which has reported colour of respondents found that 4% were black, of Afro-Caribbean origin (Simms and Smith, 1986). If this percentage is accurate, black teenage women of Afro-Caribbean origin may not be disproportionately more likely to become mothers early in their life course than white teenage women. However one study cannot provide conclusive evidence on the interrelationship of 'race' and early motherhood.

In both Britain and the USA 'race' and 'class' are interlinked so that black people (and Hispanic people in the USA) are more likely to be poor than white people. In the USA black children and Hispanic children form 15% and 9% respectively of the USA child population. Yet if the number of children estimated to be living in poverty are considered, black children form 31% of poor children, and Hispanic children 16%. Black people in Britain are similarly overrepresented in categories of poverty (Brown, 1984).

As a result of the interlinking of 'race' and 'class' it is difficult to disentangle race effects and class effects. Analyses which compare black teenage mothers and white teenage mothers may actually be using 'race' as a proxy for social class.

Marital status

Whether teenage women are married or single makes a difference to their likelihood of becoming pregnant and to how pregnancies are resolved after conception. The majority of conceptions and births to women under 20 are to those who are single. This is partly because very few women under 20 now marry. In Britain in 1986 only 2% of teenage women were married. The minority of teenage women who are married, however, are more likely to become pregnant and, once pregnant, less likely to have abortions than their single peers.

Almost a third (31%) of married women under 20 gave birth in 1986 (a higher proportion than the fifth of married 20–24 year olds who gave birth in 1986). This compares with only 3% of single women under 20 who gave birth in 1986. Once conception has occurred it is unusual for married under 20s to have abortions. Figure 2.5 shows that in 1986 only 4% of married teenage women who conceived had abortions compared with 38% of single pregnant under 20s.

The most dramatic change in the British pattern of births to teenage women over the last three decades has been to do with their marital status. In 1960 only 19% of births to the under 20s were to single women. In 1980 the figure was 43%. From 1980 onwards there was a rapid rise in the proportion of births to single teenage women. By 1985 65% of women under 20 years of age who gave birth were single, and by 1987 the comparable figure was 73% (see figure 2.3). Some of this increase can be accounted for by the accompanying

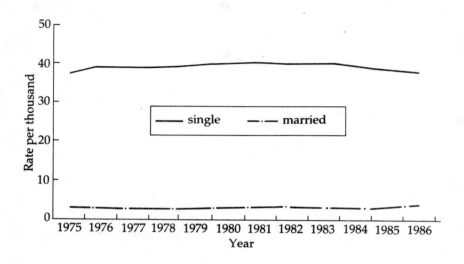

Figure 2.5 Percentage of conceptions aborted in single and married under 20s in England and Wales (Source: OPCS)

decrease in 'shotgun marriages' to women in this age group. Figure 2.6 shows that between 1964 and 1986 there has been a substantial decrease in the percentage of single women who marry once they have conceived, but before they give birth (from 44% to 9.5%).

It is also possible that some of the increase may be accounted for by an increase in cohabitation at the expense of legal marriage over the last decade. Between 1971 and 1986 there was a decrease in the proportion of women under 20 marrying for the first time. Whereas one in ten 16–19 year olds married in 1971, only one in fifty did so in 1986. The majority of single teenage women are not, however, cohabiting with their children's fathers (Moss and Lav, 1985). Non-cohabitation is not necessarily indicative of lack of contact between mothers and fathers, or lack of interest on the father's part. In 1986 a third (33%) of births to single teenage women were jointly registered. Since joint registration requires that fathers and mothers both go to the registration office to record their child's birth, it can

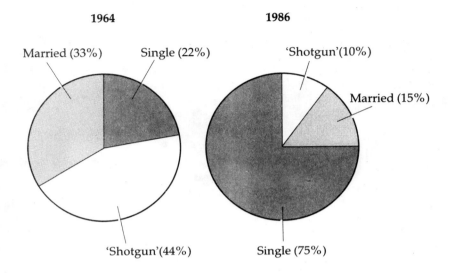

Figure 2.6 Change in percentage of births to mothers under 20 in England and Wales (Source: OPCS)

be assumed that a third of mothers under 20 are at least in contact with the fathers of their children. The percentage of joint registrations for the under 20s is not much less than for the 30–34 age group (who at 39% have the highest rate of joint registrations of births to couples who are not married).

Women who become mothers before they are twenty are the first age group of mothers who are more likely to be single than to be married when their children are born. There has, however, been a marked increase in births to single women in all age groups in Britain (see figure 2.3). A third (31%) of women in the 20–24 age group, for example, were single when they gave birth in 1987, compared with 6% in 1961. Over the same timescale rates of single motherhood in the 25–29 age range more than tripled from 4% to 14%. It seems that the under 20s are leading a trend into increasingly single motherhood, but since 1976 have constituted a smaller proportion of all births to single women. In 1977, for example, 36% of births to single women were to women under 20. In 1987 the comparable figure was 27%.

An increase in rates of births to single women who are under 20 years of age is apparent in most countries, with highest rates being in Scandinavia. Sweden, for example, has a much lower rate of marriage for the under 20s (at 1%) than any of the six industrialized countries studied in depth by Jones et al. (1986). Thus, although Sweden has one of the lowest birth rates for under 20s in industrialized countries, it has the highest rate of births to single women, at about 80%. In contrast with Britain, however, 60% of Swedish women are estimated to have cohabited with a man for some time before they are 20 (Jones et al., 1986).

In the USA, as in most other industrialized countries, the proportion of births to single women under 20 years of age has increased over the last two decades so that in 1984 more than half (56%) of all births to teenage women in the USA were to single women. This increase has been entirely confined to young white women. There has been a decrease in birth rates to single black teenage women in the USA (Jones et al., 1987). Thus, although black rates of single motherhood are much higher than white rates, the trends for black and for white mothers under 20 years of age are in opposite directions.

Age distribution

The use of the blanket term 'teenage mother' might be assumed to imply that early motherhood is uniformly distributed throughout the teenage years. This is in fact not the case. Teenage mothers tend to be predominantly 18 and 19 years old. In England and Wales in 1980, 18 and 19 year olds accounted for nearly two-thirds of mothers under 20 years of age, and those under 17 years of age accounted for less than a fifth.

An increase in the rate of births at each successive age point in the teenage years is characteristic of most countries (Jones et al., 1986).

A greater proportion of pregnancies to younger rather than older teenagers are aborted. In 1986 more than a half (54%) the pregnancies of those aged 15 years and under in Britain were terminated, compared with only a quarter (26%) of pregnancies of those aged 19 years (Francome, 1986).

Trends in pregnancy for younger teenage women (under 17 years) differ from those for older teenage women (age 18 and 19 years),

Table 2.3 Live births to mothers under 20 in England and Wales, 1986

Age of mother	Number of births	% of total
Under 14	120	0.15
14	809	1.0
15	3,293	4.16
16	8,933	11.29
17	16,101	20.35
18	22,456	28.38
19	27,419	34.65
Total	79,131	100.0

Source: OPCS series FMI 15

with 17 year olds occupying an intermediate position. In Britain, between 1980 and 1983, conception rates for the under 17s increased while pregnancy rates for women aged 17 and over decreased. For the under 17s abortion rates increased more than conception rates. For the over 17s the birth rate fell, but this was not due to increased abortion since abortion rates for the over 17s also fell (OPCS, 1985). Between 1983 and 1985 there was a general increase in the rate of teenage pregnancies, but this was highest for 17 and 18 year olds (OPCS 1987). Over the 1980s there has been a slight shift in the proportions of births to the 16s and under and those to the over 16s. In 1980 less than one in ten births to the under 20s were to women under 17, but by 1986 the proportion had risen to almost two in ten.

In the USA births to women aged 15 years and younger stayed roughly stable between 1971 and 1983, but dropped for other age groups of teenage women (Jones et al., 1986; Pittman, 1986). Pregnancy is relatively rare in women under 16 years of age in western countries. However the USA has a higher rate of births to the under 16s than do other western countries (Jones et al., 1986).

The differences in pregnancy, abortion and birth rates between younger and older teenagers suggest that teenage women who become pregnant are not a homogeneous group.

Summary

Early motherhood is now less common in most developed countries than it was two decades ago. Part of the reason for this decrease has been the introduction of legal abortion in many countries. A significant proportion of recorded pregnancies in women under 20 years of age are now legally terminated.

The circumstances in which young women give birth have also changed over the last two decades. In many developed countries there has been a marked reduction in the proportion of births to married under 20s. Relatively few teenage women now marry when they are pregnant, and marriage itself has declined in popularity among the young.

The decrease in the rate of teenage pregnancies and an increase in the proportion of births to single mothers are common to many western countries. Yet there are marked intercountry differences in relative rates of conceptions and births to women under 20 years of age. Of particular note is the fact that the USA is unusual in having a markedly higher rate of motherhood in the under 20 age group than most other western countries. This must partly account for the volume of literature on early motherhood produced in the USA.

'Young mothers' are often referred to as if they are a homogeneous group. In reality, however, the term 'teenage mother' masks differences in age distribution (relatively few younger teenagers become mothers), marital status, and 'race'. The main feature that teenage mothers share tends to be their material position. Early motherhood is predominantly a feature of the working classes. A consideration of the structural context in which early motherhood occurs is therefore essential to an understanding of it.

While motherhood in the under 20s has many demographic features which differentiate it from motherhood in other age groups, trends in all age groups tend to follow similar patterns. Thus, for the under 20s, rates of birth tend to decline and increase either in parallel with, or slightly after, those of older women. Mothers over 20 in Britain are less likely to be single at birth than those under 20. They have, nonetheless, also experienced dramatic increases in rates of births to single women (particularly those in the 20–24 age group).

3

How the Women came to be Mothers

By the time that they are 20 most people will have had their first experience of heterosexual intercourse (Farrell, 1978; Jones et al., 1986; Francome, 1986). Only a minority become pregnant, and fewer still go on to become mothers before they are 20. Many studies which attempt to explain why teenage women become pregnant focus on reasons that young women give for not using contraception (Simms and Smith, 1986; Chilman, 1980; Bury, 1984). Lack of knowledge about contraception is a popular focus for explanations of non-use or inefficient use of contraception (Ineichen, 1986). Sexually active teenagers (pregnant or non-pregnant, and of both sexes) have been reported to be uninformed about contraceptive methods other than the pill and to be generally unreliable users of contraception (Morrison, 1985).

The 'contraceptive knowledge' theory is not, however, sufficient to explain why teenage women become pregnant. 'Knowledge . . . is not successful in reducing the chances of out-of-wedlock child-bearing' (Hanson et al., 1987). Using data from their extensive cross-country study, Jones et al., (1986) concluded that 'knowledge of how conception occurs and how to avoid pregnancy is virtually universal even among those aged less than 18'. It seems then that most young women who become pregnant are not ignorant about either how conception occurs, or about the existence of contraception.

In most industrialized countries pregnancy does not inevitably lead to motherhood. Once young women are pregnant they have opportunities to disrupt the process of becoming mothers by either having abortions or by giving their infants up for adoption. In Britain rates of abortion to the under 20s have increased since the 1967 Abortion Act was put into operation, and over a third of pregnancies to the under 20s are resolved through abortion. The trend in abortions to teenage women is similar in most western countries (although the 1989 USA supreme court decision to give rights to 20 week old foetuses and forbid public funding of abortions and abortion counselling is likely to restrict the availability of abortion, particularly to poor women). The availability of legal abortion together with reduced stigma associated with single motherhood has made giving children up for adoption increasingly less popular over the last three decades. It is now only a small minority of mothers (of any age group) who give their children up for adoption.

An account of how young women come to be mothers has to consider not only why they became pregnant, but also why they decided to continue with their pregnancies, and to keep their children. This chapter uses data from the Thomas Coram study to address these issues.

Women's orientations to pregnancy before conception

Two pervasive and conflicting stereotypes of how teenage mothers came to be pregnant will probably be familiar to many people. The first is that teenage women become pregnant 'accidentally', because they have been too ignorant or indigent to use contraception properly. The second is that young women become pregnant in order to get council housing (in Britain) or welfare benefits (in both Britain and the USA). It is not, of course, simultaneously possible to become pregnant accidentally and to 'plan' to become pregnant for material gain. The logical inconsistency between these two social constructions of teenage motherhood has not prevented both from gaining widespread currency and hence being the subjects of research investigations.

It might be assumed from interest in young women's motivation for becoming pregnant that, in contrast to women under 20, all women beyond their teenage years 'plan' their conceptions. Yet some women who give birth in their teenage years report that they 'planned' to become pregnant (Simms and Smith, 1986) while some older women report that their pregnancies were 'accidental' (Oakley, 1979; Brannen and Moss, 1988).

With regard to the popular assertion that young women become pregnant for material reasons, Simms and Smith (1986) report (on the basis of data from their national survey) that 'occasionally the desire to have a baby had an ulterior motive' (p. 12). They quote one young woma who said that she wanted to have a baby in order to obtain council housing. In the Thomas Coram Research Unit study, however, no one mentioned such an ulterior motive. Nor did they in Clark's (1989) study of 38 teenage women with children. When asked directly if they had become pregnant in order to obtain housing many 'expressed derision or disbelief . . . It seemed laughable and tragic to them that anyone would "use" a baby to get a flat or house' (p. 11).

Wilson and Neckerman (1987) reviewed studies of family structure and poverty in the USA and concluded that women do not seem to become pregnant in order to get welfare benefits because births to young women living in poverty (particularly those who are single) do not increase and decline in line with changes in welfare policies and payments.

> Nonetheless, the findings from Ellwood and Bane's impressive research and the inconsistent results of other studies on the relationship between welfare and family structure, and welfare and out-of-wedlock births, raises serious questions about the current tendency to blame changes in welfare policies for the decline in the proportion of intact families and legitimate births among the poor. (Wilson and Neckerman, 1987, p. 81)

While young women do not have children in order to obtain welfare benefits, their individual circumstances obviously influence their decisions to enter or to defer motherhood. An analysis of British data (the OPCS Longitudinal Study which studied 1% of the population enumerated in the 1971 census) showed that 17–19 year old women who were unemployed at the 1981 census were twice as likely as their employed age peers to go on to have a child within the next five years (24% cf. 12%) (Penhale, 1989). This effect was independent of factors like social class and housing tenure which (as would be expected from previous studies) were also related to early motherhood.

In late pregnancy, the 79 women interviewed in depth in the Thomas Coram study were asked a series of retrospective questions about how they had felt about the possibility that they might conceive. Only 18% (14) said they had been 'trying' to become pregnant. The majority (82%, 65) had not 'planned' to become pregnant, but their attitudes to possible pregnancy (their preconceptual orientations) and hence their reasons for not having used contraception varied.

It was possible to identify four pre-conceptual orientations to pregnancy which had a bearing on whether women had used

Table 3.1 Orientation to pregnancy at conception by age at birth

Age	Wanted to conceive	Did not mind	Not thought about it	Important not to conceive	Total
16	0	2	2	5	9
17	3	4	4	4	15
18	5	4	5	9	23
19	9	10	3	10	32
Total	17	20	14	28	79

contraception or not (see table 3.1). Some women had wanted to conceive (22%, 17), some had not minded whether or not they conceived (25%, 20), others had not thought about the possibility that they might conceive (18%, 14), and the largest group (35%, 28) had considered it important not to conceive when they did.

Women who had wanted to conceive

Women who had wanted to conceive cannot be said either to have become pregnant accidentally or to have failed to have used contraception properly. But since early motherhood is socially stigmatized why did they feel ready to have children when they did? Had they used contraception regularly when they first started to have sexual intercourse? Or did they start having sex after they had decided to try to conceive?

Although many researchers consider it reasonable to ask why women who are still in their teenage years should want to have children, it is difficult to establish why women of any age want children.

> People do not have clear motives so far as having children is concerned; few organise their lives according to some overall plan. The subject of having children provokes ambivalent feelings, so that 'planning' is a euphemism for allowing one particular feeling or pressure to gain an upper hand ... Despite its complexity, the question 'did you want/plan a baby?' may be easier to answer than the parallel question 'why did you want a baby?' This taps a vast minefield of unexplored or half-explored motives and reasons. Some women have never asked themselves this question, or when they do the answer is framed in terms of 'always' having wanted a baby; others describe a long process of critical self-examination. (Oakley, 1979, pp. 32–3)

Women have difficulty teasing apart their motives for either having or not having children and feelings about having children fluctuate. (Dowrick and Grundberg, 1980)

In the study reported here most women had always wanted to have children, and did not perceive their age to be a limiting factor. While only 29% felt that they were having children at an age they considered ideal, only 21% considered that the ideal age was more than a couple of years older than their current age. Early motherhood was common in the women's social networks, and their own mothers had similarly had their first child earlier than average: 40% of the mothers of the women in the sample had their first child while they were still in their teens, and only 18% had their first child after 25.

Table 3.1 shows that women who had wanted to become pregnant were more likely to be older (18 and 19 years old) than younger (16 and 17 years old). Only three women were under 18 when they conceived. All were 17 when they gave birth (although one had been 16 at conception). They were also more likely to be living with male partners than to be single (see table 3.2). At conception nine were married, four were cohabiting and four were single. Just over half the married women in the study had wanted to conceive, compared with less than a tenth of the single women.

Women who lived with their parents were less likely to report either that they had wanted to become pregnant or had 'not minded' becoming pregnant (see table 3.3). A third of those who had wanted to become pregnant or had not minded doing so were living with their parents when they conceived compared with 79% of those who had considered it important not to become pregnant. Six women (all married) were living in their own mortgaged homes when interviewed. Four of them had wanted to have children, one had not minded whether she conceived or not, and only one (who owned

Table 3.2 Orientation to pregnancy by marital status at conception

Marital status	Wanted to conceive	Did not mind	Not thought about it	Important not to	Total
Single	4	12	13	24	53
Cohabiting	4	2	1	2	9
Married	9	6	0	2	17
Total	17	20	14	28	79

Table 3.3 Orientation to pregnancy by living with parents at conception

	Wanted to conceive	Did not mind	Not thought about it	Important not to	Total
No. who lived with parents	6	6	10	22	44
% of each orientation	35%	30%	71%	79%	
% of all who lived with parents	14%	14%	23%	50%	56%

her house jointly with her siblings) had felt that she was not yet ready to have a child.

Age, marital status and living with parents were interrelated. Older teenagers were more likely to be married, and less likely to be living with their parents than were younger women. They were the women who were most likely to have 'planned' their pregnancies or to have no objections to becoming pregnant.

Some women who had wanted to become pregnant were living in circumstances which (apart from age) are constructed as ideally suited to the rearing of children; being either married or cohabiting, living in their own homes (whether council or mortgaged) and having employed male partners. Only one married woman and two cohabiting women who had wanted to become pregnant had male partners who were unemployed. One married 18 year old with an employed husband and an owner-occupied house expressed this as 'I've done things the right way'. Other women were not concerned that they were, for example, single or living with their parents. Single women did not necessarily consider marriage to be necessary to the rearing of children. Neither did they consider that being single confined them to raising their children single-handedly. All except two women had made the decision to conceive jointly with their male partners.

> When I used to work in the nursery I used to take like 3 children home on my weekends . . . and he loves kids as well, so we used to . . . babysit for 'em – play mummy and daddy sort of thing, and then we decided it would be best to have our own instead of taking other people's kids, cos I used to feel a bit sad you know when I had to

bring 'em back. So we decided to have our own. (19 year old single woman)

Those who lived with their parents expected to be rehoused by the council after their child was born. In one case a 17 year old woman and her partner had 'planned' the pregnancy in order to be allowed to marry, and in another case a 19 year old married woman was on the brink of buying her own home.

Table 3.4 shows that none of the women who were in training or education became pregnant because they had actively wanted to. Being in employment did not, however, prevent women from wanting to become pregnant. Roughly equal numbers of women who wanted to become pregnant were employed as were unemployed. This was the only group in which no one was in any form of education, or on any government training schemes.

Table 3.4 Orientation to pregnancy by employment status at conception

Employment status	Wanted to conceive	Did not mind	Not thought about it	Important not to	Total
Employed	8	4	7	7	26
On MSC scheme	0	1	2	1	4
Unemployed	9	13	2	11	35
In further education	0	0	0	5	5
At school	0	2	3	4	9
Total	17	20	14	28	79

Women who did not mind whether or not they conceived

At first sight it may seem irresponsible for women to claim that they are indifferent about whether or not they bring another person into the world. But women who had not minded whether or not they conceived definitely wanted children at some time and did not feel that early childrearing would be particularly disruptive to their lives.

I don't think I was really bothered to be honest because I didn't have any immediate plans for the future. (17 year old single woman)

After we got married I thought I'm going to go in for a baby but I just didn't know when, and then I said to myself – well I don't care if I fall or not now because I'm married. I don't care what people think. (19 year old married woman)

I just stopped taking the pill because I'd been taking it for such a long time – one and a half [years] is a long time – and my husband said if it happens it happens. We didn't exactly say we want a kid. He said if you get pregnant you get pregnant. (18 year old married woman)

I didn't mind. Not once I turned 16 I didn't mind. (16 year old single woman)

The phrases 'I wasn't bothered' and 'I didn't mind' were common for this group of women, as indeed it was for a minority of Simms and Smith's (1986) interviewees. 'Not being bothered' and 'not minding' seemed to indicate that young women would not be upset if they did not immediately conceive, rather than that they were indifferent to having a child.

In some ways women who did not mind whether they became pregnant were similar to women who wanted to become pregnant. More of them were 18 and 19 years old than were 16 and 17 (table 3.1) and a minority lived with their parents (table 3.3). They were more likely to be married than women who either did not mind, or had not thought about the possibility of becoming pregnant (table 3.2). But in comparison with those who reported that they had wanted to become pregnant, fewer were married at conception. Only two of the husbands of women in this group were employed, and no cohabiting male partners were. This was also the group with the highest proportion of unemployed women.

Women's perceptions of their employment prospects influenced their orientations to pregnancy. Many had experienced difficulties in obtaining jobs and most (83%) had experienced unemployment at some time. It is not surprising then that even women who were employed before they conceived did not feel that they had employment careers which would be damaged by childrearing. As a result both employed and unemployed women considered that there was no good reason for them actively to defer motherhood.

Yes I sort of planned it … I was thinking that if I do – I'm not definitely going out of my way to get pregnant, but if I do get pregnant well, I'm happy and I'm keeping it because I love kids and I couldn't see myself waiting until I'd eventually settled down and that because it seemed a long way off … because I seemed to be having it difficult by not finding jobs easily like I used to before and, you know, everything. So I was thinking, I might as well I'd get settled down now. (19 year old single woman who had not minded if she became pregnant)

Similarly, an unemployed married woman whose husband was long term unemployed had been trying to become pregnant because 'We had no reason to wait.'

Women who had considered it important not to become pregnant

Women who had considered it important not to become pregnant formed the biggest group in the study (35%). They were mostly single and living with their parents (tables 3.2 and 3.3). More than half the 16 year olds were in this orientation, as were a third of 19 year olds (table 3.1). The majority of women who were in full time education had not wanted to become pregnant when they did. Fourteen women in the study became pregnant while using contraception. Most of these (11) had been using contraception because it was important to them not to become pregnant when they did. (The other three had not minded becoming pregnant.) Two women who had considered it important not to become pregnant conceived the first time they had sexual intercourse.

The main reason that women did not want to become pregnant was either because they had no independent living accommodation or because they lacked money. Only one woman (a single 17 year old) who had not yet had a job mentioned employment as a limiting factor: 'I really wanted to have my working life . . . before I wanted to have a child.' A single 19 year old felt she 'wanted to go out' instead of having a child and a married 19 year old (of Italian origin) had only had a registry office wedding, and knew that her father would be furious if it became apparent that she had had sex with her husband before she had had her white Italian style wedding.

Women who had not thought about the possibility of conception

Most women who had not thought about the possibility of becoming pregnant had conceived early in their sexual careers, but one woman became pregnant when she briefly resumed her relationship with her boyfriend, and another when she started to cohabit and sex became less frequent. Roughly equal proportions of 16, 17 and 18 year olds, but relatively fewer 19 year olds had not thought about the possibility that they might become pregnant (see table 3.1). This group were more likely than any other to be in employment.

The influence of previous conceptions

If women had previously been pregnant, they generally wanted to have a child.

Table 3.5 shows that nine women in the study had been pregnant before, and that two-thirds of them had been trying to become pregnant this time. Three were 19, two 18 and one 17. Only the 17 year old was neither married nor cohabiting when she conceived this time. None of the 6 had ever had abortions. Five had miscarried, and one had given her child up for adoption. None had been married or cohabiting when they conceived for the first time, and when they had initially started having sexual intercourse, none had been using contraception. Their sexual and reproductive careers were not, therefore, qualitatively different from those of single pregnant women who were a year or two younger when they conceived.

Table 3.5 Orientations to pregnancy by previous pregnancies

	Wanted to conceive	Did not mind	Not thought about it	Important not to	Total
Previous abortion	0	1	1	1	3
Previous miscarriage	5	0	0	0	5
Previous adoption	1	0	0	0	1
Total	6	1	1	1	9
% of each orientation	35%	5%	7%	4%	11%

Contraceptive use

Those who had felt that it was important for them not to become pregnant were the most likely to have been using, and to have considered using contraception when they conceived. While the majority of those who reported contraceptive failure were in this group, most women (61%) who had felt that it was important for them not to become pregnant did not use contraception. Yet two-thirds of the sample (52) had used contraception at some time before they became pregnant. Only 12 women had, however, used contraception regularly from when they first had intercourse until they either became pregnant or decided they wanted to have a child. Four were married when they conceived, and eight were single. None were 16 year olds, although two 16 year olds and a 17 year old were intermittent users of contraception throughout their sexual careers.

Two-fifths (7) of those who had wanted to become pregnant had used contraception when they first started to have sexual intercourse. Only four of them had, however, used contraception regularly early in their sexual careers. Three of them had had sex for the first time after they married, and had been advised by their relatives or GPs to start taking the pill before their weddings. The other was a 19-year old single woman who had decided to take the pill on her own initiative. These four had all continued to use contraception regularly until they decided to become pregnant. For some women, however, the change from not wanting a child to wanting one was not marked by any change in contraceptive behaviour.

Influences on contraceptive use

'The decision to use contraception is not an absolute one – it is not a decision that is taken once and for all' (Bury, 1984, p. 41). Women moved in and out of contraceptive use during their sexual careers in response to changes in their circumstances or changing attitudes to particular methods of contraception. The following sections will consider what influenced women to use or not to use contraception at particular times.

CONTRACEPTIVE KNOWLEDGE   Most women in the study (88%, 67) had received some contraceptive education. However of those who had, only two-thirds had found their discussions about contraception useful. Most of the sample (72%, 57) had received some contraceptive education from school. Only 29% (22) said their mothers had discussed contraception with them. However women tended to be less happy with school coverage than with their mothers' discussion of contraception. A third (35%, 7) of those whose mothers had discussed contraception with them did not find it useful. This compares with half of those who received contraceptive education at school. Many had been embarrassed to discuss contraception in large, sometimes mixed-sex groups and often giggling and general merriment had disrupted classes.

My mum was the best source. School did it, but you know what it's like. [What?] People were really silly about it. [In the class?] Yeah. It wasn't very good. The teacher just gave up in the end. (18 year old)

Well they [school] tried on numerous occasions, but every time they came with sex education I mean it was such a big laugh that we didn't learn anything anyway because everybody was messing about and they tried putting the guys out. You couldn't get on with the lesson because they kept interrupting trying to see and hear and things like that so they just gave up . . . (18 year old)

Despite the unsatisfactory nature of school sex education, most women knew which contraceptive methods were available. In answer to the question 'Which contraceptives do you know?' 90% mentioned that they knew the pill, two-thirds mentioned the coil or intra-uterine contraceptive device (IUCD) and nearly three-fifths named the sheath. The cap, however, was only mentioned by a third of women and only 1 in 20 mentioned withdrawal. It proved difficult to persuade women to itemize all the methods they knew, and this descending incidence of mention reflected the order in which contraception tended to be mentioned (as well as its popularity with the sample).

A few (7%, 5) of the sample refused to itemize any contraception and simply said that they knew all methods. This *may* partly have been because respondents found this section of the interview embarrassing to discuss. But other, equally embarrassing issues were discussed without diffidence. It may therefore be that many women could not be bothered to answer 'examination' type questions.

Asked if they felt they had needed more information or advice on sex and contraception, three-quarters of the sample (73%) said they had not. Most women did not become pregnant because they were unaware of the existence of contraception. Nonetheless there was evidence that women who experienced contraceptive failure on low dosage contraceptive pills (12 women) had some confusions about how it should be taken and how efficient it was (see the section on contraceptive failure). In addition two women thought that the cap needed to be inserted hours in advance.

ATTITUDES TO THE METHODS AVAILABLE   Two-thirds of the women interviewed had used contraception at some time before they became pregnant. Most had taken the pill (although four women who had taken it had not used it for contraceptive purposes). Only three women (4%) had had an IUCD fitted, and 19 women (24%) had been in relationships where male partners had used the sheath. Many women reported themselves to be worried about the potential side effects of taking the pill or using the IUCD. One-third (34%, 26) said that they did not like the pill as a contraceptive method, and 44% (33) did not like the IUCD. Concerns about side effects of contraceptive use had been noted in other studies of teenage women (Herold and Goodwin, 1980; Jones et al., 1986).

Reluctance to use the contraceptive pill or the IUCD was sometimes because respondents knew women who had, or had themselves, suffered side effects with these forms of contraception.

> I had to go to hospital because it was disorganising my organs. I was sick and coughing up blood . . . and it was too strong. They gave me a too strong tablet. I decided from then I'm not taking it. (19 year old single woman who had been trying to conceive, and whose side effects while on the pill may have been caused by her sickle cell disease)

> I was taking the pill and it didn't agree. That's what they reckoned caused it [lump in her breast] . . . When I discovered the lump in my bust they took me off it so I didn't use anything since then. (19 year old cohabiting woman who was trying to become pregnant)

Other reasons cited for discontinuing pill use were weight gain, headache, nausea, being scolded by clinic staff for not having taken the pill properly, the end of a relationship and having taken the pill for 'long enough' given that it could cause ill effects.

The three women who had been fitted with IUCDs had all had them removed for medical reasons. Two single 19 year olds developed infections, and a married 19 year old had experienced continuous, debilitating pain:

> I was on the pill but then I stopped because it used to make me feel sick . . . Before I got married I had the coil fitted for about five months but I couldn't sit down – I used to have terrible stomach aches. (19 year old single woman who had not minded if she became pregnant)

Concern about IUCDs was not usually based on first hand experience. But some women had relatives or friends who had been adversely affected by IUCDs:

> Some of them [contraceptives] are all right but . . . when you have the coil and things like that I don't approve of that 'cos my cousin had the coil and later on it affected something so she had to have her womb taken out. (16 year old)

The sheath had been more widely used than the IUCD. However

11 of the 19 women whose partners had used the sheath expressed disapproval of it. Nine further women (11% of the sample) had no experience of the sheath but also disapproved of it. Most women who mentioned the sheath as a contraceptive method they knew of said that their partners either did not like to, or would not use it and that they did not like it either. A few women questioned its reliability as a contraceptive method.

> We did try that [sheath] together. At the clinic they gave me some for the meantime – but it doesn't feel the same. I don't think it's very fair. (19 year old married woman)

> Oh! Great big caps they look horrible. The durex [laugh] they busted up. They're no good . . . Wasn't worth it [laugh]. Just gave up in the end. (Cohabitee who had wanted to become pregnant)

The sheath was generally only used for short periods, early in women's sexual careers, or at the start of new relationships. Only one woman's male partner had used it continuously (but not on every occasion) from the beginning of her sexual career (at 14) until she became pregnant (at 16).

The cap was the least favoured contraceptive method (together with the safe period). Only 32% of the sample (24 women) mentioned the cap when asked to itemize contraception, and 75% (18) of them disapproved of its use. No one had actually used one, although one woman was considering its use after birth. Apart from stating a general aversion to barrier methods as being 'messy', most women were not very forthcoming about why they did not like the cap. However some considered it to be as invasive of the body as the IUCD, and referred to both as 'things you put inside you' while others considered it unattractively inconvenient.

> They say that now you've got to put it up and after 24 hours, or is it 12 hours you're meant to take it out and then I think of all the horrible you know what I mean – washing it and then you've got to put it away and keep it clean just in case if you put it back in you it's not clean then you get an infection. That's why I'd just rather use the pill . . . (19 year old cohabitee who had been having fertility checks)

There were indications that some women mistakenly believed that the cap had to be inserted several hours before it was used and was thus an impracticable contraceptive choice.

Well, you can't work by an appointment system. And if you've got to put it in 8 hours before . . . ! (19 year old single woman who had considered it important not to become pregnant, and had been taking the pill)

With the cap you have to put it in a certain amount of hours before you have intercourse. And with my boyfriend he doesn't say 'well in two hours time Sheila, be in bed.' It's impulse. It's something he wants at a second's notice. I can't do that you're joking! Put it in every night. That is it! (18 year old single woman who had considered it important not to become pregnant)

In reality the cap can be used fairly flexibly because it can be inserted either just before, or *up* to eight hours before intercourse occurs. It does, however, have to be kept in place for eight hours following intercourse. Women who made comments like those above had, therefore, either not fully understood what health workers or the media said about the cap or had been misinformed by friends, partners or relatives. As a result they did not have sufficient information to make informed choices about which contraceptives to use.

Dislike of barrier methods may be linked to social class and age (Skinner, 1986). Older, middle class women may be more likely to use them than younger, working class women. However young women may be averse to barrier methods because the health professionals they encounter are not positive about them. Many GPs, for instance, do not fit the cap and do not consider that young people will be sufficiently motivated and organized to use the sheath. Since many GPs are negative about the use of barrier methods, it is not surprising that few women are enthusiastic about their use. It is, however, possible that there may be an increase in the use of the sheath by the under 20s as a direct result of publicity about AIDS and 'safe sex' (Carroll, 1988).

GENERAL ATTITUDES TO CONTRACEPTION   Worries about or dislike of particular contraceptive methods did not make the women in the sample feel generally opposed to contraceptive use. Asked what they thought about contraception in general most replied that they approved of it and considered it to be useful and a good idea. Only 13% (10) were opposed to the use of contraception. For five of them (four Catholics and one Jewish woman) this opposition was for religious reasons. Worries about particular methods may, however, have influenced their feelings about using contraception.

In late pregnancy some women who knew they did not want further children in the next few years were already wondering which contraceptive methods to use after birth. There was some feeling that the disadvantages of most methods left them little real contraceptive choice.

> Well it [contraception] will be used in the future, because now I know I can make a baby and that it could happen again. And I don't want it to happen again in the near future. [?] I don't think I'd use the pill for a long time. It's OK for a while but after a while you get side effects . . . It doesn't seem right having something inside you all the time [cap and coil]. (19 year old who had not thought about the possibility of pregnancy because she thought she was infertile, and who had started to cohabit in pregnancy)

> The pill, they say it can affect you with cancer and that. And you don't know what to do. That's the safest one, the pill. But the coil – my sister fell pregnant with the coil this time, so they're not really that safe, them things. So I really don't know what to go on after. It frightens me a bit. The doctor can give you a weak pill, but is it strong enough ? The coil – I wouldn't use that because it's dangerous. And the cap and the creams I wouldn't use those. (17 year old single woman who had not wanted to conceive)

> And then the coil. I hear that's meant to give you heavy bleeding and pains and that. My mum had it and she had . . . very bad pains and heavy bleeding and she had to have it taken out of her . . . The only thing I wanna use is the pill. I mean that's what I've got to sort out after I have the baby because if it's gonna affect me again then I don't know what I'm gonna use 'cos if he won't use the sheath then – and I won't use the coil or Dutch cap and I don't want to fall pregnant again. So therefore something has to come to an arrangement. (19 year old cohabitee who had been having fertility tests)

RELATIONSHIPS WITH MALE PARTNERS   Attitudes to, and use of, contraception were influenced by women's relationships with their male partners. Many women said that their own male partners considered that contraception was 'up to the woman', and wouldn't use it themselves. This effectively rules out the sheath for these women's partners. Seven of every ten women said that they thought that men were less concerned about contraception than women, while only 3% (2) thought they were more concerned. This compares with four in every five who considered that responsibility for contraception ought to be shared equally. Women's reports of male concern about contraception differed by age: 18 and 19 year olds were more likely than 16 and 17 years olds to say that men were concerned about contraceptive issues. This may be because older teenagers were more likely to be married and to have relationships which had lasted longer. Some married women, however, also felt strongly that men are not as concerned about contraception as are women.

> Because if you leave it down to the men half the time they would say they're using contraceptives, but they're not really. You really don't know. (Married woman who did not mind whether she became pregnant or not)

In this study young men were not interviewed about their attitudes to contraception. However the findings of an American study indicate that young women may be accurate about young men's attitudes to contraception. Finkel and Finkel (1975) found that over half of the 421, 12–19 year old males that they studied felt that only women should use contraception. Over half of the women in the Thomas Coram study had partners who were 21 or over, but younger women were equally likely to have relationships with men who were over 20 as with men who were under 20. One 16 year old's male partner was 38, and the only married 17 year old was married to a 26 year old.

Many girls still grow up expecting that they will not initiate sexual intercourse or take a lead during its course. In order to continue to see themselves as 'nice girls' rather than 'slags', sex has to be something which is not pre-planned and which happens to them, for which they take no responsibility (Crabbe, 1983; Lees, 1986). This poses a dilemma for young women who are not 'trying' to become pregnant. Using contraception defines them as pre-planning sex, yet not using contraception may result in their becoming pregnant. Griffin (1985) found the same contradictions between the desire for spontaneous sexual intercourse and planning to use contraception. These contradictions make young women reliant on their male partners' use of the sheath. Since the sheath is generally unpopular with men as well as with some women the chances are that young women will sometimes have unprotected intercourse.

> First time we went out we used that [sheath]. Nothing happened . . . Then after he never used it . . . (19 year old single woman who had not minded becoming pregnant)

> I didn't really think. I just listened to [boyfriend] but he just thought about himself. (16 year old who had not thought about the possibility of pregnancy)

Age and marital status are relevant here. Younger women are more likely to be sexually inexperienced than older women. It is probably more difficult for women who are just beginning to have sexual intercourse to have the confidence to insist that their partners use sheaths, for example, than it would be for more sexually experienced women.

Skinner (1986) found that young women in what she calls 'integrated relationships' with their boyfriends are more likely to use contraception than those in less 'committed' relationships. Bury (1984) similarly suggests that young women are least likely to use contraception at the start of a new relationship. This is probably for two reasons to do with the nature of male–female relationships. Firstly, women in established relationships can more readily admit that sexual intercourse is likely to occur. If they do not want to become pregnant, this facilitates use of the pill or the IUCD. Secondly, increasing confidence about sexual activity is likely to facilitate use of methods like the sheath and the cap which require situational control.

> I think it's an easier thing to go on the pill. For me to take it rather than to use anything else. Especially when . . . you don't know someone like I know [him] now. It's less embarrassing I suppose. (19 year old single woman who had been on the pill because she had considered it important not to become pregnant)

In addition men in such relationships (if only for fear of censure from friends and relatives) may feel more committed to ensuring that pregnancy does not occur before they have both decided that it should. Less than half the women who were married when they became pregnant had used contraception when they first had sex. Seven used contraception regularly and one intermittently. Eight women had not had sex before they married. Four of them had used contraception regularly at first, and one sometimes.

The difficulty of using contraception in a new sexual relationship places young women in a paradoxical situation. At the time in the life of the relationship that it is most important to prevent pregnancy, it is also most difficult to take active precautions against it. Young women who have taken the pill in one relationship are likely to stop taking it once the relationship ends, and are so unlikely to be using contraception when they start a new relationship (Bury, 1984). In that situation women in their late teens may become unintentionally pregnant as readily as younger teenagers.

I just stopped taking it because I wasn't going with anyone at the time then I just forgot about it and just threw them away and that was it. (18 year old single woman who had considered it important not to become pregnant)

Two sexually experienced women who had not wanted to become pregnant conceived early in new relationships. One had previously taken the pill following an abortion. She stopped taking it when her relationship ended but conceived the first time she had sex with a new boyfriend. The other had been taking the pill, but stopped taking it when she stopped seeing her boyfriend. She became pregnant when they (briefly) resumed their relationship. Luker (1975) suggests that women weigh up the costs and benefits of contraception against the unknown risks of pregnancy. With gender relations as they currently are, the start of a relationship is generally a time when contraceptive use is, for some women, more costly than running the risks of pregnancy.

CHANCE AS AN INFLUENCE ON CONCEPTION   The difficulties inherent in the management of early sexual intercourse explain why substantial numbers of young women use no contraception when they first have sexual intercourse (Skinner, 1986; Johnson, 1986). The sheath is the form of contraception most likely to be used in early intercourse (Zelnik and Shah, 1983). Young couples are unlikely to use contraception at first intercourse if male partners are opposed to using the sheath.

Two-thirds of women in the Thomas Coram study used no contraception when they first had sexual intercourse. Nineteen year olds were the year group most likely to report having used contraception when they first had sexual intercourse. A higher proportion of women who used contraception in early intercourse were married than single. Having used contraception initially was no guarantee of future use. Two women (both single 19 year olds) who had used contraception early in their sexual careers had later become pregnant and had abortions.

Some women who did not use contraception when they first had sexual intercourse then went on to use contraception regularly until they wanted to become pregnant. For this reason it is unsatisfactory to dichotomize women who become pregnant as either contraceptors or non-contraceptors. Chance alone may have prevented some 'non-contraceptors' from being 'contraceptors'. If they had not become pregnant when they first started to have intercourse they may well have become regular contraceptive users. Four women (all single) became pregnant the first time they had sex. One was 17, two 18 and one 19 years old. Two had thought it was important for them not to become pregnant, and two had not thought about the possibility that they might become pregnant.

> The thing what happened is – the first time that we ever did have sex I got pregnant, but I didn't know. So that was it. And I said, 'Let's stop. I don't want to do it any more . . . until I actually go . . . [to the family planning clinic]. (16 year old)

Most women who did not initially use contraception did so later. Two-thirds had used contraception at some time, even if only for a short period.

> Q–Why didn't you use any contraception when you first had sex?
> A–I don't know. I was stupid really, but I just didn't think of it.
> Q–Were you aware you were taking chances?
> A–In a way, but I had gone so long without using anything – you know with the withdrawal method that I wasn't worried about it. I thought it was quite safe. Like we didn't use anything for six months and everything was all right. I never dreamed I'd get pregnant really.
> Q–Why did you start taking the pill then?
> A–Just in case I *did* fall – I suppose you could make mistakes. That's why.
> (Married 18 year old who had been trying to become pregnant)

The above respondent had then taken the pill regularly for two years before deciding to try to become pregnant.

If women did not become pregnant after a period of sexual intercourse in which they had not used contraception, they often thought that they were unlikely ever to become pregnant. They were then unlikely to start using contraception.

> Because I went for two years with not getting pregnant I thought that I wouldn't. At one point I was worried – I thought that I couldn't have children – I couldn't fall for any. And then this one come along. (18 year old)

> First time we went out we used *that* [sheath]. Nothing happened. We used the sheath. Then after he never used it. So nothing happened. It was like, you know, I still saw my periods so I thought well, nothing can happen, so (laugh) just carried on using nothing. (19 year old)

This is similar to Oskamp and Mindick's (1983) finding that nearly a sixth of the pregnant teenagers they interviewed agreed with the statement, 'If a girl has intercourse for a month or so without getting pregnant, this means she probably isn't likely to get pregnant for a while.'

It is not unusual for women who do not become pregnant after a period of sex without contraception to worry about their fertility and for some deliberately to test it (Bury 1984). The invisibility of the reproductive system and of the process of fertilization together with the knowledge that it is possible to be infertile can also generate curiosity, and sometimes fear in women. Uncertainty about whether they are physiologically able to become pregnant may lead some women to want to test their fertility without necessarily wanting a child at that point (Pines, 1978; Luker, 1975). Similarly women who do not necessarily want to have a child can gain some happiness from knowing that they are fertile (Bury, 1984).

> I didn't know whether to laugh or cry because I was happy because I felt like I could actually produce a child of my own and that, and I was actually having my own. (19 year old)

Prior to pregnancy more than a fifth (17 of woman said that they had thought that they could not become pregnant. Kantner and Zelnik (1973) found that more than a quarter of their national probability sample of US 15–19 year olds had not used contraception because they thought they could not conceive. The reasons Kantner and Zelnik's respondents gave for this belief included infrequency of intercourse and being too young. The reasons given by respondents in the present study were related more to their experience/knowledge of their reproductive system than to general beliefs. These reasons included irregular periods (one women) tubal infections (two women) and failure to conceive after a period of intercourse without contraception (nine women). Four women said they 'just thought' they would not become pregnant and a married 19 year old said that she had erroneously thought that it was necessary to try and try to become pregnant.

> It used to worry me a lot [being infertile] and I used to talk to Joe about it, and he used to say that it didn't matter . . . It was him that persuaded me to go and see someone [gynaecologist] about it [irregular periods]. (19 year old single woman who had considered it important not to become pregnant)

> I didn't know you could get pregnant so easily. I thought you had to try and try to get pregnant. And it was so quick. (19 year old married

Two women who had both been trying to conceive for over a year were so worried about the possibility of being infertile that they had initiated the process of fertility investigations. One of them became pregnant between having a fertility test done and starting treatment.

> I didn't get pregnant for about a year and I had some tests done and they said I wasn't releasing any eggs. (18 year old)

Young women do not necessarily ovulate when they first menstruate. Lack of ovulation may account for the fact that some do not conceive when they are first having sexual relations but not using contraception. Teenage women may, therefore, become convinced that they are infertile, and need never use any contraception. In reality, however, they are only temporarily infertile or subfertile and are likely to become pregnant if they continue not to use contraception.

Obtaining and storing contraception

Once women have decided that they wish to use contraception, they have to get contraceptive supplies from chemists, GPs or clinics. Contraception is available free of charge in Britain and young women can obtain it without having to inform their parents. The process of obtaining contraception is, however, frequently difficult and sometimes daunting for young women, as the following two respondents make clear.

> I dunno. I think I sort of feel a bit embarrassed as well going to the chemist or going to the doctors. I wouldn't be able to say a thing. (17 year old)

> I didn't want go innit. I felt kind of embarrassed, but I still went. (18 year old)

Nearly a third of the 20 women who had attended clinics and the 31 women who had consulted GPs for contraception were unhappy about the treatment they had received. This was frequently to do with the manner in which they were treated, but was sometimes, as in the following example, because of what was actually said.

She was saying like – 'how old's your boyfriend?' And I told her. 'He's a bit in the baby woods' she said and it was nothing to do with her, and I was answering. I was telling her everything . . . I was really upset. (17 year old single woman)

In this example the woman on her mother's advice changed her clinic, but some other women who were unhappy with the way they were treated never collected further contraceptive supplies.

But I stopped going up there because she told me off for not taking the pill properly. (18 year old single woman)

More than half (56%) of the women were living with at least one parent (more often their mothers than their fathers) when they became pregnant. Some single women living with their parents felt reluctant to use contraception like the pill or the sheath which has to be stored somewhere. They worried that parents would find their contraceptives and be displeased to learn that their daughters were sexually active. This finding differs from that in other studies which suggest that parental attitudes towards contraception 'have little impact on adolescent's contraceptive use' (Morrison, 1985). In the Thomas Coram study parents influenced their daughter's contraceptive behaviour indirectly because living with parents was felt to be a constraint on storing supplies of contraceptives. One woman, for example, reported that she had obtained supplies of the contraceptive pill long before she became pregnant, but had never taken them because she was worried that her mother might find them.

In trying to ensure that young women had sufficient contraceptive supplies, family planning clinics were sometimes insensitive to the problems of storage and embarrassment that some young women may face. This is made graphically clear in the following description.

He said 'what about the sheath?' And I didn't really know about them then. And he said 'I'll give you some of them and you can see if you like it'. So he gave me a card and I went to the reception area where you get your tablets and things. And there were all these men sitting there with their girlfriends and things, and they gave me 100 boxes of Durex! Oh God, I nearly died on the spot. I could feel my face going bright red. So I shoved them into a carrier bag and put my pill in, and I walked out and felt such a clot. I felt, I can't take 100 Durex home, my mum will go mad! So I slung 'em. And a bloke behind me picked them up and said, 'I think you've lost these!' I quickly shoved them in a dustbin when I got further down the road. (18 year old)

Some parents (or parent substitutes) did actively encourage their daughters to use contraception rather than risk pregnancy. Almost one woman in every six reported that someone (usually but not always their parents) had put pressure on them to use contraception. If women wanted to use contraception they welcomed encouragement to do so.

> Because they [parents] thought we [respondent and her older sister] should go onto it last year . . . and we took notice and we went on it. (Single woman who became pregnant while taking the pill, and who had thought it was important for her not to become pregnant)

> Well I was [living] with my nan and like I spoke to her once and I said – because my mum had me very young [at 16] and I said to my nan I don't want to ever fall pregnant and she said well you're not going to because you haven't got a boyfriend and she took me to the clinic and she said she's not going out with anyone at the moment but she wants to have the pill . . . (19 year old married woman who had mot minded whether she became pregnant or not)

It should be noted, however, that some felt uncomfortable or even angry at suggestions that they should take contraception when they were not yet sexually active.

> At first I felt funny because I was going out and she thought that I was doing things and I wasn't. (17 year old single woman who had not minded whether she became pregnant)

> Oh she told me to go on the pill [laugh]. Anyway I told her I wasn't doing anything so I don't know what she's talking about . . . Because she knew I had a boyfriend she . . . just used to jump to conclusions . . . I goes to her 'What do I want the pill for? Am I doing anything?' . . . She went out and she flung the slippers at me . . . [This episode then developed into a full blown physical fight.] (18 year old cohabitee who had been trying to become pregnant this time, but who had miscarried the previous year after becoming 'accidentally' pregnant)

Three women received domiciliary contraceptive services (arranged by their mothers) and were very satisfied with this method of obtaining contraception.

Contraceptive failure

Contraceptives are not failsafe, and some women conceive while using contraception. Francome (1986) found that over a third of the women (of mixed ages) in his abortion survey reported that they had used contraception regularly when they conceived. One-fifth of Simms and Smith's (1986) nationally representative British sample of mothers under 20 also said that they had been using contraception when they conceived.

Most pregnant women interviewed in this study had not been using contraception when they conceived, but nearly two-fifths of those who had considered it important not to become pregnant said they had been using contraception when they conceived (see table 3.6). Four of them had not always used the contraceptives as they had been directed to, and therefore felt that they had run the risk of becoming pregnant. One had relied on her male partner's use of the sheath and the other three had been taking oral contraception.

> I used to take it before I went to work . . . One morning – oh I'm late for work and I just rushed off – you tend to forget about it by the evening time with all the people you see – I just forgot about it. (17 year old)

The other ten women who had been using contraception when they became pregnant reported that they had used it correctly. Nine of them had been taking the pill, and one had been using the sheath regularly (although not with spermicide). While it is theoretically possible to separate contraceptive failure from failure to use contraception as recommended, in practice it is difficult to distinguish them.

For example two of these ten women became pregnant the first month after IUCDs (which were causing them problems) were removed. Both women were then prescribed low dosage contraceptive pills which failed. Since low dosage pills are unreliable in the first two weeks of use, it is possible that these women had not followed manufacturers' recommendations on use stringently. They could also, however, have been misinformed or not informed about those recommendations and not been able to understand manufacturers' leaflets. In any event the two women mentioned above were

Table 3.6 Orientation to pregnancy by contraceptive use at conception

	Wanted to conceive	Did not mind	Had not thought about it	Important not to	Total
% of sample	0 (–)	3 (4%)	0 (–)	11 (14%)	14 (18%)

absolutely certain that they had taken the pill properly. One was furious with her doctors for not telling her that the antibiotics prescribed to clear up the infection caused by her IUCD could make the pill less effective.

> And they took it [IUCD] out, and gave me the pill and an antibiotic. And the antibiotic counteracted the effects of the pill and thanks to the doctors I ended up pregnant! I mean they never said anything to me. They just gave me the pill . . . (19 year old single woman who had considered it important not to become pregnant)

The period of transition from one type of contraception to another, or from one type of pill to another, seems to be when contraception is more likely to be reported to have failed and also to be less effectively used (Francome, 1986).

> She gave me a different pill and it turned out to be a weaker dose and that's why I got pregnant. (19 year old)

> I was watching some programme on TV about the pill and cancer. So I went to the doctor to change the pill to get another pill – it was a lower dosage and when I was changing onto that I was mixing myself up and that's when I fell pregnant. This pregnancy was in between changing pills. (18 year old)

Women who reported that they had been using the pill regularly were angry that they had become pregnant. They felt that their doctors had omitted to give them necessary information about oral contraception.

> I didn't know there was any different dosages you know what I mean? And when I went for the pregnancy test I went to a youth advisory centre, and I went to see a doctor there for the first appointment and she said to me, 'What pill were you on?' And I told her, and she said, 'I have had so many people, so many girls in here that have been on that pill and have come to me in here pregnant.' I couldn't believe it. I was so angry because I'd been careful. (18 year old)

Whatever the reasons that women conceived while using contraception, some who were taking low dosage pills felt puzzled about why they had become pregnant. They needed more information than they had apparently been given about how the pill works, and when it should be taken.

I don't know how it [pregnancy] happened. My doctor said it was a low dosage pill and it hadn't got into my system, which is probably why. (19 year old who had considered it important not to become pregnant)

Decisions after conception

Once women realize that they are pregnant they either have to go ahead with their pregnancies or to decide to have abortions. If they give birth they can keep their child or give it up for adoption. These decisions are affected not only by how women feel about being pregnant and about abortion and adoption, but also by the reactions of significant people in their lives. Since the study reported here is of women who all gave birth and kept their children the discussion of decisions made after contraception does not apply to women who decide to terminate their pregnancies or to give their children up for adoption.

Initial reactions

Figure 3.1 compares women's reactions when they first realized that they were pregnant with their later reactions. Initially over half reported that they had some positive feelings about being pregnant: 28% reported only positive feelings. A further 11% had a few small misgivings but were predominantly positive, while a further 15% reported both positive and negative feelings. Women who had wanted to become pregnant were most likely to report positive feelings. But women from the other orientations described above (i.e. who had 'not minded', not wanted to or not thought about the possibility of becoming pregnant also said that they had felt positive. The 15% of women who initially reported mixed feelings about being pregnant came from all four pre-pregnancy orientations.

Women who were unhappy to be pregnant were mainly those who had considered it important not to become pregnant. Two-fifths of the sample (42%) said that they felt miserable once they realized that they were pregnant: 29% felt nothing but misery, while 13% were mainly miserable. They described feelings of upset, anger, misery, negativeness and fear. None of the women who were married at conception described her initial feelings in this way.

Studies of teenage mothers often treat ambivalent or negative feelings on discovery of pregnancy as if they are worrying precursors

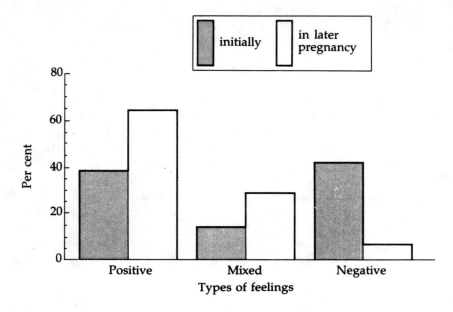

Figure 3.1 Women's feelings about being pregnant

of poor outcome for mothers and their children. Yet ambivalent and negative initial reactions to pregnancy are common in any age group of mothers. Indeed pregnancy itself is a time of rapid developmental change.

> The psychological work which takes place is not necessarily conscious, although it is well known that during pregnancy there is a tendency for women to become more introspective. Pregnancy is a time for reassessment of the past and for thoughts about the future . . . Imbalance and disorganization often precede times of greatest change. And so in pregnancy a woman may feel that her world is being turned upside down . . . During the *first months of pregnancy* a woman has to come to terms with being pregnant. Even when planned, the decision to have a baby and the conception, whether immediate or not, are followed by conscious or unconscious misgivings. These first months are filled with doubts, confusion, regrets, anxieties and disbelief. (Birksted-Breen, 1986, p. 23)

A married woman pregnant with her first child should be 'absolutely thrilled'. But many have far more complex reactions . . . So strong is this cultural imperative to be overjoyed at the news of pregnancy that a woman who reacts differently may puzzle the professionals and be labelled abnormal ... Cultural images of pregnancy portray such [mixed/negative] reactions as abnormal. Yet many women, who become ordinary loving and caring mothers have them ... (Oakley, 1979, pp. 40–41)

Women's initial reactions to pregnancy were related to their personal circumstances. Most women were affected by their perceptions of how their male partners and parents would react. It was rare for women in the Thomas Coram study to worry that their employment prospects would be affected adversely by early motherhood.

I didn't really want to be because when I thought of all the things you know. How it would set me back in my career [as a clerical officer] and things like that you know I was a bit upset about that ... At the time it didn't enter my head. It was afterwards I started thinking 'Oh my God, what have I done?' (18 year old single woman who had not thought about the possibility that she might become pregnant)

I really wanted to have my working life ... before I wanted to have a child. (17 year old single woman who had been unemployed when she conceived)

It did matter to me because of my work [as an accounts clerk] ... (a 19 year old single woman who considered it important not to become pregnant, but became pregnant the first time she had sex)

Single women who lived with their parents sometimes seemed more concerned about how their parents would feel when they learned of the pregnancy, than about how they felt about it. Such concern was not surprising since parents had the power to make their daughters homeless. Only one woman was eventually made to leave home (and go into a mother and baby home) by her father, but fear of a harsh reaction made some women reluctant to tell their parents that they were pregnant.

I wasn't sad and I wasn't happy. It wasn't a shock to me. I was just scared about what might happen at home. That's what I was fretting about. (16 year old single woman who had considered it important not to become pregnant, and whose father did make her leave home)

Alright. A bit scared, but I got over it ... Scared at first of telling my mum (Cohabiting woman who had wanted to become pregnant and was living in her mother's house; 16 at conception, 17 at birth)

Some women feared a more adverse reaction from their fathers than from their mothers.

> I thought he'd kick me out straight away, hit me. (17 year old single woman who had not minded whether she became pregnant or not, but had been on the pill)

> I thought my dad would hit my boyfriend and beat him up. (17 year old who had been on the pill and had considered it important not to become pregnant)

While women who lived with their parents were more likely than not to be anxious about what their parents would say, some were not perturbed that their parents did not like the idea of them having a child and a few knew that their parents would support them whatever happened.

> To me it wasn't [important]. But to my parents it was. (18 year old single woman who had not thought about becoming pregnant)

> It wasn't really bothering me if it happened. I always knew I'd have support from my family. (19 year old single woman who had not minded whether she became pregnant or not)

Initially women reported that over a quarter of parents (27% of mothers and 30% of fathers) were pleased that their daughters were pregnant while nearly a half of mothers (47%) and almost three in ten fathers (28%) were reported to express nothing but displeasure (see figure 3.2). Most other parents apparently took news of the pregnancy calmly, but were not delighted that their daughters were pregnant. There were marked age and marital status effects. Parents of older, married teenagers were more likely to be pleased that their daughters were pregnant than were parents of younger, single women. But some parents with older, married daughters living in circumstances socially constructed as ideal for the rearing of children thought their daughters should have waited until they were older to become pregnant.

> She said I was very silly to let myself get pregnant, and how could I want to have a baby when I was this age – I had no life, you hadn't done anything together. She was quite upset for quite a while actually. (19 year old married woman who had wanted to become pregnant and who, unusually for this study, was an owner–occupier)

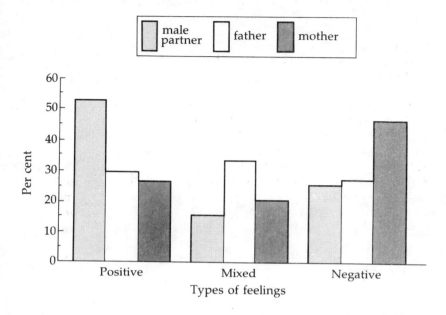

Figure 3.2 Other people's initial feelings about women's pregnancies

> Everybody wasn't as enthusiastic as I thought they'd be at first mean-
> ing parents and parents-in-law ... My father kept saying you should
> have waited a while ... (18 year old married woman who had been having
> fertility checks, and owned her own house)

Older, married teenagers were more likely than younger, single
ones to report that their male partners (like parents, and like the
women themselves) were pleased that they were pregnant. But male
partners were more likely to be pleased that they had fathered a
child than were women or their parents (see figures 3.1 to 3.3). Over
half (53%) of male partners were said to be pleased when they first
learned that women were pregnant, and only just over a quarter
(26%) had no feelings of pleasure at first.

Women who lived with their male partners were keen that they
should be pleased, but those who lived with their parents often felt
more concerned about how their parents would take the news than
how their male partners would.

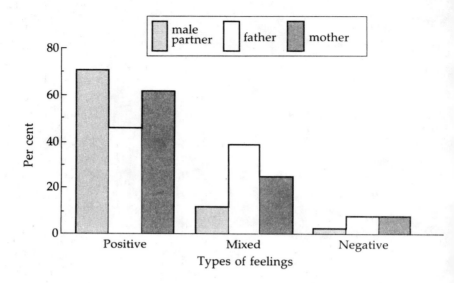

Figure 3.3 Other people's feelings in late pregnancy about women's pregnancies

Q–How did you feel when you first suspected that you were pregnant?
A–What was my mum going to say! [Laughs.] I wasn't really worried about him [boyfriend] knowing. It was my mum, mainly, and my dad. Because my mum had her son when she wasn't married, and she just always said how hard it was bringing him up herself, and things like that.
(19 year old single woman who had not thought about the possibility of pregnancy)

Abortion and adoption

Women who are immediately pleased to be pregnant and whose families and male partners are also pleased are unlikely to want either to have abortions or to consider giving their child up for adoption. Women who are unhappy to be pregnant or who have mixed feelings about it may however consider abortion or adoption.

Alternatively women may be persuaded into having abortions by their parents or male partners.

The design of the Thomas Coram study precluded interviews with women who actually had abortions because the sample was selected in late pregnancy. It is unlikely that women would have agreed to be in the study if they were intending to give up their child for adoption. One woman approached at antenatal clinics gave this reason for refusing to be in the study. Various studies indicate that young women who become pregnant and have abortions differ on various characteristics from young women who go on to have children. They are likely to be of higher social class, have better academic records, and to be more ambitious than those who go on to have children (Phipps-Yonas, 1980; Bury, 1984).

The discussion of abortion and adoption presented here relates to a group of women who did not either have abortions or give their children up for adoption. They cannot, therefore, be claimed to be similar to women who made different decisions. Nonetheless a tiny minority of women had previously had abortions and one had given up a previous child for adoption and some women thought very hard about whether to have abortions or choose adoption in the pregnancy discussed here.

When asked about their general attitudes to adoption and abortion it became clear that neither were popular options with women (see table 3.7). Opposition to adoption was not as vehement as opposition to abortion. Less than half the sample (41%) reported that they were mostly or completely opposed to adoption. Yet few women gave the possibility of having their child adopted serious thought. Only five women (6%) had considered that they might have their child adopted, and only one (who was 16 at conception and 17 at birth) actually got as far as asking a social worker about adoption (see below). One woman (who was 17 and single and had wanted to conceive this time) had a child adopted three years previously. Her family had handled her pregnancy by hiding it, and pretending

Table 3.7 Attitudes to adoption and abortion

	Completely opposed	Mostly opposed	Mixed feelings	Mostly in favour	Completely in favour	
Adoption	35%	6%	12%	33%	14%	(N=66)
Abortion	58%	20%	7%	7%	9%	(N=76)

nothing had happened after the adoption. The woman was still hoping that she could get her son back at some time.

Three women interviewed had previously had abortions. Two were 19 and one 18 when they conceived this time. The 19 year olds were single, but the 18 year old was cohabiting. One 19 year old had had two previous abortions, but had not minded whether or not she became pregnant this time. She had been having difficulty finding jobs and saw no reason to defer motherhood. The other 19 year old became pregnant the first time she had sex in a new relationship, when she had not yet thought about the possibility that she might become pregnant. The 18 year old cohabitee had been taking the contraceptive pill because she considered it important not to become pregnant while living in her boyfriend's parents' house. Only the woman who had not thought about the possibility of becoming pregnant was not immediately pleased when she realized that she had conceived, but none of these three women considered abortion or adoption as possible courses of action during this pregnancy.

Most women interviewed reported that they were opposed to abortion except in specific circumstances, such as if a foetus was known to be affected with a disorder, or if a woman had been raped. More than four-fifths expressed some opposition, and nearly three-fifths claimed that whatever the circumstances, they could not condone abortion (see table 3.7).

> I just don't think it's right killing a baby. It's like killing yourself. Getting pregnant and then killing the baby is not right. It's not worth you having sex. If you have sex you know you're going to get pregnant. What's the sense killing it . . . (17 year old single woman who had considered it important not to become pregnant)

Women who have strong anti-abortion feelings are unlikely to terminate even pregnancies they are unhappy about. However some women who reported that they were opposed to abortion did consider having one. Twenty two women had considered having an abortion when they first realized that they were pregnant and 13 had actually gone along to their GPs or clinics to get information and advice about abortion. As would be expected from the national trend for pregnant teenage women who are married to give birth rather than have abortions, only single women had considered abortion. Most of these were 16 and 17 year olds. Their consideration of abortion was often inspired by parents. Some parents actually suggested abortion to their daughters but some daughters considered abortion because they feared their parents' anger.

> Well my mum said to me [suggested abortion]. She doesn't like them at all. She's against it really, but where I was so young – she thought – she was in two minds . . . and she did decide to leave it up to me but I don't think I could do that. [You said no?] I wanted to say 'no' straight away but it . . . weren't just for my sake it were for my mum and dad's sake as well as for me to live here, but they said to me 'look if you don't want one we'll stick by you' and everything. But I didn't want one really. (17 year old who became pregnant while taking the pill, and had considered it important not to become pregnant. Her older sister became pregnant two months before she did)

> No we went there [to the abortion clinic] but I wasn't going to have it [the abortion] anyway . . . My mum hadn't told my dad, so I was a bit worried about him finding out . . . but then I just came back and said, well I don't want it [abortion] and she said all right. Told my dad and my dad just said we were a bit mad and that was it . . . (17 year old who had had a previous child adopted and who had become pregnant in order to persuade her parents to allow her to marry. She did marry in late pregnancy)

Other women were also prepared to show themselves willing to accommodate their parents' feelings by considering abortion if necessary. In most cases parents left it up to their daughters to decide whether to have abortions or not, and given the option most women did not have abortions.

One 16 year old came close to having an abortion. She was actually anaesthetized and taken to theatre, but then not aborted because the doctors estimated that she was too advanced in pregnancy. Her parents had told her that it was up to her whether she had an abortion or not, and she expressed anti-abortion views. This apparent inconsistency of views and behaviour was because she believed that, although her parents were not insisting that she had an abortion, they would prefer it if she did. She said 'I was doing it for them' and reported herself to be relieved when she found that she could not have an abortion. Her parents were opposed to her having the child adopted so when abortion proved impossible the whole family began preparing for her child to be born.

Some women reported that abortion was suggested to them at hospital antenatal clinics. The following two examples illustrate how, if clinics suggest abortion, young women can use delayed disclosure of pregnancy to ensure that they are not pressurized into having abortions they do not want.

I was just in there having a check up. This was about the second visit, and a tall nurse came in, and she saw my age and saw that I was going to be a one-parent and she said about my job – how am I going to be able to cope and bring it up by myself. And she said I should have an abortion. And I was really annoyed. I just cried. I didn't answer her. I couldn't. My mum did mention it – but I was too far gone. That's why I didn't want her to know [sooner]. (19 year old single woman who had not thought about the possibility that she might become pregnant)

At the clinic they said would I like an abortion, and I didn't know what to say – but then when they said that my mum would have to sign this and this, and that's when I didn't go to the clinic again at all – until they [family] found out. (16 year old who had not thought about the possibility that she might become pregnant, who resisted her family and friend's pressure to have an abortion, and later to have the child adopted)

Male partners who were unhappy that women were pregnant sometimes made it clear that they did not want a child just yet, but it was rare for them to attempt to force women to have abortions.

He kept saying he didn't want it, and he still says it now. [Why?] Because he doesn't have the money to look after a kid, or me come to that. [?] He says he'll still love it, and look after it. (17 year old who had not minded if she became pregnant, but who had been taking the contraceptive pill)

When he found out that I was four months pregnant he didn't want to know me. And then one day he come up and he turned round and said I should have an abortion because he doesn't want a baby. (17 year old single woman who had not thought about the possibility that she might become pregnant)

An 18 year old woman who became pregnant the first time she had sexual intercourse suspected that her male partner would be negative about her pregnancy, and broke off the relationship before he had a chance to suggest abortion to her.

When I found out, I didn't tell him, and I broke off the relationship. And I knew the only answer he would give me would be 'Go and have an abortion.' It would be a very uncaring attitude, and I didn't want to be involved in that situation – being kicked when you are down . . . I just didn't want to know anyway. (18 year old single woman who had not considered the possibility that she might become pregnant)

Two women wanted abortions because they felt that they could not cope with children in their situations, rather than because their parents felt they should not have a child. One (17 at birth, but 16 at conception) was undecided about having an abortion until it was too late to do so, but when seen in late pregnancy was very disapproving of its availability, saying 'It's given too freely and it shouldn't be like that.' Once she decided against abortion she began thinking of having her child adopted. She was the only person in the sample to start the process of getting her child adopted rather than just considering it without taking any action.

> When I thought I'm not going to have the abortion, I thought to myself, Jane, you just can't keep it. And I said well I'm going to have it adopted. And the social worker said to me 'if you have it adopted, there's no way you can see it again.' And I thought to myself, Jane, why the hell are you having a child, and you're not going to get no benefit or anything out of it ... (17 year old who had considered it important not to become pregnant, but became pregnant the first time she had sex)

The other woman who initially wanted an abortion because she did not feel that she could manage to look after a child was an 18 year old single woman who became pregnant while drunk, and had not realized that she had ever had sexual intercourse. She considered having an abortion but did not consider adoption because she felt that there was no point in going through with childbirth and then 'giving the child away'.

> I said well I wouldn't be able to keep the child, because I'm unemployed, I haven't got a job, I haven't got a flat. I haven't got anything. So it would be unfair to bring a child into the world ... I said 'I'm afraid I'll have to have an abortion so he gave me a letter for the hospital ... and then I decided that I couldn't go through with it. (18 year old single woman who had not thought about the possibility that she might become pregnant)

Reactions in late pregnancy

It is sometimes assumed that women who are initially unhappy to be pregnant are unlikely to want their children. Yet psycho-analytic writers consider negative feelings to be a normal part of early pregnancy, and pregnancy itself to be a period of coming to terms with transition to motherhood (Pines, 1978; Birksted-Breen, 1986). Negative reactions have been reported for some women who are over 20 years of age (Oakley, 1979; Brannen and Moss, 1988) as well as those who are under 20 (Simms and Smith, 1986; Skinner, 1986). As pregnancy progresses women are generally reported to become more positive about being pregnant, and this is also the case for women who are under 20 (Furstenberg, 1976; Simms and Smith 1986).

In the study reported here, most women said that they recognized themselves to be pregnant in the first trimester, and four in every five got a doctor to confirm their pregnancies then. More than a third reported that they had their first hospital antenatal appointment before they were three months pregnant. Nearly all (90%) had been to antenatal clinics by the end of the second trimester. Asked how they had felt about their antenatal visits, four fifths expressed some dissatisfaction about waiting times, the way they were treated, or not being given sufficiently clear explanations. Yet over three-quarters never missed an antenatal appointment. These findings run counter to studies which find that mothers under 20 are likely to be late bookers and erratic attenders at antenatal clinics.

Only one woman did not disclose her pregnancy until just before she gave birth and, therefore, did not attend antenatal clinics at all. She was a white woman who was frightened to tell her parents she was pregnant because her child's father was black and her parents, particularly her father, were she reported 'prejudiced'.

Women's feelings in late pregnancy were related to how they perceived that pregnancy would fit into their lives, and how the people who were important in their social networks (predominantly parents and male partners) responded. Only one of the six women who were eligible for maternity leave wanted to take it. She was a 19 year old who was apprenticed to a traditionally male trade and still had a year of training to run in late pregnancy. She had wanted to become pregnant, and did not regret her decision to try to conceive. She intended to complete her apprenticeship. Other women felt that employment and motherhood were not compatible and that motherhood was more important. For example a single 19 year old who qualified for maternity leave strongly disagreed with her mother's desire for her to return to her job as a cashier in a supermarket.

Figures 3.1 to 3.3 show that as pregnancies progressed women themselves, parents and male partners became happier about the child to be born. In late pregnancy only 8% of mothers and the same proportion of fathers were still displeased that their daughters were pregnant. Women's mothers were slightly more likely to be positively enthusiastic about the pregnancy than were women's fathers.

> She said it's up to me. You can do what you like. It's your life now. She was a bit negative to start with, and my dad hit the roof. [Now . . . ?] She's great now. She's very helpful. And my dad's better now. It's as time goes on, nearer I get to having it the more excited they're getting. Because this is their first grandchild. They don't like the circumstances much, but they're still excited. (19 year old single woman who had previously had an abortion, but became pregnant the first time she had sex in a new relationship)

> Um she was shocked. She was crying and things like that . . . Now she's all for it. She's always running out the street buying me this and buying me that. She's just like a normal mother I suppose. (16 year old who had not thought about the possibility of pregnancy, and had still been at school)

By late pregnancy nearly three quarters of male partners (72%) were happy about their partners' pregnancies, and only 13% still felt predominantly negative about it. It continued to be the case that a greater proportion of male partners were enthusiastic about women's pregnancies than either the women themselves or women's parents. This may partly be because the men who were most upset to learn that their partners were pregnant were no longer in relationships with them in late pregnancy. Fifteen single women stopped having relationships with their children's fathers during pregnancy. Five of these pregnant women reported that their male partners had stopped contacting them without saying that the relationship was over. Three women said they had ended the relationship because men had either reacted badly or were anticipated to react badly to news of their pregnancies. The other seven relationships had reportedly ended for reasons that were less clearly related to the fact that women were pregnant.

As other people in women's social networks became more enthusiastic about the child to be born, so too women felt increasingly pleased to be having a child. In late pregnancy 66% of women were very pleased to be pregnant. Only one person (the 16 year old who had been forced by her father to leave home) felt that, while she was looking forward to having a child, there was nothing good about being pregnant. By late pregnancy when everybody in women's social networks knew about the impending births, women were in a position to weigh up what childrearing was likely to entail for them instead of mainly concentrating on how friends and relatives would react. Far from being unrealistic about what mothering was like, women recognized that childrearing was sometimes difficult, and that there were losses as well as gains involved.

> Oh yes, all the plans I'd had for myself went out of the window. I was faced with a different sort of life to the one I'd thought about. I had to sit down and think about what I had to do, what I was going to come across. I knew that it wasn't going to be a bed of roses. I knew there would be hard times. (18 year old who had not thought about the possibility of pregnancy)

> I would have preferred not to, but now I don't mind. Maybe I could have gone out and found a career for myself, and maybe we could have got things a little more organized first. I'd like to have been a bit older, but I don't think now it's going to make a lot of difference to my life. I will try not to make it. (19 year old single woman who had considered it important not to become pregnant).

> I think it's quite good. It depends on what mood I'm in whether I'm positively happy. [Any regrets?] Sometimes I think it might be a tie . . . That's what I'm afraid of. And with my family . . . like the women – they just had their children and stayed in all the time – and I'm afraid of falling into that. Because I've seen different things you can do – I don't want to fall into that. (17 year old having twins, who married in pregnancy and had not minded whether she conceived or not)

> I regret it at times, thinking, we could have had our own place by now, or we could have had the wedding we wanted, a bigger wedding. But it's a case of having to. We've got a child coming which we're over the moon about, and it's one of those facts of life we've got to face. But I do sometimes think it could have been better than this. (18 year old who had been cohabiting in pregnancy but not thought about the possibility that she might become pregnant)

Although they recognized that mothering would not always be easy, most women were looking forward to having their child by late pregnancy. Even those who said they had initially been miserable about being pregnant felt keen by then.

> And I'm really looking forward to it you know. I've come to terms with it. It's taken a long time, but . . . (18 year old single woman who had considered it important not to become pregnant and had been taking the pill)

> I'm quite happy about it. (18 year old single woman who had considered it important not to become pregnant, but became pregnant, without having a relationship with the child's father, the first time she had sex)

I decided that I was gonna have the child and I'm happy now that I'm gonna be a mother. I've always loved children . . . (18 year old who had conceived while drunk, and had no idea that she had ever had sex)

Parents were invaluable in providing support for women who had initially been unhappy about being pregnant, or whose male partners had left them. The fact that women in such circumstances were looking forward to childbearing owed something to parental enthusiasm about having new grandchildren.

Conclusions

Most women knew which contraceptive methods were available, and many had used contraception at some time. They had not, therefore, conceived because they lacked knowledge about contraception. Nor did any woman report that she had wanted to become pregnant in order to get housing or welfare benefits. Contraceptive use and non-use depended on a number of complex factors, and women sometimes had conflicting feelings about it. For example some women felt that they did not wish to become pregnant, yet were afraid or embarrassed to go to a doctor or clinic in order to obtain it.

Other factors which deterred women from regular contraceptive use included fears of potential health risks; of breaching socially accepted gender relations; of parents finding out that they were sexually active; and queries about fertility (sometimes because prolonged periods of sexual activity without contraceptive use had not resulted in pregnancy).

Some reasons for not using contraception are more relevant to teenage women than to older women. For example gender relations, parental influences and difficulties with obtaining contraception are more likely to affect teenagers than older women. Other reasons are relevant to all age groups of fertile women. Fears of potential health risks, for example, are related to the nature of the contraceptive methods currently available. Queries about fertility are frequently based on women's own experience of their reproductive physiology, and are not necessarily age specific. It is, however, possible that some young women who did not become pregnant after more than a year of having sexual intercourse and not using contraception may not have been ovulating yet.

Most women were not 'trying' to become pregnant. But nearly one in five reported that they had been 'trying' to become pregnant.

These women together with those who said that they had not 'thought about' the possibility of becoming pregnant as well as those who were 'not bothered' whether or not they became pregnant did not perceive contraceptive use to be relevant to them.

Programmes designed to reduce teenage pregnancy frequently stress the need 'to give sexually active teens the access they need to contraceptive services and counselling' (Pittman, 1986). If, however, some teenage women do not consider contraception to be relevant to them, this strategy is clearly insufficient. Pittman herself recognizes that the 'problem of teenage pregnancy' is one 'that stretches well beyond sex education and contraceptive services.'

A number of studies report that young people have a general dislike of contraception (see the review by Morrison, 1985). In this study, however, women disliked particular contraceptive methods for specific reasons. These reasons were usually to do with concerns abou the effect of contraception on women's health. Yet these specific dislikes of particular contraceptive methods did not generalize to all contraceptives. Relatively few women were in principle negative about contraception.

There were clear differences between older and younger teenagers, with older teenagers being more likely to be trying to become pregnant or to have been using contraception, and with younger women being more likely to have considered it important not to conceive. Older teenagers were more likely than younger teenagers to be married or cohabiting, and marital status was also related to orientation to pregnancy.

Contraceptive use changed over time. Women were less likely to use contraception at the start of sexual relationships than when relationships were well established. So although women who had wanted to become pregnant seemed different from the rest of the sample at conception, their sexual careers had often followed similar paths, and only chance had prevented most from conceiving earlier. Women's reasons for becoming pregnant are more complex than stereotypes that they become pregnant through ignorance or for material gain would suggest.

Once they realized that they were pregnant, those who felt pleased to be pregnant and those who felt unhappy about it were roughly evenly divided. Most women's parents and their male partners were not initially pleased that they were pregnant. The upset generated by news of the pregnancy was usually less if women were married, and if they were in their late, rather than early teens. Most women declared themselves to be opposed to abortion, and only a minority had considered having an abortion. Even fewer considered having their child adopted although less opposition was expressed to adoption than to abortion.

Over the course of the pregnancy women and significant people in their social networks gradually became more enthusiastic about the child to be born. In late pregnancy only one woman (the only woman to be thrown out of her home by her parents) said that there was nothing positive about being pregnant. Yet even she was looking forward to having her child. By the time they were six months pregnant the majority of women were attending antenatal clinics regularly even though most did not enjoy their clinic visits.

4

Men and Marriage

In Britain and the USA single motherhood has become progressively more common over the last 20 years. In both countries it is now normative for teenage women to be single when they give birth. The most common reactions to this trend toward single motherhood are consternation and concern.

> Moreover teenage motherhood is associated with illegitimate births . . . and this in turn is associated with all kinds of deprivation. (Simms and Smith, 1986, p. 2)

> These trends are of concern because early parenthood and illegitimacy are associated with lower educational and occupational attainment, marital instability, closer spacing of subsequent children, larger completed family size, and poorer mental and physical health of the mother and child. (Robbins et al., 1985, p. 567)

In his 17 year follow up of mainly black mothers who had given birth when they were 17 years old, Furstenberg et al., (1987) found that less than a sixth (14%) had never had a marital or cohabiting relationship which lasted at least six months. Only 16% were, however, married to the father of their child when that child reached 17. Simms and Smith (1986) suggest that 'the condition of being "separated" . . . may not necessarily be a permanent one' (p. 50) since two of the four women in their study who were separated soon after birth had reunited with their husbands a year later.

The recording of marital status at one point (birth) presents a static picture of a status which is dynamic for many people. Most women do marry at some time and so it is likely that teenagers who are single when they give birth will marry at some later date. Conversely teenagers who marry have high rates of divorce and are likely to remarry later. Perhaps more importantly, cohabitation is not recorded at registration of birth and so there are no accurate records of the proportion of teenage women who are living with their children's fathers. Furthermore we do not know why there have been such dramatic increases in rates of single motherhood in most age groups, but particularly to the under 20s.

This chapter aims to provide basic information about changes in women's marital status during pregnancy and over the first two years of their children's lives. It also discusses possible reasons for increases in single parenthood of mothers under 20. It does so by describing the characteristics of men who father children with teenage women. It then documents changes in the marital status of women interviewed in the Thomas Coram study. Young women's professed views about men and marriage are also discussed. It is argued that women's negative feelings about marriage are partly responsible for the reduction in marriage rates in mothers under 20, but that marriages are not likely to occur if male partners are unable to make adequate economic contributions to their households. The relationship between marital status, emotional support and social support are discussed in the following two chapters, which also discuss reasons for relationships either ending or being stressful.

The male partners of mothers under 20

More has been written about fatherhood than is generally acknowledged by writers on fatherhood (Lewis and O'Brien, 1987) but relatively little is known about the male partners of women who become mothers before they are 20 years of age. There have, however, been studies of or which have included male partners in both Britain and the USA (for example Simms and Smith, 1986; Elster and Lamb, 1986; Bolton and Belsky, 1986).

Most children born to mothers who are under 20 years of age are fathered by men who are slightly older than the women. In Britain in 1980 four-fifths of all married teenage women who gave birth had male partners who were over 20 years of age. Most of these male partners (three-fifths) were aged 20–24 years. Only one-fifth of married mothers under 20 had male partners who were over 25 years of age (OPCS, 1983).

Married women who are under 20 are a minority of the under 20s. In 1986 only 2% of teenage women were married (cf. 0.6% of teenage men; OPCS, 1988). Complete official figures for the male partners of single mothers under 20 years of age are not available. But Simms and Smith (1986) found that four-fifths of the male partners of women in their nationally representative sample of mothers under 20 were at least 20 years old. Single mothers of any age group are now more likely to register their children's birth jointly with their children's fathers than to register them alone. A greater proportion of the male partners of women who are in their teenage years are older than them compared with the male partners of older women. For example, two-thirds of fathers who jointly registered their children's births with single mothers under 20 in 1986 were aged 20 or over. Less than a half of women aged 20–24, however, had male partners who were in an older age group (OPCS, 1987).

In the Thomas Coram study over half women's male partners were 21 years old or more at birth (see table 4.1). They ranged in age from 16 to 38 with the most common ages being 20 and 21 years. More than seven in every ten were over 20. Women who were aged 19 were more likely than any of the other age groups to have male partners who were in their late 20s or in their 30s. But the only 17 year old who was married at conception had a male partner who was 26 years old, and a single 16 year old had, for two years, been having a relationship with a 38 year old male partner. Women who were single at conception were as likely to be having relationships with older men who were in their late 20s and 30s as were married women.

Table 4.1 Age of women's male partners by women's ages in pregnancy[a]

	Male partners' ages									
	17	18	19	20	21	22	23	24	25	26+
Women's ages										
16	0	2	3	2	1	0	0	0	0	1
17	2	3	4	3	0	2	1	1	0	1
18	1	2	4	5	1	3	2	2	2	1
19	0	0	1	3	4	3	4	3	1	8
Total	3	7	12	13	6	8	7	6	3	11
										(N=79)
% of total	(4%)	(9%)	(15%)	(17%)	(8%)	(10%)	(9%)	(8%)	(4%)	(14%)

[a] Three women did not know their children's fathers' ages

In the USA the male partners of mothers under 20 are more likely to themselves be under 20 than is the case in Britain. This may be because a greater proportion of teenage mothers in the USA are under 18 years old than is the case in Britain (Jones et al., 1986). Male partners are still, however, more likely to be over than under 20. Just under 40% of children born to USA teenage women are fathered by teenage men (Elster and Lamb, 1986).

The majority of male partners of women who become mothers before they are 20 come from similar backgrounds to the women they impregnate. Simms and Smith (1986) found that male partners tended to come from disproportionately large families of origin (two-thirds had three or more siblings); the majority (four-fifths) were from the working classes. A third of them had mothers who had themselves been teenagers when they had their first child. They were also one-and-a-half times more likely to be unemployed than men in their age group: 12% of the Simms and Smith's fathers were unemployed at the time of interview. Most (87%) had manual occupations.

The male partners of women in the Thomas Coram Research Unit study of 16–19 year old mothers also came from similar backgrounds to those of the women themselves. A third of them had four or more siblings. Two-fifths were unemployed during the women's pregnancies. The fact that many more of our sample were unemployed than Simms and Smith's study reflects cohort effects (because youth unemployment increased dramatically between 1979 when their study was done and 1983/4 when this study was done) and possible area effects (since the Thomas Coram study was a local one and the Simms and Smith study was a nationally representative one). Where male partners had been employed, their usual occupations were mainly in skilled and unskilled manual work. A similar picture emerges from American work on fathers who are under 20 years of age (Lamb, 1987).

Overall then, the fathers of children born to teenage women are more likely to be over than under 20. Yet because they have high rates of unemployment a substantial minority are unlikely to be able to make material provision for their children or children's mothers.

The marital career over time

Most women do not marry in their teenage years. But women who become mothers before they are 20 are more likely than their childless age peers to marry in their teens. When they gave birth in 1983 and 1984, a third of women in the Thomas Coram sample were married, compared with 3% of women in their age group. Within the under 20 age group marriage is age related, so that 19 year olds are more likely to be married than any other age group of teenagers (Simms and Smith, 1986). No 16 year olds in the Thomas Coram study were married when they gave birth, while more than two-fifths (44%) of 19 year olds were.

Trends in marriage and cohabitation

DURING PREGNANCY Over the course of pregnancy there were two noticeable trends in women's marital careers. Firstly there were increases in the numbers of women married or cohabiting (see table 4.2). At conception a fifth of the sample (22%, 17) had been married, and a tenth (11%, 9) cohabiting. By late pregnancy a third (33%, 26) were married. The numbers of women cohabiting stayed the same between conception and birth, but in fact three (4%) started to cohabit in pregnancy (three had moved from cohabitation to marriage over the same period).

The second notable trend during pregnancy was for relationships with male partners to end. While only two of the women interviewed in late pregnancy had had no relationship with their child's father

Table 4.2 Change in women's relationships between conception and late pregnancy

Relationship	At conception	In late pregnancy
No relationship	2 (3%)	17 (22%)
'Visiting' relationship	51 (64%)	27 (34%)
Cohabitation	9 (11%)	9 (11%)
Marriage	17 (22%)	26 (33%)
Totals	79 (100%)	79 (100%)

when they became pregnant, a further 15 (making 22% altogether) relationships ended before birth.

AFTER BIRTH Attrition was relatively high in the Thomas Coram study. Information on changes in the relationships of some women who were given lengthy interviews in late pregnancy is not, therefore, available. Conversely information on changes in relationships is available for some women from whom only basic information was collected in pregnancy. It may be that women who were interviewed 21 months after birth may have been those from the original samples (long interview and short interview) who were most likely to continue having relationships with their children's fathers. For example, one woman who continually deferred the 21 month interview had moved away from her husband, and another who had left her own council flat to her child's father and had not left a forwarding address, did so in order to get away from her cohabitee. Nevertheless the relationships of women who were sucessfully seen underwent a number of changes in the first two years after birth.

Table 4.3 shows the various sorts of changes that occurred in

Table 4.3 Patterns of relationships from conception to 21 months

Pattern	Age: 16	17	18	19	Total	% of total
M throughout	–	1	4	11	16	(24%)
C throughout	–	1	–	1	2	(3%)
S throughout	6	3	6	4	19	(28%)
S–M	1	4	2	2	9	(13%)
S–C	–	3	2	4	9	(13%)
C–M	–	–	1	–	1	(1%)
C–S	–	2	1	1	4	(6%)
S–C–S	–	2	–	1	3	(4%)
S–M–S–M	–	1	–	–	1	(1%)
C–S–C	–	–	1	–	1	(1%)
C–M–S–C	–	–	1	–	1	(1%)
C–M–S–M	–	–	–	1	1	(1)%
S–C–M–S	–	1	–	–	1	(1%)
Total	7	18	18	25	68	(100%)

Key: M = married; S = single; C = co-habiting; – = change to
Note that the category 'single' includes women who are in relationships with male partners and women who are not.

women's relationships with their male partners in the two years after birth. Between birth and when their children were a year old, one-sixth experienced changes in their relationships with their male partners, and over the following year a fifth did. Thirteen patterns of relationship were evident. Three women who were cohabiting at 21 months (and one who had previously cohabited) were semi-cohabiting. They were a 17, an 18 and a 19 year old who had their own flats where their male partners (in one case not the child's father) regularly stayed some nights a week and contributed to the household as if he were resident when there.

Twenty-one months after birth a minority of cohabiting or married women reported that their relationships with male partners were either troubled or had ended. Seven women who had been in cohabiting relationships at some time were no longer in them at 21 months. Two married women separated from their husbands after birth and were still separated when interviewed for the last time at 21 months. One was 17 and the other 18 at birth. The 18 year old later started cohabiting with her husband's stepbrother.

When relationships went through difficult phases cohabiting and marital relationships sometimes ended temporarily. For example, one woman stopped cohabiting with her child's father during pregnancy when she still lived in her parents' home. Later, however, when she was rehoused by the council she agreed to let him live with her in her own flat in her child's second year. Similarly two married women (one 17 and one 19 at birth) allowed their husbands to return to the marital home after short separations. Neither of these women had been married when they conceived.

None of the women who married before they were pregnant really separated in the first two years after birth. Their relationships were not, however, necessarily stronger or happier than those of women who married after conception or after birth. One woman (18 at birth) had packed up and gone back to her parents for a day when her child was a year old. Another two had been unhappy in their marriages and had been thinking of separating since birth, but had not done so. At least one other wanted to leave her husband, but did not have sufficient money to make this possible. Several women expressed dissatisfaction with their marriages or cohabitations. In one case a 17 year old was unsuccessfully trying to persuade her cohabitee to leave their home.

Although it was not uncommon for women to move into or (more rarely) out of cohabitation and marriage, it was more usual for them to remain in the marital status they had been in at conception.

Overall more than half the women (55%) had not changed their marital status between conception and 21 months after birth. But more than two-fifths (45%) had had at least one change in their relationships with their children's father. These changes were both into and out of cohabitations and marriages as well as out of relationships altogether. The lability of women's relationships is not surprising since marriage is still a popular enough institution for most people to marry at some time, and marriage (and presumably cohabitations) contracted early are less likely to last (Rimmer, 1981).

Reasons for being single, cohabiting or marrying

In order to try to explain why many women's relationships with male partners were not static, the rest of the chapter will focus on the nature of these relationships, women's feelings about men and marriage, and the circumstances in which marriages have and have not occurred.

Attitudes to men and marriage

Table 4.4 shows that women were not uniform in their views about the advantages and disadvantages of marriage for women, but expressed three sorts of views. More than a quarter of those asked in late pregnancy about advantages and disadvantages of marriage were unequivocally negative about marriage, seeing it as having only disadvantages for women. A second group of comparable size (just under a quarter) thought that there were only advantages for women, but the largest group (nearly two-fifths) did not think of marriage in terms of advantages or disadvantages to be gained and said either that they could think of none, or that there

Table 4.4 Reported advantages/disadvantages of marriage for women

Neither advantages nor disadvantages	36%	
Advantages only	23%	
Disadvantages only	26%	
Both	12%	
Undecided	3%	(N=69)

were neither advantages nor disadvantages for women.

By way of contrast women were more likely to think that men benefited from marriage (table 4.5). A third thought that there were only advantages in marriage for men, and only 7% of women thought that men gained only disadvantages from marriage. Over 40% could think of neither advantages nor disadvantages in marriage for men. Asked which partner gets the better deal from marriage, 40% of women said that men and women benefited equally. However nearly as many again said that men benefited more, while only 7% thought that women benefitted more. These accounts fit with Lees' (1986) findings that young women expressed mostly negative views about marriage.

The majority of women who were already married (82%, 18) felt that marriage had been a good idea for them at the time they married. One (4%) felt that marriage would have been a good idea for her if she had left it until later, but three (14%) were not sure whether marriage would ever have been a good idea for them. None of them said that it would definitely never have been a good idea for them to marry. Women who were cohabiting were no more likely to think that marriage would ever be a good idea for them than were single women.

Table 4.5 Reported advantages/disadvantages of marriage for men

Neither advantages nor disadvantages	32%	
Advantages only	34%	
Disadvantages only	7%	
Both	18%	
Undecided	9%	(N=68)

Although married women were unlikely to say that marriage was disadvantageous to women when they were asked directly, their accounts often highlighted the costs of marriage for women and the benefits for men. The following woman, for example, had said that there were only advantages for women in marriage.

Q.–What are the advantages of marriage for women?
A–They [women] feel sort of, they, maybe you feel you've got someone to rely on, you've got someone that's there, you've always got someone to turn to, that's with you. So, it's not very nice at first having to clean and wash and that, but you've always got someone that's there . . .
Q–What about advantages for men?

A–They got someone to cook and clean and I think they rely on you
and that's their benefit, they rely on you, and they think you're their
slave. Well they don't think you're their slave, but they rely on you
to wash and that, so they really haven't got any worries, I don't think.
That's it, you've got to wash and make the dinner and that's hard
luck if you don't because I can't.
(17 year old married woman who became pregnant in order to be allowed to
marry; husband present for the interview)

The costs to women and benefits to men described by this respondent were identified by many women. Women's role in marriage
was perceived to entail drudgery, while men were perceived to have
a more relaxed time through women's hard work. If they were lucky,
women could expect support (material and emotional) and security
from the marriage.

Men know they have to go out to work and the women are looking
after them. Especially in Jewish life the women are giving a lot more
– I don't mean to say that the men don't give to the women – but the
women are looking after the men. But he on the other hand gives
other things – like support. (19 year old married woman)

Someone to depend on. Like me before I'd get paid, but then half
way through the month my money would run out and I'd have
nowhere to turn. But now I'm married and I'm happy giving my
money to my husband and he'll deal with it. And every worry you've
got you share. You've got someone there. (18 year old married woman)

The price of such security in marriage was often considered to be
restrictions on women's, but not men's, personal freedom. Cohabitation was perceived to be qualitatively different from marriage in
this respect. Women who were cohabiting (as well as single women)
felt that marriage would be more restrictive than 'just living together'.

It ties you really if you're married. Like I can get up and just go to
me mum's, but if you're married you've got to explain yourself. (16
year old cohabitee)

They can't go out with their friends because their husbands don't like
it. (16 year old single woman living with parents)

Boulton (1983) suggests that it is having children, not marriage,
which restricts women's freedom relative to men's. When they were
pregnant, however, women in this study were more likely to say

that marriage would curtail their freedom than that children would.

Despite its reportedly restrictive nature, marriage was not perceived to guarantee men's fidelity or that relationships would last.

> I mean I've always been told that a man's meant to be faithful to you if you're married and that . . . I feel sorry for some of these women who are married and then their husband's – he's no good and that, and I don't think it's any better for women who are married. I think it's just luck if you stay together. (19 year old cohabiting woman)

It was because marriage was considered to entail many disadvantages for women that nearly a third (18) of those who had an opinion about whether or not marriage was a good idea for women said that they considered women to be generally better off not married. More than a third (21) felt that it depended on the individual relationship whether marriage was a good idea for women. Just over a quarter (16) felt that marriage was, in general, a good idea for women.

It is not unusual for teenage women to express negative views about men and marriage. In a study of 100 women aged 15 and 16 years done in 1980, Sue Lees (1986) found predominantly negative reactions to the idea of marriage and the burdens it imposes on women. Despite their negative views, however, most of Sue Lees' respondents expected that they would marry at some time in the future.

Table 4.6 shows that more than half the women in the Thomas Coram study who were either single or cohabiting in pregnancy (56%) said that marriage would be a good idea for them in the future. More than two-fifths of women who thought that it would be a good idea for them to marry at some point considered that they would ideally like to marry in their mid 20s, while a third thought that somewhere between the mid 20s and later would be preferable.

Table 4.6 Single and cohabiting women's intention to marry[a]

Never intend to marry	24%	
Not sure if they will marry	20%	
Not sure when	14%	
Before 20	12%	
Early 20s	12%	
Mid 20s	4%	
Late 20s or older	14%	(N=50)

[a] Data for three single women are not available

The rest were undecided about the ideal timing of marriage.

A fifth of those who were neither married nor cohabiting were undecided about whether marriage would ever be a good idea for them. But a quarter were adamant that they would never marry. This was for the reasons already described: that they don't want to service men's needs and that they do not want their freedom to be restricted. It is also, however, because they have seen other people's marriages, (parents, other relatives and friends) end in acrimony: 35% (28) of the women in the study had parents who had separated. Some women had been deeply affected by this.

> I've seen what happened to my parents and I wouldn't want that to happen to me. (18 year old single woman)

> The majority of people I know haven't got nothing out of it [marriage] ... To me I could never get married because I've sat down and watched my mum and dad's marriage fall apart and I wouldn't like to go through that myself ... I mean they [men] come home, find the kitchen clean, food waiting ... They get a little slave. (16 year old single woman)

Griffin (1985) suggests that however anti-marriage young women are the pressures of 'compulsory heterosexuality' are likely to result in their eventual marriage or cohabitation. Single women in the Thomas Coram study who did not want to get married did not necessarily rule out cohabitation for themselves. Fifteen (about a third) of the single women said that they would consider living with their child's father without marriage being a future consideration. A further two women said they would consider living with a man other than their child's father on the same terms. There can be a further mismatch between attitudes to marriage and later marital status. Mansfield and Collard (1988) found that some women reported that they had married earlier than they had anticipated they would.

> Yet a feeling of unrealised intention is indicated by the fact that the great majority of those who gave an ideal age range (93 per cent of men and 88 per cent of women) had relinquished their freedom prematurely – indeed, a quarter of women had married as much as five years or more before their ideal age. (Mansfield and Collard, 1988, p. 58)

The majority of single women subscribed to the view that children should live with both their mothers and fathers: 80% (37) said that it was better for mothers to live with their child's father, while only two women (both 17 year olds) thought it was better for them not to, and only six (13%) thought that whether it was a good idea or not depended on circumstances.

In late pregnancy the picture that emerged was one in which most women stressed negative aspects of marriage for women. Yet most single women thought they would marry at some time. Even if they were adamant about not marrying, many women expected that they would cohabit in the future. Most women held normative views about children being reared in households with both parents.

As we have already seen there were enormous changes in women's marital status over the two-and-a-half years from conception until their children were 21 months. To some extent the variability in women's marital status was a consequence of the diversity of their views. Women who were sure that they did not want to marry could refuse to do so, but obviously simply being in favour of marriage could not guarantee that marriage would take place.

> I get a bit depressed sometimes. Especially as all my friends are pregnant. And they're all sort of settled with someone. They're either married or they're settled with someone, and I feel a bit sort of left out you know . . . Because like – I mean I know women because like they've got a couple of kids and they still like – cos to me – I really want to get married, and they still manage to sort of find someone, whereas I tend to get blokes who either don't wanna know because you've got a child, or they think you're really easy because you've got a baby . . . You have to be so careful – like whenever I meet someone I always think will they be good to Robert . . . (woman who was 18 years old at birth speaking 21 months later when she was having a relationship with a married man)

Reasons for marrying

Since many women are negative about men and marriage, why had some women married before pregnancy, and why did additional women marry during pregnancy and after the birth?

Women did not mention love as a reason for marriage, but they may have taken it for granted that in current western societies love is the most common and acceptable reason for marrying. Four general reasons (which were not mutually exclusive) for marrying were evident and these applied both to women who married before they conceived and those who married later. As will become apparent later, no one said that pregnancy or having a child was their primary motive for marrying.

1. NORMATIVE EXPECTATIONS Some women had always expected, and/or been expected to marry early. This was sometimes because early marriage was usual in the women's social network. Women from social classes IV and V are more likely to marry in their teenage years than women from social classes I and II (CSO, 1988). Additionally a few women mentioned that there were cultural reasons for their early marriage.

> Like I said, I got married at 16, and when I left [school] at 15 I had in mind I'll be getting married at 16. (19 year old)

> I mean Turkish girls ... they have to be married before they *are* ... 22 or something like that. (19 year old)

> I always wanted to get married at about 18, 19 and to have children straight then – once you get married. (19 year old)

2. HAVING A FAMILIAR AND RELIABLE PARTNER Some women had known their boyfriends for some time and felt that they would be reliable marriage partners. The following respondent had cohabited with her partner from 15 years (at her parents' home) and married at 16 years.

> We don't argue over anything ... It's great really. That's why I'm so happy about it ... If I weren't so sure about it ... that I'm gonna be with him for the rest of my life, I wouldn't have got pregnant ... (17 year old)

3. IN ORDER TO IMPROVE THEIR CIRCUMSTANCES Women who married could legitimately leave home with their parents' blessing. Marriage could also be an act of defiance against parents who were attempting to break up a relationship.

> If I had a choice I would have been brought up differently to start with which probably meant I wouldn't have got married so young because I would have been able to have a *proper* relationship. I wouldn't have wanted to get married so quick. Well I mean it could have changed the whole of me life really ... (18 year old)

> When we got married me and my husband forged the signatures of

my mum and dad because I was under age. We just went and got married. His mum never really liked me. We're second cousins, me and my husband, and she used to say that you'll have mental children and things like that, so ... the more she tried to push us apart, the more we got closer together ... (19 year old who married at 17 years; second interview)

There were some women who did not mention that they married for such explicitly instrumental reasons who may well have married at least partly in order to improve their circumstances. The following respondent met her husband and started cohabiting with him immediately.

Well my husband took me from a shed. 'Cos I was living in a shed. That's how we met ... Then started living with him (after a week in the shed) and we just got closer and closer. It was on the ... third day we got engaged [and married three months later when R was three months pregnant]. (19 year old)

4. A MORE ATTRACTIVE PROPOSITION THAN BORING JOBS

We knew one day we would get married. I think I am more for being a mother to a family than I am to working. (18 year old)

Campbell (1984) suggested that marriage and/or motherhood provide alternatives to employment for many young working class women. It was rare, however, for women to suggest that they perceived marriage to provide an alternative to an employment career.

On the whole parents approved of marriage contracted before conception began. The exceptions were the woman who forged her parents signature, one who married a man she did not know and a woman who married at 16 in order to leave home as soon as possible. In the first case the parents never gave their consent, but in the other two cases they reluctantly gave their consent.

It was very serious. My father went mad, he wouldn't talk to me. He said to me, 'you're just marrying someone you don't know. How can you live a life with him? Probably you'll get divorced the second month.' And about going to Italy – he didn't like it. But because it would make me happy they let me go [to get married there]. But they were really upset. (17 year old)

Women who married after conception

Women who married after becoming pregnant expressed reasons for marrying which were similar to those who married before conception. This section discusses who they were and their circumstances in order to see whether they were different from those who married without being pregnant.

Once pregnant, dominant ideological assumptions about the correct situation in which to have children make single women subject to social disapproval. It might be expected, therefore, that parents would attempt to pressurize their daughters into marriage. In this study, however, few women reported that any pressure to marry had been put on them.

Fifteen per cent of the women who had been single when they became pregnant reported that someone (usually, but not always, parents) had put pressure on them to marry before they gave birth. However this pressure was resisted when women did not want to marry.

> My aunts wanted us to get married before [the baby was born] and they were literally trying to force us into marriage, but I didn't want it and he didn't want it so it was causing a bit of friction between us but we got that sorted out, and we just did what we wanted and not what they wanted us to do. (18 year old who had been engaged before the pregnancy anyway)

Nine women interviewed in pregnancy married after becoming pregnant. Three of them had been cohabiting already, and none of them felt that they had married because other people had forced them to. All except one claimed that they had been intending to marry in any case, and that pregnancy had only brought an acceleration of their plans.

> I regret it at times, thinking, we could have had our own place by now, or we could have had the wedding we wanted, a bigger wedding. But it's a case of having to. We've got a child coming, which we're over the moon about . . . But I do sometimes think it could have been better than this. (18 year old)

> Everything just happened so quickly. We did have plans for what we were going to do . . . we weren't definitely going to marry until next year, and children were never even talked about. And instead everything just happened all together. (18 year old)

In the one instance where there had been no plans for marriage prior to conception, a grandmother (with whom the woman was living) clearly put pressure on her to marry. The respondent claimed that she had wanted to get married anyway.

> So they sat me down, and my nan pushed into my hand this wedding ring and said 'you can borrow my ring, but you're getting married aren't you?' Said 'we're not trying to push you. It's up to you what you do, but you are getting married?' Which I think I would like to do anyway but I wasn't forced to. I think they would like us to. Personally I preferred to. (17 year old)

Although pressure to marry was almost exclusively applied on women by older relatives, pregnancy could be used as a means of resisting parental power to prevent under 18s from marrying. One woman reported that she and her boyfriend had wanted to have a child anyway. They realized that their parents would not want them to have a child while single and, therefore, deliberately timed her pregnancy for when she was 17 in an attempt to force her parents to allow her to marry.

Marriage after birth

Two women married after birth, but before their children were six months old. One of these women had cohabited with the child's father from before conception. She left him shortly before she gave birth, but married him when their son was three months old. She reported that she had married only for the baby's sake and at her husband's insistence. She was not happy with the relationship.

> I think maybe we'll stay together another couple of years, but then I think that will be it. (18 year old)

The other woman who married before the second interview married five-and-a-half months after the birth. Her husband is Protestant and she is Catholic. Religion is significant because both are from Northern Ireland, and the woman's mother has not spoken to her since she started having a relationship with her husband.

> We were thinking that if we got married that would make her [respondent's mother] feel better. But she wasn't pleased with it. (19 year old)

Three further women married within 21 months of the birth. One (a 17 year old) had begun to cohabit in late pregnancy and married when the baby was nine months old. They had intended to marry at some time. Another woman (a 16 year old) married a boyfriend she had known before she had a relationship with her child's father. The third woman (a 19 year old) also married when her child was one year old because she was pregnant for a second time (by a new boyfriend) and felt that it would be totally unacceptable to her family for her to have two children while single.

One woman who had planned to marry and got as far as setting a date and starting preparations, had to cancel the wedding because her mother-in-law to be became ill. She then semi-cohabited with her child's father instead.

Economic reasons associated with marriage or cohabitation

Women's perceptions of their own reasons for marrying are important to an understanding of what marriage means for them. Yet post hoc rationalizations of reasons for marriage do not provide a complete picture of why marriages occurred. Not surprisingly nobody mentioned economic reasons for marrying. Economic considerations used to be considered the most sensible reasons for contracting marriage, but love has replaced economics as the most publicly accepted foundation for marriage (Gittins, 1986; Mansfield and Collard, 1988). Yet if those who married prior to conception are compared with those who did not, there are definite economic differences between them.

Twenty three per cent of male partners who were either married or cohabiting were unemployed, while for the whole sample 40% of the male partners were unemployed. Single women's partners were therefore more likely to be unemployed than either married or cohabiting couples.

The finding that single mothers under twenty tend to be 'welfare dependent' is often taken as evidence that marriage is crucial if young women are to make adequate financial provision for their children. What seems to be the case in this study, however, is that couples follow the normatively prescribed sequence of marriage-then-conception only if their partners can fulfil the economic functions that husbands are traditionally supposed to. Many writers now link high rates of male unemployment with low rates of marriage and cohabitation (Willis, 1984; Pilcher and Williamson, 1988; Wilson and Neckerman, 1987; Daly, 1989).

The absolute shortage of men who earn enough to support families means that in many communities the primary route off welfare – marriage to a man with a job – is out of reach for a growing percentage of women.

For a long time this phenomenon has been apparent in rural America, where the collapse of the farm economy left many young men with no means to earn a living. In these communities there has been a striking increase in teenage pregnancies outside marriage and in dependence on welfare. (Daly, 1989, p. 14)

The group of 17 women who married before they became pregnant were financially better off than other groups in the sample including those who married after conception or after birth. Most (14) of the husbands in this group were employed full time, and some of the wives had been employed before pregnancy. Only three of these 17 couples were living with kin. It was only in this group that any couples were homeowners (6). All other women were either housed by the council or by relatives (usually parents). Couples who were buying their own houses all had husbands whose take home pay was high in comparison with that of other male partners in our study (£62–£250 per week, with a mean of £111). This compares with a range of £38–£150 (with a mean of £67) for the male partners of the rest of the sample.

Nine women were cohabiting in late pregnancy, and seven of their male partners were employed. At first sight they seem to be relatively affluent. Only one cohabiting couple was living with kin (the rest were renting flats) and three men were bringing home over. £100 per week. However two of these relatively well paid men had only started employment during the woman's pregnancy. The other man in this group was married to someone else and £40 of his £109 take home pay went on mortgage and maintenance for his other family. Three other employed cohabiting men took home £38, £50 and £55 per week, and so were not in a position to support a mortgage. The other employed man had been unemployed for a year and, in a determined bid to earn some money, had taken a job in Libya after his partner became pregnant. He was not making a financial contribution to his partner.

One women in the cohabiting group explicitly said that she was cohabiting without the DHSS's knowledge so that both she and her cohabitee would continue to receive supplementary benefit. She was already having difficulty making ends meet and did not feel that she could manage on less money. In that sense the DHSS cohabitation rule does provide a disincentive for women to cohabit officially (or to marry) if male partners are not earning well. Supplementary benefit for a couple was rather less than it was for two single individuals (Wilson, 1987), but the replacement of supplementary benefit by income support in the 1988 reforms in British social security legislation apparently has not improved this situation. According to the Maternity Alliance (1989) it has instead served to worsen the financial position of many parents, particularly those who are under 20.

Summary

A minority of women in the Thomas Coram study were married or cohabiting when they conceived. But some women's marital status changed over the course of the pregnancy and after birth. Some single women married, or began to cohabit, while a minority of cohabiting or married women moved into single or separated status. Relationships with male partners did not always fit neatly into the three categories, married, cohabiting or single. In pregnancy, for example, a few married women were not living with their husbands because they had no homes of their own. Later a couple of women briefly separated from their husbands. Over the two years of the Thomas Coram study some women moved into and out of a state which can best be described as 'semi-cohabitation', regularly living with their male partners for only part of each week.

It seems likely that the reduction in rates of marriage to mothers who are under 20 years of age partly results from the negative attitudes towards men and marriage that many women (more than a quarter of the sample) held. But this is not a complete answer, since some married women felt that men benefit from marriage more than women do. Yet most married women said that marriage had been a good idea for them. It is possible that married women could not admit that they may have made a mistake in marrying early, but their accounts suggested that many were pleased to be married.

It was possible to identify four main reasons for marrying. These were: normative expectations that they should marry early, having had a satisfactory period of courtship, for instrumental reasons (such as to leave home) and because marriage and motherhood had always been considered the most important careers women could have.

Women did not mention economic reasons for marrying, but there was some evidence that women who married before they were pregnant were more likely to have male partners who were relatively affluent (in comparison with the rest of the sample) than women who married later or who did not marry. In general the male partners of women in the sample came from similar backgrounds to the women themselves. They came from working class families which were larger than average, and had experienced higher than average levels of unemployment. Although relatively few women were married it seems possible that part of the reason for the decline in marriage rates in this age group may be a consequence of young men's poor economic circumstances.

5

Social Networks and Emotional Support

The previous chapter discussed women's relationships with their male partners over the first two years of their children's lives. But male partners were not, of course, the only people who were important in women's lives. A lot of literature on young women suggests that relationships with (almost predominantly female) friends and/or with their own mothers influence their attitudes to all aspects of their lives, including relationships with men, and attitudes to sex, contraception, abortion, etc. (McRobbie, 1978; Griffin, 1985; Lees, 1986; Brazzell and Acock, 1988).

Relatively little is known about the nature of young women's friendships. However school seems to be an important focus for young working class women's friendships, being where many friendships are formed and maintained. But when women start having relationships with young men, friendships with other young women can be affected adversely. Griffin (1985) found that when women started having regular boyfriends, they gradually lost touch with ('deffed out') their female friends, often at their boyfriends' insistence. Similarly McRobbie (in prep.) found that after leaving school young women who were unemployed would congregate on street corners. However their friendship groups gradually dissolved as they began to have boyfriends. Female friendships thus usually seem to be transient, generally kept up only until relationships with boyfriends were established.

Few women in the Thomas Coram study were still at school when they conceived, and all except two were in established relationships with their children's fathers when they gave birth. Most were not, therefore, in an institution which could facilitate and structure their friendships. In addition, they generally had exclusive relationships with one male partner, and so were likely to see more of his friends than of their own (Lees, 1986).

Only 3 per cent of women who are under 20 years of age give birth before they are 20 (OPCS, 1988). They are unusual among their age peers and it may be the case that mothers who are under 20 years of age are more likely to have fewer relationships with peers than young women who are childfree.

Women's relationships with their own mothers have also been found to influence their attitudes to contraception, abortion and marriage and were an important source of support after childbirth (Skinner, 1986; Brazzell and Acock, 1988; Boulton, 1983). But just how mother–daughter relationships affect young women's attitudes, feelings and behaviours is not well established (Brazzell and Acock, 1988). Relationships with fathers are generally not discussed in literature on young women (see Cunningham-Burley's, 1985, article on how new grandfathers are often reluctant to discuss grand-fatherhood, but still consider it to be important).

Social support is now generally accepted to be important in peo-ple's lives (Riley and Eckenrode, 1986; Belle, 1982). Social support will be the subject of this chapter and the one which follows. This chapter establishes the potential pool of people on whom respondents could theoretically call for support and considers women's attitudes to emotional support, and who, if anyone, pro-vided them with emotional support. The following chapter will focus on support which is more practical, namely childcare and material support.

Social networks

Women's social and support networks were constructed in two ways. Firstly, women were asked with which individuals they were in regular (at least monthly) contact, and if any of those individuals were, independently of the respondent, in regular contact with any other. Each person mentioned was presumed to have a social tie with the respondent. Recording the interlinkages between people in women's social networks gave a measure of interconnectedness or density of networks. Literature on social support suggests that the speed at which support can be mobilized, help sought, and the types of support available to an individual are influenced by the structure of the support networks women have (Gottlieb, 1981). If, for example, someone is part of a tightly knit, 'solidary' network, support can be mobilized quickly and efficiently during times of crisis, because news that help and/or sympathy are required spreads quickly among network members. For people who control few resources, like most mothers under 20 years of age, such networks are reported to enable the conservation and control of resources. At the same time such tightly knit networks may be limited in their ability to mobilize sources of support which are external to the networks (Wellman, 1981). It may also be that such tightly knit networks require individuals to shoulder more responsibilities towards network members than do sparsely knit, multiple networks (which give access to a variety of resources, but cannot provide orchestrated support).

Later on in the interviews women were asked a range of questions about:

- which individuals had provided them with particular sorts of support;
- who (if anyone) they felt they could or would ask for help with specific problems;
- whether they had either asked for, or been offered such help within the last year, and what the outcome of that request or proffer had been.

The above questions were not asked directly following questions about social networks. Instead they were asked in relation to particular issues.

It was therefore possible to establish whether women's social contacts mostly knew each other or were unconnected individuals; which individuals provided women with which sorts of support; and whether social contacts tended to be supportive or not. In addition it was possible to see whether social networks were relatively stable entities, or whether they changed over time, perhaps as residence changed, and whether the people women saw most frequently were necessarily the ones who provided them with support.

Variations in network size

Table 5.1 shows that there was a lot of variation in the number of people women had in their social networks. In late pregnancy this ranged from 2 people (for 1 woman) to 21 people (for 1 woman). The mode was 9 people (regularly seen by 12 women, 16% of

Table 5.1 Network size, linkages and numbers seen weekly

	Range in no. of people in social network	Range in no. of linkages in network	Range in no. of those seen weekly
Pregnancy	2–21	2–67	1–20
6 months	2–26	6–62	0–20
21 months	2–21	3–68	1–18

the sample). The number of interconnections between members of respondents' social networks were also strikingly diverse, varying from 2 (for the woman who regularly saw only two people who were not friends with each other) to 67 (for a woman who had a social network where most people in her social network knew most others).

Women were also asked to indicate with which members of their social networks they were in at least weekly contact. In late pregnancy this ranged from 1 person seen at least weekly (by 1 respondent) to 20 who were seen weekly (by 1 respondent). The mode was for 8 people (seen weekly by 10 respondents, 14% of the sample). Everybody in the study had regular weekly contact with somebody in late pregnancy.

Over the two years of the study the overall numbers of people in the study group's social networks stayed fairly constant. When their children were six months old, the numbers of people respondents claimed to be in at least monthly contact with ranged from 2 (seen by 1 person) to 26 (seen by 1 person); with a mode of 9 (reported by 9 people, 13% of the sample). The number of linkages between people in women's networks ranged from 2 to 62, with no obvious mode. One person was not in regular weekly contact with anyone; the range being from no weekly contacts to 20, with a mode of 4 people seen weekly by 12 respondents (18%).

When the children were 21 months old, the number of monthly contacts ranged from 2 to 21 with a mode of 13 contacts seen by 8 people (12% of the sample). More than half (53%, 35 women) regularly saw more than 10 people each month. The number of linkages ranged from 3 to 68, and the number of weekly contacts from 1 to 18, with a mode of 7.

Viewed as a group the sample social networks were fairly stable, but there were fluctuations in individual social networks. As women's circumstances changed, so too did the number of people in their networks. Most people experienced minor changes (the addition or disappearance of one or two people) in their social networks which, considered for the group as a whole, made little overall difference to network size. Dramatic changes were, however, extremely rare. A woman who experienced a large (and atypical) change in her social network over the course of the study illustrates how much social network contacts were influenced by where women lived.

Jenny was 17 when she gave birth. She had cohabited in a squat with her child's father for a few months before she became pregnant. Throughout her pregnancy she lived with her mother, four of her five siblings, and two of her ex-step father's children. She regularly saw her child's father and a brother who did not live in the family home. The family had moved from the Midlands only the previous year. Jenny had never been to school in London and as yet had no friends (other than her boyfriend). Her social network consisted of eight people, seven of whom were relatives, or step relatives, plus her boyfriend. These individuals were all interconnected, so that there were 36 linkages in her network (see figure 5.1).

When Jenny's son was 12 months, however, her mother moved back to the Midlands. Jenny decided not to go with the rest of the family, and since neither she nor they had a telephone, contact between them was sporadic and infrequent. Jenny went to see them a couple of times, and they had been to see her once (the week before the final interview, 21 months after the birth). Jenny's mother had taken Jenny's son away with them, so that Jenny could find a job, get herself established in it, and organize day care without having responsibility for the daily tasks of childcare*. Jenny's social network now consisted only of her ex-boyfriend (whom she had previously not seen for several months but who, since her mother moved out of the family flat, was now pressing her to allow him to move in) and a new friend she had made. There were no interconnections between these two (see figure 5.1).

Factors which were beyond women's control influenced the structure of their social networks. People around them sometimes moved away (as in the case of Jenny's mother) or the respondents themselves were rehoused. People who stopped being within easy travelling distance often stopped being network members because many

---

* Since Jenny's mother had taken her son to the Midlands just before the final interview, it is unfortunately not known whether Jenny did manage to find a job and then bring her son back to London.

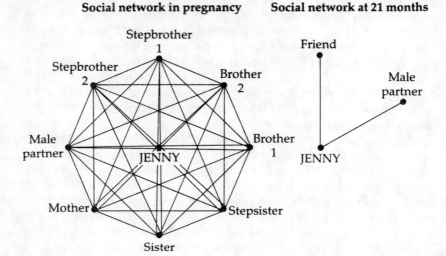

Figure 5.1 Change in Jenny's social network from pregnancy to 21 months after birth

women and many of their network members, could not afford to pay even the cheapest bus and tube fares very often. Where either the respondent or the network member (or both) had no telephones, monthly interactive communication was unlikely. Limited material resources (in the form of telephone ownership, home ownership or access to a wage) therefore diminished women's chances of maintaining continuity in their social networks.

Network size and membership

Some women had social networks which included very few people, while others had networks which had many people in them. Networks which included less than six people were unusual in the study. They are referred to as 'restricted'. It was more usual for women to have networks with ten individuals or more in them. In the following discussion restricted and extensive social networks are discussed.

RESTRICTED SOCIAL NETWORKS AND FELT SUPPORT Few women had networks which included less than six people. At the third contact only eight women (12% of 66) had such restricted networks. There were no dramatic changes from very small networks to large ones over the two years of the study (and only one dramatic change from a large to a small network) but there were fluctuations in the network size of those who had few regular contacts with other people.

For example, Mary had the smallest network size during pregnancy. She was, at the time, in regular contact with two people who were not friends with each other. One of these was a boyfriend she met during pregnancy and was now cohabiting with in bed and breakfast accommodation. The other was her cousin. She saw her father and brother very infrequently, and in late pregnancy was worried that her father would reject her because she was pregnant. Her biological mother lived abroad, and Mary had never lived with her. Her stepmother and father had separated, and since Mary had not got on well with her, they were not in contact. She saw a variety of people in the bed and breakfast hostel, and bumped into old school friends occasionally. She did not seem to mind the restricted nature of her network, or to miss having friends. She said 'Well, from the time I was in primary school I've never had best friends, because I don't think it's worth it.'

By the time her child was a year old, Mary had been rehoused to her own council flat. She was in weekly contact with her father and younger brother (she invariably went to visit them because they never visited her) and saw an aunt regularly. In addition she was also in contact with many of her boyfriend's relatives. There were nine people in her social network. Six months later there were six people in Mary's social network. She no longer saw much of her father because she had started work and found it difficult to fit in visiting him because he lived two bus rides away. Her father, who had slipped a disc, never came to see her, and neither did her younger brother. She also saw fewer of her boyfriend's relatives, but saw people at work, and was in regular contact with a social worker. Her social network had increased in size from pregnancy, when it had been the most restricted in the study, to 21 months, when it was still restricted but no longer the most restricted. Mary's boyfriend and her cousin were the core people in her network and over the two years of the study they were the only people who were continually in her network.

The woman who had the least network members six months after her child's birth was similar to Mary in that the core of her social network was essentially her husband and her brother-in-law. During pregnancy Jenny was in regular contact with eight people, most of whom were relatives. After birth, however, when, having had twins, she was rather less mobile, she saw only the two people mentioned above regularly, and was in intermittent contact with her own family. A year later she had re-established regular contact with some members of her family, and there were seven members in her social network.

Twenty-one months after giving birth Jenny had the least members in her social network (two). The two women with the next smallest networks were in regular contact with three sets of people. Olwen was 18 when she gave birth. She lived with her mother and stepfather (counted as one contact in her social network), and saw two friends regularly. There were no interconnections between the people in her network. In late pregnancy there had been six people in her network. She was then in regular contact with her child's father (with whom she had previously cohabited), she saw a cousin regularly and had four friends she was in regular contact with, two of whom 'pop[ped] round all the time'. After birth, however, she lost contact with two friends (two continued to visit her several times a week), and her relationship with her boyfriend ended. There were thus three contacts in her social network.

Yet Olwen felt that in general she had been given sufficient support. She would have liked more babysitting help, but was satisfied with the support she got from all but the (then) DHSS. Her small network size did not seem to worry her. She said that she sometimes felt lonely, but felt that her social life would be improved if she had a better job and had her 'own place' rather than by simply having more social contacts.

The other woman with only three people in her social network 21 months after the birth was 16 when she gave birth. June had been in council care since she was a year old because her mother could not look after her. Her mother died when she was six years old, and although she had six siblings, they were not brought up in the same institution and did not maintain any meaningful relationships. Her father now lives in the USA. June had a strong relationship with a housemother from the children's home in which she had been brought up, but this 'aunt' had moved to Ireland soon after June became pregnant.

In late pregnancy June was living in a mother and baby home because the staff at the hostel for adolescents in care where she used to live had been 'unpleasant' once they realized she was pregnant.

Her social network consisted solely of her boyfriend (whom she had known for a year) and his father and brother. She was not quite as isolated as she might have been because she had access to help from the staff and use of facilities at the mother and baby home. There were also other young women around who were either pregnant or had young children.

Six months after the birth June was still in the mother and baby home. Her 'aunt' from the children's home had returned from Ireland, and now played a crucial part in providing childcare while June went out in the evenings. June had also started visiting her aunt and two cousins, and had re-established contact with two of her friends. She still saw her boyfriend, but had (that week) told him she wanted to end the relationship because he never took her out. She had stopped visiting his father and brother, but despite that the number of contacts in her social network had increased from three to seven largely unconnected contacts.

During the next year June went to live with a foster mother, with whom she did not get on. She still saw the 'aunt' from her old children's home each week. This 'aunt' often babysat while June went out with her (the aunt's) 18 year old daughter. June saw her child's father infrequently now, but had a new boyfriend she saw regularly. Her contacts with her own aunt and cousins had also become infrequent and irregular. There were, as in late pregnancy, three contacts in her social network, but they were different ones.

Overall June felt that she had received little support from anyone since she became pregnant. She did not feel particularly close to anyone, and had no one to whom she felt she could disclose personal problems. At the same time she said that she liked being on her own, and felt that her social life would be improved if she had her own accommodation.

EXTENSIVE SOCIAL NETWORKS AND FELT SUPPORT Where women had extensive social networks their networks generally included several interconnected members of their family. For example, Chris lived with her mother, stepfather and siblings in late pregnancy. Chris came from a large family. She had three siblings, but her mother had seven siblings, all of whom Chris saw regularly. There were 21 individuals in her social network. Fourteen of them were her own family, and five were her child's father and his family. Only two were girlfriends. Her network was so densely interlinked that there were 60 interconnections in her network. She said, 'We're a very close family . . . We always phone each other, go to each other's houses you know. We're very close.'

When Chris was rehoused 14 months after birth she maintained the family connections so that, although she saw her family less, she was still in more than monthly contact with them (although employed full time). Yet despite the enormous size of her network, there were only four people to whom Chris felt she could, would and had turned to for different kinds of support. These were her mother, her child's father (with whom she was cohabiting by the end of the study), her sister, and her cousin (who was the only person she felt she would turn to for support with a personal problem). The support, as opposed to social side of her network, was fairly restricted.

Julie also had an extensively interlinked social network. She lived with her parents, brother and sister, and was in regular contact with four other members of her family. She also had eight friends in her network who were interlinked because they (and Julie) were all still at school together. Together with her child's father whom she saw regularly, there were 17 people in her social network, and 67 connections between them in pregnancy. (In Julie's case the interconnections fell into two groups; school and family, whereas Chris's was one main interlinking of her family and her child's father's family.)

Yet Julie felt that there was no one in whom she would confide if she had a personal problem. She simply said 'I don't like it' when asked how she felt about confiding. In general she found it difficult to contemplate accepting help from anyone, but felt that she would turn to her mother for help if she ever needed it.

By the end of the study Julie had left school and become employed. She continued to live with her family and her familial connections remained the same. Her child's father had stopped coming to visit their son, and she had lost touch with three friends. Her social network now consisted of 13 people, and 45 interconnections. She still maintained that 'I like keeping it [personal problems] to meself', but said that her mother had been very supportive to her in providing childcare help.

Individuals in women's networks

The more people that women saw regularly once a month, the more they were likely to see each week, and network members were more likely to have relationships with each other independently of the women being studied. The number of linkages in a network, the number of people seen each week and network size were all highly correlated.

This was partly because women with the largest number of people in their social networks were those who had regular contacts with relatives. Those women with the smallest networks were those whose mothers were not available to them. Twenty-one months after birth, only three women (all described in the previous section because they had small social networks) had none of their own relatives in their social networks. The majority of women (48, 76%) had three or more relatives in their social networks, with more than a quarter (26%) having seven or eight. Whether women lived with their child's father or with relatives made no difference to either their network size or the number of interconnections between network members.

Twenty one months after birth women were more likely to see their own relatives at least once a month than to see their child's father regularly each month. Sixty-five women's (96%) social networks included relatives, compared with only two-thirds (42) who included their child's father. Similarly girl friends were more likely to be in women's social networks than were members of the child's father's family. Over a third of the sample were not in regular monthly contact with any members of their child's father's family – more than double the 15% (10) of those with no girlfriends in their social networks. (Hardly any women counted any men among their social network members.)

The relationship between women's social networks and their feelings of being supported

The number of contacts in a woman's social network was not related to her feelings about motherhood, or to how supported she felt. There was, however, a highly significant relationship between the number of people in a woman's social network and how she felt in herself. The more people with whom women were in regular contact, the more likely they were to report having felt happy and cheerful in the previous month. Conversely, the fewer people with whom women were in regular contact, the more likely they were to report that they had felt anxious, depressed or irritable in the previous month. But this relationship did not reach significance.

The relationship between women's emotional state and the number of people they saw regularly is probably related to whether women felt lonely or not. The fewer people with whom women were in weekly contact, the more likely they were sometimes to experience feelings of loneliness. Loneliness and emotional state were related. Simply being in contact with people was therefore important to women's well being, although it made no difference to how they felt about themselves as mothers.

Just as small networks did not necessarily signify that women would be lonely and lacking in support, so large social networks did not necessarily signify extensive channels of support. Neither the total number of contacts in women's social networks nor the density of linkages in the network was signficantly related to women's feelings about whether they had been sufficiently well supported. Similarly (although it approached significance) the number of people women regularly saw each week was not related to satisfaction with support.

Women were significantly more likely to report satisfaction with the support they had received if they were also satisfied with their social lives, and if they never felt lonely. Feelings, of loneliness and satisfaction with social life, were however not related to the number of people women saw regularly, although they were related to the number of people seen weekly.

People were included in women's social networks only if women said that they were in regular interactive (phone or personal) contact with them at least once a month. Therefore more women than recorded here were in contact with their children's fathers and even considered themselves to have relationships with them. While it seemed reasonable to exclude people who were either seen sporadically or less than monthly from social network membership, women themselves did sometimes consider people excluded on this criterion to be important sources of support.

For some women, frequency of contact with network members was not a defining characteristic for presence/absence from social networks or support networks. The woman whose mother moved back to the Midlands (Jenny), for example, experienced a marked reduction in contact with her mother as well as her siblings, and presumably a qualitative change in the nature of the support her mother could give her. Yet she felt that her mother was a continual, network member and an important source of support. Her mother's absence removed the negative aspects of having her mother in her social network. It was no longer necessary to provide daily practical support to her mother. Support is recognized to be a complicated interlinking of privileges and obligations (Belle, 1982; Riley and Eckenrode, 1986).

When asked whether she was happy with her social life, Jenny replied, 'I suppose it could be better, but I wouldn't say I'm not happy.' She felt that she would like to get to know more people, but hoped that employment would give her the opportunity to do so. She also felt that she never got bored now. 'Well the last time you came, I said I got bored then, but now I can play with Alex. He's you know – he's old enough for me to play with him now.' Asked directly whether she ever felt lonely, she said, 'No not really. Cos if I see my family too much I get sick of 'em. They get on me nerves.'

This last response indicates how large social networks are not necessarily only beneficial. When interviewed in late pregnancy, Jenny had explained how, although she now got on with her mother well, they had previously argued a lot because Jenny felt that her mother was going out and leaving her to look after the four younger children too much. For Jenny, the disadvantage of living with her mother was having more childcare responsibility than she otherwise would, and having lots of people and noise all the time. The advantage of living separately from them was that she had no such responsibilities, and could live in comparative peace, tending only her own child, and the puppy she had chosen to get. Jenny's example neatly illustrates that it is only possible to understand how social networks influence people's lives and feelings by viewing them in the context of the responsibilities as well as benefits they entail.

Yet although Jenny's mother was no longer within her social network she was clearly still a major source of support. Her intention in taking Jenny's son to stay was to facilitate Jenny's attempt to obtain employment. A rather different, and less satisfactory, picture may have emerged if Jenny had been faced with a stressful life event with her mother so far away, or if she did not experience her mother as still being part of her network.

Just as there was no one-to-one correspondence between social support and network size, so social support was not simply related to particular individuals' presence or absence from the social network. How well supported women felt depended more on whom women lived with than on who was in their social networks.

When their children were nearly two years old, women who lived with a spouse or cohabitee were much more likely than those who had not, to say that they had not received sufficient support in the last year. The longer women had cohabited, the more dissatisfied they reported themselves to be with the support they had received. The reverse was true if women lived with relatives. But the relationship between reported satisfaction/dissatisfaction with support and whether women had relatives or spouses in their networks, did not approach significance. Shared household was more important than presence in a social network.

What do these findings mean? A possible explanation is that most married or cohabiting men were not contributing enough emotional, material or childcare help to make women feel generally satisfied with the support they gave. Another explanation may be that women expect more support from the men they set up home with, than from their own families, and would be more grateful for support from their own families than from their cohabitees. They would, therefore, be more disappointed by lack of support from male partners than from relatives. Alternatively, many women's relatives may have provided them with such enormous amounts of high quality support that male partners found it difficult to match.

In late pregnancy most women had expected that their male partner, if sharing a household with them, would make substantial contributions to 'bringing up their child'. Their expectations may well have been dashed by the actual experience of cohabitation (including marriage) once their child was actually born. The following section, and the next chapter, discusses the support that women received from different people.

Emotional support

Even if the people in women's social networks were unable to provide them with material resources or childcare support, they might provide emotional support by listening to women's problems or concerns and being supportive about them. Successful provision of emotional support requires that the person to be supported considers such support to be useful and has someone from whom she is prepared to request and/or accept it. It also requires that the person providing support recognizes when support is necessary. This section aims to explore whether the mothers interviewed were likely to be receiving emotional support, and whether they considered it to be important. It concentrates mainly on women's attitudes to confiding their feelings.

Confiding and emotional support

Chapter 3 discussed how some women found it difficult to disclose the fact that they were pregnant to their parents and male partners. It might, therefore, seem reasonable for women to have confided in their friends. Friends could possibly provide empathy, calm discussion of the options available to a young pregnant woman, and perhaps mediate between women and their parents or male partners if news of the pregnancy was unwelcome. Yet few women chose friends as confidantes once they realized that they were pregnant. There were only seven women (10%) for whom friends were the first person told about the pregnancy. Perhaps more surprising is the fact that three-quarters of the women (56) never directly told their friends that they were pregnant.

It is possible that for young, single women the revelation of pregnancy to non-pregnant peers is (particularly because it indicates sexual activity) embarrassing and unpleasant. But this was not the whole story. Asked whether any of their friendships at school had been close ones, only two women (3%) said that their friendships had been close.

> No they wasn't any close friends – just convenience. (17 year old woman who married in pregnancy)

> At first it was about four or five of us. Then as we got older people went their separate ways, so I used to spend more time with my cousins. (19 year old woman who started cohabiting after birth)

Many women did not like the idea of disclosing personal information (see table 5.2). A third of those asked (23) said that they thought it was better to keep personal problems and worries to themselves. Of those who felt that it was a good idea to 'turn to others with personal worries or problems' more than a third had no experience of personal disclosure. Some had never felt the need for such self disclosure, while others reported that they did not feel such disclosure would be a good idea for them personally. Less

Table 5.2 Attitudes to confiding personal information

Negative	36%	
Positive, but has never confided	16%	
Positive generally, but negative for self	11%	
Positive	37%	(N=64)

than two-fifths (37%) were both positive about confiding, and had themselves confided personal problems to anyone.

> It's a good idea to talk to someone cause otherwise you keep it bottled up and you get in a state in the end. [?] If I got any I go straight to me mum. (18 year old single woman living with her mother)

The number of people in women's social networks was not statistically related to whether or not they felt they had someone in whom they could confide. Some women with many people in their social networks felt they had no one in whom they could confide. Similarly women who had someone in whom they felt they *could* confide if they chose, and women who did not have a possible confidante were equally likely to say that they were reluctant to confide in anyone.

One reason given for reluctance to confide was fear (sometimes based on experience) that confidantes would not maintain confidentiality or would exact too high a price for listening to confidences.

> Most of them (friends) are stupid. If you tell them one thing, they go and tell everyone else, so I never used to bother telling. (17 year old single woman)

> Cos all these people you think you've known for a long time they've got such big mouths. You can't really talk to them anyway. (16 year old single woman)

> . . . As far as friends are concerned – because right they were . . . people that I could talk to and if they wanted anything they'd sort of say 'Come on Di, lend me this, lend me that'. And then I started to lend them my clothes and all that lot and . . . they never brought them back and all that lot . . . (16 year old single woman)

But some women simply preferred to keep their own counsel, particularly on subjects they considered to be really personal.

> I don't like it [confiding] . . . [?] Yeah, my sex life. I would never discuss that. (16 year old single woman)

> I can't do it [confide], even with closest friends. (16 year old single woman)

> Talk to me mother about some things, but not other things. [?] Me and Tom I think. I don't talk to her about that. (17 year old single woman)

Mothers were much more likely than friends or fathers to be

confided in, if women felt they had to confide in someone (see table 5.3). In fact only four women said that they would be prepared to confide in their own fathers. This rather marginal status of women's fathers with respect to disclosure of personal information has been found in other studies. Elizabeth Monck, for example, found that only three of 121 young women she studied could be said fully to confide in their fathers (Monck, in press). More women said that they would confide in their male partners than in their mothers. This may have been because women considered sexuality to be the most personal issue, and many felt that if they ever discussed it with anyone it would be with their male partners.

The hypothetical 'would confide' was usually never put into practice. On the basis of the accounts they gave in late pregnancy, women were rated for whether or not they had anyone with whom they felt they could freely discuss anything. Only a quarter of the sample (19) were rated as having such a relationship. Of these, only two women felt close to friends (one of these friends being an older nextdoor neighbour) while ten were rated as having an open relationship with their child's father, and seven with their mothers. The fact that nearly half of the sample (44%) were either married or cohabiting in late pregnancy when the data for these ratings was collected suggests that women did not necessarily perceive cohabitation or marriage to include the exchange of confidences.

Women did not feel more able to confide in their male partners after their children had been born. When interviewed just before their children were two years old, three-fifths of women (40) were married or cohabiting. Yet only 22% (23) said that they would discuss a personal problem with their child's father. This compares with over 50% (36) who would discuss such a problem with a relative (almost always their mothers). A minority of women expressed pleasure about being able to talk freely to their child's

Table 5.3 People in whom respondents would confide

Father	6%	
Friend	27%	
Mother	40%	
Male partner	50%	
Other	25%	(N=68)

Note: Some respondents reported that they would confide in more than one person.

father, but even some of these felt that they had received as much or more support from their own relatives.

> He's great ... which really made me feel happy you know what I mean – the fact that I could actually talk to him like that ...
> Q–Who has given you the most support?
> A–Me nan and me sister. Me mum's been ill so I don't really bother her.
> (17 year old)

Many women did not comment on this lack of confiding. However a few felt that inadequate communication within the relationship caused tensions and strains. Both the women reported below have considered leaving their husbands. The first (who did briefly return to her parents when her child was one year old) reported that she had had postnatal depression, and felt strongly that her health visitors and general practitioner would have been better able to discuss it with her husband than she could.

> I think perhaps if somebody had talked to him about it, it would've perhaps got him to understand a little bit better like what's involved and things like that. Because as nobody ever acknowledged the fact that I had postnatal depression, I think perhaps he didn't believe me and he thought that I was just being silly or whatever 'cos he didn't understand ... But er I think perhaps if somebody had talked to him he *might* have been a little bit more understanding. But he *was* really quite good about it. (18 year old; second contact)

> He's a very quiet person. I don't like that. I'm getting a bit annoyed with it. Cos I go out too much – I see people laugh – and to just sit in the house. It's so boring. I get so annoyed with it. Why won't he talk more? He only likes coming home, sitting down and folding his arms [laugh]. I can't stand it. (19 year old at birth; third contact)

Another woman (19 years old when she gave birth) interviewed six months after birth complained that her husband was too uncommunicative. She did leave her husband some time in her child's second year but continually deferred the 21 month interview, and was not eventually seen.

Friends, and relatives other than mothers, were rarely confidantes. Feelings of closeness to other people did not necessarily correspond with being able to confide in them freely. Few women felt able to confide, and even fewer actually did in practice, yet many more felt they did have at least one close relationship with someone. Perhaps significantly in this context, after birth a few women reported that their closest relationship was with their child.

Many women did not define 'support' as having an emotional component. Asked whether they had been given enough support, equal numbers of women with and women without someone with whom they could discuss personal problems reported themselves to be satisfied. Nor were women likely to feel lonely if they had no one to whom they could confide personal problems. There was no relationship between feeling lonely and availability of a confidante for personal problems. The disclosure of personal problems was not of central importance to many women.

Since many women did not define their friendships as close ones and were not in the habit of disclosing personal information to their friends, it is easily understandable that most friends (even those who are said to be close) are not told about early pregnancy.

> Yeah I got a close friend . . . I've known her all my life so I go round with her. [?] I tell her everything. I didn't tell her I was pregnant though. She found out herself. (16 year old)

The profile of friendships which emerged from women's accounts indicates that, on the whole, friends were not primary sources of emotional support. In part this was because they were not privileged with confidential information, but it was also because mothers and male partners were more important in women's lives than were friends. Support was not perceived necessarily either to include or to entail disclosure.

The disclosure of pregnancy was an unusual instance of confiding, in that women's pregnancies would eventually become evident even if they were not disclosed and (particularly for single women living at home) having a child would potentially affect women's parents and male partners. Male partners were the most likely people for

Table 5.4 First person to whom pregnancy was disclosed

Fathers	3	(4%)
Mothers	12	(17%)
Other relations	8	(11%)
Male partners	32	(44%)
Friends	7	(10%)
Others	2	(3%)
Never disclosed	9	(12%) (N=73)

women to tell initially that they were pregnant (see table 5.4). This is to be expected since the child conceived is shared with the male partner, and for single women the male partner was sometimes the only person other than the woman who knew that she had been sexually active. More than a quarter of the women interviewed did not directly tell anyone in their social network that they were pregnant, but instead waited until the pregnancy was noticed. Women who did not tell their own friends or relatives that they were pregnant did, however, generally go to their GPs and register at antenatal clinics before it became obvious to those around them that they were pregnant. Some mothers discovered their daughters were pregnant when they found their daughters' antenatal appointment cards.

Part of the reason parents were frequently not told about the pregnancy immediately is that many women had a lot to lose if parents were angry with them. Nearly half the sample lived with their parents when they conceived. For some the fear associated with disclosure of early pregnancy was that they would be forced by angry and ashamed parents to leave home.

For some women pregnancy led to changes in relationships with male partners. Eight couples married, while 15 stopped having relationships. By comparison, only one parent (a father) refused to have anything further to do with his daughter once he realized that she was pregnant. In some cases, therefore, parents provided stability and support that male partners did not.

> I reckon I'll just stay with my mum and dad. I suppose I feel a bit wary [about the thought of living with a man]. I mean it's stable here. I have a stable relationship with my mum and my dad. (19 year old)

Despite some women's initial reluctance to disclose that they were pregnant, and the misgivings that some parents and male partners initially felt when they learned that women were pregnant, most parents and male partners were eventually emotionally supportive of women. By late pregnancy parents, and male partners with whom women were still in contact, were almost all enthusiastic about the fact that they were to have a grandchild or child. Friends were all reported to be immediately supportive of women once they realized that they were pregnant, even if they were initially surprised about it or thought that women should not keep the baby.

Emotional unsupportiveness

It is already apparent that members of social networks can be unsupportive as well as supportive. Friends, for example, may disclose information women consider to be personal, male partners may refuse to discuss issues considered important, parents may react angrily when they learn that their daughters are pregnant. This section discusses a few other ways in which parents and male partners could be emotionally unsupportive.

Although many women did not expect a great deal of emotional support from anybody, and did not consider that marriage or cohabitation necessitated close, confiding relationships, those who considered that there were any benefits to marriage were likely to report that these were things like providing them with company and security. After they had given birth a few married or cohabiting women began to comment on the fact that their male partners were free to go out whenever they wished, while they had to spend most of their time at home with their children.

In addition a few women felt that their male partners had started to behave in unacceptable ways. Relationships with other women were, for example, always upsetting. For some women this was enough to finish the relationship. Other women put up (albeit unhappily) with the situation.

The reason Leslie and I did split up is because he was having an affair with his sister-in-law and his brother found out and caught them in bed . . . and I told Leslie I weren't standing for it . . . (18 year old married woman who separated from her husband when her child was five months old)

Oh I'm used to him going off. He always does it . . . I can't trust him any more. He goes and picks up different women and lives with them in hotels in Victoria when he goes off. And then he comes back to me when he feels like it . . . I don't care any more as long as he doesn't come near me, 'cos it's dirty. (married woman, 19 years old at birth; third contact)

Well he *is* seeing a girl . . . but he says there ain't nothing to worry about you know. Us two can still be together or whatever, but I don't see how you know. I'm not that kind of person . . . (single woman, 16 years old at birth; second contact)

Well he lives three doors away, but I don't talk to him or nothing 'cos he's got two other babies now. And I just think that that's a dead loss, so I've just forgotten about him. (same woman; third contact)

I nearly killed him – he did silly things, coming home smelling of perfume, plus one of his friends told me [that he had fathered another child]. I knew of the seven month old one and I put up with it, but I threw him out over the three month old one. (Woman had cohabited with her child's father; 18 years old at birth; own child now nearly two years)

Me mum told me to pack him in [because he was having an affair] . . . And then we sorted it out together and got back together. (18 year old cohabiting woman)

Since infidelity was not asked about, these reports of it were spontaneous. There may have been other women whose partners also had affairs, but who did not mention it. Infidelity was considered to lessen the feelings of security that women felt in their relationships. Since this was one of the benefits of marriage and cohabitation that those women who reported any had mentioned (see chapter 4), it is perhaps not surprising that they reacted strongly against it. (See also chapter 8 for examples about women being depressed by the state of their relationships with male partners.)

If women lived with their parents, their parents could exercise control over who visited them at home. When they were pregnant, a few, younger women reported that they had either been forbidden from seeing their male partners, or that it was too awkward for them to continue visiting. Six months after birth, for example, one 16 year old woman reported that she had re-established a relationship with her child's father, but that her mother did not know. Similarly, the only woman to conceal her pregnancy until a few days before birth did so because she knew her father would not approve of the fact that her child's father was black. A major reason for her leaving her parents' home (despite anxiety about being the only wage earner there) when her child was a year old was that it was awkward for her male partner to visit her at home. Similarly another white woman had to stay in hospital postnatally until the council found her accommodation because her father forbade her from bringing her black baby back to his home. After birth she almost always visited her family when he was at work, and he never visited her. All three examples cited here were of white women whose children's fathers were black. Not all such women were emotionally unsupported by members of their family, but they did seem to be at the receiving end of more anger than many other women.

Summary and conclusions

Women's networks varied in size and density, but there was no one-to-one correspondence between the number of people in women's networks and how supported they felt. Sometimes people with whom women were not in regular contact were still important members of their support networks. This was especially likely to be the case for family members. Women who reported that they had someone with whom they could discuss personal matters did not feel more supported than those who did not have such support available.

It made no difference to the numbers in women's social networks whether women lived with their parents or male partners. But the longer women had lived with male partners, the more likely they were to say that they were unhappy with the support they were being given. Similar relationships did not hold for the length of time they had lived with relatives. Feelings of loneliness were important, because if women felt lonely they were likely to have feelings of depression or irritability, to feel that they were not receiving enough support and to be dissatisfied with motherhood. Women who did not see other people regularly each week were likely to report that they felt lonely.

Most male partners did not provide the mothers of their children with the close, companionate relationship that modern couples are said to desire. Apart from the disclosure of pregnancy, young women were more likely to turn to their own mothers than to their male partners for emotional support.

Single women were more likely to be worried about disclosing that they were pregnant to their parents, and to their male partners, than married women. Male partners were most frequently chosen as the first person to whom to reveal pregnancy. Yet while male partners were more likely than parents to be happy initially about the pregnancy, almost all parents eventually rallied round to support their daughters. A sizeable minority of relationships with male partners came to an end during pregnancy. For some women, therefore, parents provided welcome stability and continuity of relationship. Since most women relied on their parents for some form of support, many were concerned to maintain a good relationship with them.

For many women, friends were not very significant sources of emotional support. The context of most women's friendships was such that few had any close friendships, and those who did were not prepared to confide in their friends. Relatively few women were prepared to confide personal information at all. All sources of emotional support could behave in ways which women did not consider to be supportive.

6

Practical Support

The previous chapter discussed the people in women's social networks and the emotional support provided by different individuals. This chapter is concerned with the material and childcare support that women receive from individuals in their social networks. Social support is recognized to be an important mediating influence on the way individuals experience stressful situations (Gottlieb, 1981; Brannen and Collard, 1982). Social support may be a protective factor, acting as a prophylaxis against the onset of stress; a buffer against stress; or amelioratively after stress has been experienced. Beneficial effects of social support have been reported for both physical and psychological health.

If social support is a protective factor, it should be an important influence on how mothers fare. Motherhood is socially constructed as marking or emphasizing women's transition to adulthood. Yet, paradoxically, it is often a period of increased emotional and economic dependence as well as reliance on others for practical assistance with childcare. This increased dependence makes social support particularly important for many mothers. Teenage mothers are a socially stigmatized and marginalized group of mothers. Awareness that they are socially devalued may make motherhood a more stressful experience for them than for older mothers. In addition, the material circumstances of most mothers who are under 20 years of age are usually impoverished. Social support may, therefore, be a critical influence on how they fare.

This chapter discusses the ways in which, and by whom, support is or is not provided in relation to:

- childcare;
- housing;
- material resources.

Childcare support

A fashionable media image is of the 'New Man' willingly playing his part in an egalitarian relationship with his female partner. The 'New Man' looks after his children and does housework with practised competence. Yet research studies which have examined what fathers actually do with regard to their children find that over the last two decades there has been very little change (Lewis and O'Brien, 1987; Henwood 1987).

When their children were six months old women were asked who had performed various childcare tasks in the previous week (see table 6.1). Two-thirds of male partners had not changed nappies or fed their infants. Three-quarters had not bathed their baby. In each case relatives (usually mothers) had done substantially more than male partners. Relatively few children had woken in the night in the week before the six month interview. Other than the respondents, only five people had got up to see to them. Asked whether anyone had looked after the child in the previous week while the woman went out, just under a sixth of women reported that their male partners had looked after the child. This compares with eight women who reported that the child's father's relatives had done so; 12 whose friends had provided childcare, and 30 whose own relatives had. Male partners were said to have provided short periods of childcare (minutes, or at the most a couple of hours at a time)

Table 6.1 People other than the respondent who had done any childcare tasks in the previous week at six months

	Male partners	Relatives	Friends	Others	
Bathing	26%	30%	9%	8%	
Nappy changing	37%	52%	12%	9%	
Feeding	35%	56%	16%	6%	
Childcare	16%	45%	18%	18%[a]	(N=67)

[a] 'Others' for childcare help includes male partners' families and nurseries.

whereas relatives were reported to have provided more extensive care.

This greater involvement of relatives than male partners cannot simply be explained by looking at women's living circumstances. When interviewed six months after the birth, nearly a third (31%, 26) were living with their parents and over half (51%, 43) were living with male partners.

When women were asked whether they were satisfied with the amount that other people did for and with their children, just under a third (31%) expressed some dissatisfaction (see table 6.2). Only a quarter (25%), however, said they felt they needed more childcare help (all except one of these wanted the extra help from their child's father). Since men provided much less help than relatives, why were more women not dissatisfied with their male partners' contributions to childcare?

The answer lies partly in the conflicting ideologies surrounding male–female relationships. On the one hand the current ideology of 'mutuality' gives women a vested interest in seeing their relationships as ones in which tasks and resources are equally shared. On the other hand many women subscribed to the longer established ideology of asymmetrical relationships, with women being responsible for childcare and housework.

Acceptance of asymmetrical male–female relationships leads women to have very low expectations of help from male partners. As a result they consider any childcare contributions, however little, from their male partners to be good.

> A mother's satisfaction with the amount of help her husband gives her with the baby depends in part on her own expectations of what he *should* do. Husbands, on the whole, should do so much and no more. Sometimes satisfaction is expressed in terms of the husband being 'very good' or 'marvellous' whereas in fact he does very little (Oakley, 1979, p. 214).

Women can, therefore, report themselves to be simultaneously

Table 6.2 Satisfaction with childcare help at six months

Positive	28%	
Uncritical	41%	
Mixed feelings	9%	
Negative	22%	(N=65)

dissatisfied with lack of childcare help and satisfied with their male partners' contributions (Brannen and Moss, 1987).

When their children were nearly two years old women were asked who helped them with childcare. These questions were, however, more general than they had been at six months after birth, and women were not asked to specify what had happened in various childcare situations over the previous week (see table 6.3). More than half the 68 women interviewed (36) reported that they received regular help from someone with childcare tasks. A third (23) said that they received regular help from their male partners (40, 59% lived with male partners), whereas a quarter (17) reported that they received regular help from a relative (12, 18% lived with relatives, 9 being their own parents, 1 a foster parent, 1 a brother and the other a female cousin). Few women felt that they got as much help as they would ideally have liked (11), but nearly half those interviewed (33) simply said that the amount of childcare help they got was 'all right', or that they were 'quite happy with it'. Just under a third felt that they definitely did not get enough help (20). Ten of these women said that they would like more help from their child's father, one from relatives and one from daycare provision. The other 8 women did not specify from whom they wanted more childcare help.

The picture of help with childcare tasks seemed to have changed in the period of just over a year between interviews. Even though a minority of women wanted more help from their male partners, men were now reported to be providing more childcare help than mothers or other relatives. This change is arguably, however, an illusory one for two reasons. Firstly women's expectations of their female relatives, particularly their mothers, and of their male partners were different. Whereas men were not really expected to do much to help (particularly if they were not cohabitees), many women's history of dependence on their families was such that relatives were expected to provide any support necessary. Mothers'

Table 6.3 People reported to help regularly with childcare tasks at 21 months

Male partners	34%	
Relatives	25%	
Friends	1%	
Others	4%	(N=68)

help, for example, was almost taken for granted while male partners' help was more remarkable. A general (rather than specific) question about childcare help was therefore likely to elicit overstatements of men's contributions and underreporting of contributions from relatives. This methodological difference between specific and general questions is obvious in some responses.

Q–Does anyone regularly help you with [childcare tasks]?
A–No. I do all that.

(Later in the interview):
Q–Who else has looked after [baby] this week?
A–When they [younger sisters] come home from school they do the care whether I am here or not. . . If he needs changing they just change him. If it's time for bed they just take his clothes off and you know put his pyjamas on and wash him. . . I mean my sisters they're better mothers than I am. . . They're excellent. I mean I think if it wasn't for them two I'd've really been stuck. . . .
(17 year old at birth; third contact; woman had been single on giving birth, cohabited later, but chose to return to her parents)

The second reason for the apparent change in the relative contributions of male partners and relatives to childcare is to do with changes over time in the nature of the father–child relationship. Many men began to play more with their children as they grew older, and women included playing as a contribution to childcare.

Q–Does [husband] ever look after her [baby]?
A–Yeah he does probably more than what I do half the time.
Q–How much help does he give?
A–Um the actual looking after her in the sense of feeding her – that's me. Whereas entertaining her, amusing her and putting her off to sleep it's him.
Q–How do you feel about the amount of help you get?
A–Oh I'm pleased, yeah. I'm probably doing a lot better than what most people are. . . probably getting enough [laugh].
(Married woman; 18 year old at birth; third contact)

Boulton (1983) also found that women expressed satisfaction with the help their husbands gave with childcare when in fact help was mainly based on playing with the children.

There is little evidence from this study, therefore, to suggest that the sharing of child care between husband and wife is now widespread. Instead, what sociologists of the family. . . see as an increase in men's involvement in domestic matters may be little more than an increase in their interest in and enjoyment of their children. This is quite different from their sharing in responsibility for their children and does not necessarily presage any marked increase in their more practical help. (Boulton, 1983, p. 145)

When asked, in late pregnancy, about the relative benefits of marriage for both sexes, some women asserted that women gained only benefits from marriage. In further discussion, however, they went on to talk about only unpleasant aspects of marriage for women and benefits for men. A similar process occurred in discussions of men's contributions to childcare. Many women said that they were satisfied with what their male partners did, but then indicated that they would really like him to do more.

> My husband could do more, but that's the way it is. He is at work a lot and he will do things if I ask him. (Married woman; 18 years old at birth; third contact)

> Well I'd like a bit of help looking after her. . . He does play with her, but not often enough I reckon. I mean I can't blame him. He comes in tired, but she doesn't know that does she? (Married woman; 18 year old at birth; third contact)

> [Husband] will change her nappy now and again for me. . . Oh I don't ask him. If I asked him he would do it. . .
> Q–How do you feel about the amount of help you get?
> A–I'm quite happy. . . I like doing it myself. . . Cos I mean I can do it myself. I'm not an old woman.

> (Later in the interview):
> I wouldn't depend on him looking after her. I would expect more, but you couldn't depend. (Temporarily separated married woman; 19 years old at birth; third interview)

> I think Patrick could have done more. He is one of those blokes who thinks he shouldn't do anything – that it is my job to do everything. (19 years old at birth; third interview)

Nonetheless some women clearly felt that childcare was really their responsibility.

> I could do with more help. [Childcare. . . ?] Oh no. That's my job innit? (18 year old married woman who had two children and wanted to leave her husband by 21 months)

Even when married women who have had their first child later than their teenage years are employed full time outside the home, men usually do less childcare work than women.

Support and housing

Most women interviewed came from working class backgrounds. Over a quarter of their parents were unemployed when their daughters were pregnant, and many lived in council housing. Most women could therefore expect little material help with housing from their families.

Relatively few women in the Thomas Coram study lived in owner-occupied housing. Less than a third (29%) of the women interviewed when their children were 21 months old had been in mortgaged or outrightly owned houses in late pregnancy. The majority (64%) were dependent on rented accommodation, most of which (five-sixths) was council accommodation.

Since more than half the women we saw lived in their parents' homes (56%) and another 14% lived with relatives, many of their relatives must have been dependent on public provision of housing. Younger women (16 and 17 year olds) were more likely than older women (18 and 19 year olds) to live with relatives. Older women were more likely than younger women to live on their own, or with male partners (5% and 17% respectively).

During pregnancy the majority of women were living in houses (56%) with most of the rest living in flats and maisonettes (34%). A minority were, however, living in bedsits, bed and breakfast accommodation or mother and baby homes (9%). Most women (94%) were living on the second floor or below, in other words below the council's recommended fifth floor maximum level for households with young children.

For many women pregnancy and the first two years after birth were periods of change in living arrangements. Some of this change was not by choice. There was frequently insufficient space in which to squeeze a new baby. A few women had to move because landlords and landladies did not want babies in their property. In other words, factors beyond women's control often dictated where they could live.

Many women were not, however, simply swept along by circumstances. Some women subscribed to the social construction of motherhood as signalling adulthood and independence, and made definite decisions to push for independence by leaving their parental home. Others decided that they were not yet ready to leave the support their parents would provide for them.

> If I stay at home my mum is gonna do everything for me and I'm gonna. . . just automatically rely on her so when I do eventually get my flat I won't be used to doing things. So I prefer to stay independent and *be* independent. (16 year old)

> I just want to stay at home with me parents that's all. I haven't applied for council accommodation. (17 year old)

In late pregnancy nearly half (49%) the women expected to move at some time. All except one of these women expected to be rehoused by the council. There was therefore little they could do to facilitate that process since, to a large extent, it was beyond their control. Women were, therefore, dependent on local councils, as dispensers of public housing, for much of their housing support.

Women in the Thomas Coram study became pregnant just prior to government legislation authorizing the sale of council housing. The boroughs in which they lived were able to rehouse most respondents who requested rehousing during the two years of the study. As a result there was a sharp increase in the percentage of women who were either householders on their own, or who were joint householders with male partners between conception and 21 months after birth. With changes in housing law, however, this group of women is likely to have been the last generation of mothers under 20 to have obtained council housing relatively quickly.

Table 6.4 shows that between pregnancy and 21 months after birth

Table 6.4 Change in tenancies for women interviewed at 21 months after birth

Tenancy	Conception	Birth	12 months	21 months
Own	5%	8%	30%	41%
Spouses/cohabitees	13%	22%	23%	24%
Joint	3%	6%	17%	16%
Parents	56%	49%	21%	10%
Other relatives	8%	8%	5%	3%
Male partner's relatives	6%	3%	3%	3%
Friends	3%	2%	0%	0%
Other	6%	2%	2%	3% (N=67)

there was a substantial increase in the percentage of women who held their own council tenancies (alone or jointly with a male partner). At conception only 5% of those who were successfully interviewed 21 months after birth held their own tenancies, while 13% lived in accommodation for which their husbands or male partners held the tenancies and 3% shared tenancies with male partners. By 21 months post birth 41% held tenancies on their own, 24% lived with male partners who held tenancies and 16% were joint householders with male partners. Only 10% (mostly the youngest sample members) still lived in accommodation where their parents were the householders, and only a quarter of the sample had stayed in one address throughout the period of the study.

Over the course of the study the percentage of women living in accommodation where their husbands or cohabitees held tenancies only in their names increased (from 13% to 24%). This was not generally because men could obtain independent housing. Most men who held independent tenancies were living in council housing and obtained housing only because they were living with, or intending to live with, women and children. In a few instances women were too young to hold tenancies themselves when they first moved into their homes, but in most instances where men were sole householders couples seem to have decided that men should be responsible formally for family accommodation. By the end of the study, however, a greater proportion of women than men held tenancies independently (41% compared with 24%). Joint tenancies were rare by comparison (at 16%).

Moves to independent living usually provided women with more space than they had previously had, but there were some drawbacks involved. An increasing number of women moved into council housing (54% at the beginning of pregnancy, compared with 69% at 21 months). A correlate of increased dependence on council housing was a move to less attractive housing. The proportion of women in houses and women in flats largely reversed over the two years of the study. In pregnancy three-fifths were living in houses, and one-quarter in flats. By 21 months after birth three-fifths were living in flats, and one-quarter in houses. This change involved losses of gardens and moves to high rise occupation. Whereas only 6% lived on the third floor or above before they had a child, one-fifth (21%) did so at some point after birth.

Despite these disadvantages most women who wanted to be rehoused had been so within the first two years after birth. Yet council housing departments were not entirely popular with women.

Nearly half (44%, 19) of those who had attempted to get council accommodation in their child's second year had some negative feelings about the experience, reporting that they had had difficulty in getting council accommodation.

> Um, well they say they've got no places, but like today we came up on the bus. . . we seen 15 houses that were empty. . . [?] Well I mean why ain't they filled up. That's what we ask them when we go down but they say because there's other people on the list. I mean if there's other people waiting they should get a place there, where the houses are empty. Seems as if they're not even bothering [pause]. And we just got to be grateful for what we got at the moment. (19 year old married woman living in a bedsit with her husband)

The perceived difficulty of obtaining council housing led some young women to feel that they were in competition with other people who wanted council housing. It was not uncommon for them to berate the council for housing 'less deserving' people.

> It's like I really have to beg to them or beg for somewhere to live and. . . you know, that's bad because some of the girls I know that get their flats, they get nice flats and all fully furnished you know with their first babies just like I'm expecting mine and where they offered. . . me. . . depressed me. . . seeing what those other girls have got and the only reason that they've got is because they actually pressured them and you know shouting and make a lot of commotion. . . and because I don't do it, you know. (19 year old living in her mother's council house)

For some women it was only a short step from dissatisfaction with council housing policies in general, to expressed dissatisfaction with allocation of council housing to black people. Although some council housing departments have been found to be racially discriminatory towards black people (CRE, 1984), some white respondents said that black people were treated unfairly well when it came to getting council housing.

> *Q*–How do you feel about council housing departments?
> *Respondent*–I can understand that there's lots of people like us, but I can't understand when they're told – this is not because I'm prejudiced because I'm not – this is when they're told 'oh this couple's come over from abroad, and they've got to have this flat before you, otherwise they're going to sue us for being prejudiced', well I don't think that's fair.
> *Q*–Is that what you were told?

Respondent–Yeah.
Spouse–I think they should wait their turn.
Respondent–I don't see why they can't be put into one of those bedsits and we can have a flat until another one comes up. I don't see why they should always jump it.
Spouse–A coloured girl moved into the bedsit where we was, now she was – I don't think she was pregnant as what you was, and also she wasn't married, now she managed to get – she moved in, you take it in turns as she explained, now we was living there before her. She got a two bedroomed place and she was out before us. And she lived on her own, she wasn't married and she got a two bedroomed place.
Respondent–But we've got to live, there's more of us and we have to. . . so there's definitely a fiddle in the council. . .
(17 year old)

Fearing that they would have to wait years to obtain council housing, a few women slightly misstated their circumstances to the housing department.

I reckon if we told the truth the way that we was before, we'd wait much longer yeah cos we told the council that we was living separate and our families didn't allow us to be together and that's how we got a flat really. But otherwise if we'd told them that we had room at the mother-in-law's we wouldn't have got a place. (19 year old married woman)

Other women made themselves 'homeless' and tolerated living in bed and breakfast accommodation so that they would be rehoused more quickly than otherwise.

Q–Why did you make yourselves homeless?
A–Because we wanted a place, because if we lived with our mums, we'd have a roof over our heads and you can't get a council flat, you have to be homeless to get one quick or you have to go on their waiting list for as long as it takes, well you have to live at home a year and then go on their waiting list, and then you can wait how long it ever took, if you go homeless you usually get one quickly, so we had to go homeless. . .
(17 year old married woman)

A few parents were prepared to assist their children to get housing by telling the council that they were evicting their children and making them homeless.

I just went down there and they said they would put me in a hostel, because I said my mum was throwing me out. My mum wrote this letter saying she was throwing me out from such and such a date, so they put us in the hostel. (16 year old cohabitee)

Efforts such as these to speed up the process of obtaining council housing did not lead to instant success in being offered a council flat. Women had to be prepared to go into the least desirable council accommodation, bed and breakfast hostels, for a period first. Once there, there was no guarantee that women would not have to stay for up to two years. They therefore gambled on relatively short term discomfort for long term gain.

It was evident that women were not passive victims of 'the system'. They quickly learned, from family, friends and citizens advice centres and bureaux, how best to facilitate their attempts to get council housing, and took action to manipulate the process. Many parents were supportive of their children's attempts and would accompany them to council housing offices when they were able to. This may partly be because rehousing was in parents' as well as women's interest if the parental home was overcrowded, but parents of women who already lived independently also tried to help.

Male partners were scarcely mentioned in attempts to get council housing. This seems largely to have been because bearing a child was the factor which made young women eligible for council housing, and therefore women were central to the process. Many male partners became dependent on women to get council housing and to allow them to move in. For many men, fatherhood thus provided them with a rare opportunity to leave their own parental home or to leave unsatisfactory housing.

Although women generally moved to less desirable housing than their parents' over the course of the study, there was wide variation in the quality of the housing and the neighbourhoods in which women were offered housing. Some were offered small terraced houses in quiet, residential streets, while others were offered flats high in tower blocks on vast estates. Satisfaction with allocated housing also varied. Some women envisaged staying in their allocated accommodation for the foreseeable future and were pleased to do so, while others were keen to move as soon as possible.

One woman arranged two swaps for herself in order to improve the quality of the council housing she obtained. Within the two years of the study she moved four times. Yet when her daughter was two years old she was still in poor accommodation and was very unhappy with it. She did not, however, think that she would move again in a hurry.

> Q–How do you feel about your flat?
> A–No. I mean it's got no heating. Plugs don't work properly and there's a lot of decorating and they're not giving me money to decorate and people knock at the door how much hours a night [to see previous tenant]. . . It's just like whole lot of problems. I mean the front door if you push it too hard it just flies open and there's people writing on the doors. . .
> (16 year old single woman whose friend was living with her at 21 months)

Dissatisfaction with the housing stock was not the only reason for wanting to move house. Women who were rehoused a long way from their families were sometimes keen to arrange flat swaps which would take them nearer their family home. Council housing departments played little part in the organization of swaps, leaving the major effort to the individuals concerned. Nonetheless, some women managed to organize them. One couple, for example, exchanged a ground floor flat on a lowrise estate for a flat on the 14th floor in a less pleasant estate, in order to be within walking distance of both sets of parents. The woman they exchanged with also wanted to be near her family. The couple who arranged the swap disliked their new flat so much that they immediately wanted to move to another flat in the same area so that they could continue to visit their families each day without having to pay any bus fares.

> I'm right at the bottom of the [council housing] list. They said if I find my own exchange, then I can exchange, but it's finding someone who will go up to that height and I don't know. (18 year old married woman)

Desire for geographical proximity to families of origin is hardly surprising since in general women had little (if any) spare money for bus fares, and found it difficult to manoeuvre buggies and babies onto public transport. Maintaining social network contacts with both family and friends required being in relatively close proximity to the area in which the women had grown up, and was important to them.

> We'd prefer to – to move like further down in Townside or further away. It all depends. But a little nearer to me mum and his mum. Cos it's. . . the walking. . . Yeah cos when you've got a double buggy you can't get on a bus and you have to walk everywhere, and that's a bit

far. (17 year old cohabiting woman who had a six month old baby and her
first child of 21 months, and who very much liked the council house she had
been given. Her [white] father still did not talk to her because her child is
black)

I wish I could take my flat with me. I do want to move though. [?]
Well preferably back to — , cos that's where I come from, and I know
practically everybody there. And it's the *one* area where you can feel
safe to walk around at night. . . (18 year old single woman)

Offers of accommodation on the other side of London tended to be
turned down.

When we went to the council, they told us that they were going to
offer us places out there [other side of London] because there was
none in. . . and if we wanted to appeal against it we could. There's
no way I was going to live that far, so we appealed against it. . .
(Married woman)

Only two women in the study had access to a car they could drive
themselves. But even one of these wanted to be nearer to her family
so that they would also visit her rather than relying on her to drive
over.

Sometimes I used to feel why don't they come and visit me? But then
I realized it was because I was too far away. When I see everyone
near enough all the time they're round me mum, so they haven't got
no reason to come up here. (18 year old married woman who had organized
a swap with a woman who also wanted to be nearer to her mum)

So far council housing has been discussed as if it was the only
housing women had access to. By 21 months after birth eight women,
however, were owner-occupiers. They were married women who
married before pregnancy, most of whose husbands earned more
than was usual for male partners in this study.

Some parents were instrumental in helping their married daughters to obtain housing. Indeed one woman was unique in the study
in that about six months after birth her mother started buying her
house. This woman was exceptional in being an owner-occupier
without her husband earning well. Her husband was unemployed
throughout the two years of the study. Prior to buying her the
house, however, her mother had been paying rent for the flat in
which she lived.

Q–How much is your mortgage going to be?
A–No idea.
Q–How much is your rent at the moment?
A–Um 45 to 50 pounds. Don't know. Really don't know. My mother pays for it.
(19 year old married woman)

This woman was the only one in a couple relationship who was entirely kept by her mother. One other woman was, however, living in a house mortgaged to her father and next door to her parents' own house. Although she lived in the house with her husband, it was in her father's name, and one room was sometimes used by her brother, and was filled with his possessions.

Q–Is this your own house?
A–It's in my father's name because he pays the mortgage.
Q–How much is the mortgage?
A–I don't know... I keep the front bedroom and the little bedroom and my brother keeps the back room, but he doesn't sleep here.
(18 year old married woman)

This woman didn't have exclusive possession of the house. Yet she clearly benefitted from having desirable accommodation at no material cost to herself or her husband. She was further dependent on her father because he employed her husband in the family business. Without material support from her family, her standard of living would have been markedly reduced.

In two other instances women had some parental assistance in buying their own homes. They had lived very cheaply with their parents-in-law and parents respectively when they first began to cohabit and got married. They had thus been enabled to save money for a mortgage. One of these spouses was employed in the family clothing manufacturing business. A further set of parents contributed to the deposit for their daughter's mortgage and employed their son-in-law in their restaurant.

Material support

A pervasive theme running through this book is that women who become mothers in their teenage years have limited access to material resources. Few women interviewed found it easy to make ends meet on the money coming into their household. Yet with changes in social security legislation many mothers in subsequent generations of women who give birth in their teenage years will obtain fewer welfare benefits.

In late pregnancy two-thirds of the sample (46) were either experiencing financial problems or expected to have money problems once their child was born. Regular weekly household income ranged from nothing (for three 16 year olds living with their parents) to £250 for a 19 year old whose husband was relatively well paid. Nearly half (36) were dependent on supplementary benefit as their main source of income. Forty-five per cent had a weekly income of £50 or less.

Apparently large differentials between women with husbands or cohabitees who earned relatively well did not always reflect large differences in standards of living. This was because households with the higher levels of income were responsible for paying their own rents or mortgages, whereas, when these women had their children, the rents of those on supplementary benefit were paid in full by the DHSS (now the DSS). Also, although special-needs payments were abolished in 1986, women interviewed in this study who were on supplementary benefit were lucky enough to obtain special-needs payments for major, necessary items of equipment, like cots and prams. Women who were on supplementary benefit were, however, responsible for paying their own fuel bills from their supplementary benefit and this was a major drain on their resources. In terms of future standard of living it seemed likely that the biggest differentials were likely to be between those who were managing, albeit by struggling, to buy their own houses and those who were dependent on accommodation rented from the council.

Over the two years of the study poverty remained a dominant feature of women's lives. When their children were six months old nearly two-thirds of women (63%, 53) were dependent on supplementary benefit as their main source of income. A further five were reliant on unemployment benefit, and one on an education grant. Six were employed. Household income that women had access to (that is, excluding parental income for those living at home) ranged from £25 to £254. Just over a third (35%) had a household income of over £100 per week.

Twenty-one months after birth 14 women (21%) were employed (7 part time, and 7 full time). Less than half (40%, 27) were dependent on supplementary benefit. Household income ranged from £25 to £240. A similar percentage (34%) earned over £100 as had done at the six month interview. Most women's household income had not increased over the two years of the study. If inflation is taken into account, many women's household income had probably decreased in real terms.

Women who received supplementary benefit were united in dissatisfaction with the amount they received.

£26–80 [a week] can only just do for me. Well how is it going to do for me and the baby after? Sometimes it worries me. (17 year old single woman)

What social security is giving me I really have to struggle on it. And most of the time I'm always broke until the next money comes in but I just do without until the next money comes in. (19 year old single woman)

When we first moved in here and we first had [baby] we were getting £110 per fortnight, but then they put it down to £76. [Why?] Cos they said they were paying we're gas bills, but they're taking too much off us, cos David went up a few weeks ago and they said that they were taking too much off us and they said they were giving us a bit extra, but they have nae. (19 year old married woman)

Women were frequently dissatisfied with the length of time it took for supplementary benefit offices to process their claims, and with the way in which they were treated when they went to claim in person. Two-fifths (39%) had something negative to say about their contacts with the DHSS. Staff were often reported to be rude and unhelpful. Going to the supplementary benefit offices was felt to be an ordeal by many women because of the long waiting times and ungracious reception they received.

For example us the other weekend, our cheques hadn't arrived and we were faced with a whole weekend without any money at all. So you're in a state and if you phone up and you're confronted by someone who's rude and not understanding, it's going to make you worse... The whole system seems like that... You've got benches and benches of depressed looking people... and you have to wait for ages and ages and it's all depressing. (17 year old woman who married in pregnancy and had twins)

Yes, I had to wait so long in the freezing cold [in unfurnished flat]. Had to wait about eight weeks. She sent me money [immediately] for my bed and cooker, and that was it. I was always phoning her up every day. But I was quite quick. My brother waited months and months and months. (17 year old cohabitee)

Economic support from male partners

Furstenberg (1987) suggests that white mothers under 20 fare better economically if they marry rather than remaining single.

> For whites, marriage operates as a major recovery route, offering an alternative or, at least, an important supplement to their own earning ability. Low education and restricted job opportunities, therefore, are not quite as costly as they are for black young mothers.
>
> On the other hand, the advantages of delaying parenthood are not so great for blacks as well. As we discovered, blacks who postponed motherhood are less likely to do well economically than whites who enter parenthood in adolescence. The cruel fact is that for blacks delaying childbearing has a relatively low payoff. They are damned if they do, and damned if they don't. (Furstenberg, 1987, pp. 396–7)

Furstenberg's analyses are for the USA and are long term, following women from pregnancy until their own children are adolescent, whereas this study is of British women and only of the first two years of their children's lives. Nonetheless there was no evidence that marriage would rescue most women from poverty. For while women were more likely to have married if their male partners were employed, many married couples were struggling to make ends meet, and it was rare for them to own their own homes.

All except two (5%) of the women who were married or cohabiting when their children were nearly two years old reported that their partner had an income, and knew where the money came from. Married and cohabiting male partners were more likely than the male partners of single women to be in employment. Most men (70%, 28) who lived with women were reported to earn their income, whereas overall only 54% (37) of male partners in the sample were reported to be employed two years after the birth. Not surprisingly single women were less likely than married or cohabiting women to know how their children's fathers got their income. Nineteen per cent (13) of respondents did not know what their children's fathers' employment status was and nearly all of them were single.

According to women's reports the amount of money cohabiting or married men brought into the household ranged from nothing (one man) to £180 per week. Income levels were varied. However both the median and the mode (four men) was £100. The mean for those men who were reported to have an income was £58. The lower levels of income came from state benefits rather than earnings. Twenty eight per cent (11) of married or cohabiting male partners received state benefit (one received unemployment benefit, the others supplementary benefit). One cohabiting woman had no idea where her male partner got his money from.

Single women rarely received any income from their male partners at all. In late pregnancy one single woman had reported receiving regular sums of money (£20) from her child's father. By the time her child was two years old she no longer had any contact with him, and got no more money. At two years of age only four women who were not cohabiting received money from their children's father. This did not always increase their available income, however. If the women were dependent on supplementary benefit and declared this additional income, the amount they received from their child's father was deducted from the benefit they received. More single men may well have wished to contribute money to the mothers of their children but had been prevented from doing so by lack of money. This is particularly relevant since men with the poorest prospects were least likely to be married.

> He is on the dole as well, and he has to give money to his mum, so... [he can't give any money to the respondent]. (Single woman; pregnancy interview)

It remains to be seen whether the British schemes to ensure that fathers who do not live with their children pay maintenance for them has any impact on men who father children with teenage women. Since such men are themselves frequently living in poverty, it may be as Angela Phillips (1990) suggests that such schemes 'will make it more difficult to get reluctant fathers to acknowledge paternity at all'.

It might be thought that because women who are married or cohabiting have their male partners' incomes coming into the household, they are likely to be economically better off than single women. There are, however, two reasons why this expectation was often not met.

Firstly, if both members of the couple were dependent on supplementary benefit (or if a man earned very little money and the woman was unemployed) women were likely to be economically better off if they claimed supplementary benefit as an individual rather than if the couple claimed as a unit (Wilson, 1987). In this study for example, single women living alone received about £25.70 supplementary benefit per week in pregnancy, compared with about £22.75 per week for each member of cohabiting couples (the amount women reported that they received varied). One-parent benefit was, of course, only available to single, rather than cohabiting or married, women. Even women married to men who were earning in the top range for this sample sometimes felt that they were disadvantaged by not being able to claim State benefit in their own right.

> I don't think there's no benefits in it at all. . . I mean you lose – like if you weren't working you get less money when you're married. . . I mean before I was married. . . I was getting. . . unemployment money, but as soon as you get married, you have to give it all up don't you? . . . I think you're better off not married. (17 year old married woman; pregnancy interview)

Single women or couples who were dependent on supplementary benefit could (at the time these women gave birth) obtain special-needs payments to enable them to buy essential household and baby items when they first set up home and had their first child. Since married and cohabiting women were more likely to have employed male partners than were single women, some women who lived with male partners expressed anger about the welfare payments and grants that single women could obtain.

> The ones that do need the help never seem to get it. In my mind anyway. I mean I'm sometimes hard up enough that I don't get any shopping, but I don't get a cent from them. . . I know some of the things I'm not entitled to – the free milk, the um FIS [family income supplement] the – that sort of thing. I know I'm not entitled to it because they don't take what you have to pay out a month and what you actually have left in your pocket. They take it on what his gross income is which is relatively high, but once you've knocked out everything you gotta pay and everything, you find that you're just left – we're left with less than what people on the dole are which if they look at it that way is a whole different kettle of fish, but they don't look at it that way. They don't look at what he earns in respect to what we actually have left in our pockets each week, so I don't actually get anything off of the social security at all.
> Q–Do you think you should?
> A–Yes, yes I do. I think if they was to look into it better, although. . . I don't give anybody that right to social security money but I do think that people do tend – I'm not necessarily saying that they don't deserve it, but the ones that I know are doing a lot better than what I am on social security than what I am, going about it the right way. (18 year old home-owning married woman)

Ironically, social security revisions have served to remove reasons for the sort of discontent the above respondent was expressing by reducing welfare benefits (in terms of payment of rent, special-needs payments and in some cases weekly income) to unemployed parents and their children. These reforms are likely to increase differentials between couples where men are earning relatively well and those where men are unemployed, and will, therefore, have deleterious effects on families with children.

The second reason that cohabiting women are not necessarily better off than single women is to do with control of household resources. It is increasingly being recognized that resources which enter a household are not equally distributed among household members (Brannen and Wilson, 1987). Men in couple relationships tend to consume a disproportionately large quantity of household resources, and to have greater control of how resources are used (Graham, 1986; Wilson, 1987). In cohabitation or marriage it is still usual for welfare benefits to be paid to male partners (although women have been able to receive it since the end of 1983) and, after childbirth it was unusual for women to be employed. Women living with their children's fathers were, therefore, dependent on their husbands or cohabitees distribution of earnings or benefits. The following example is unusual in this study because the husband, who was present at the six month interview, answered questions about how the couple organizes money within their household.

> If she needs anything, like if she said to me I need something. . . Like, you see I do work on the side right, now and again and it depends on whatever I earn. But if I had £100 I should give her £30 and say 'Go and buy some clothes'. The other money would go on the house. Like last week I gave her £75 to buy clothes for herself and the baby, and she spent it all. By the night time I was skint, and I didn't realize. Spent £85 in the pub! I was in company. I only went out for half a lager to tell you the truth. . . I was in a lot of company. (Spouse of woman who was 18 years old at birth who married after birth)

Feelings about men's financial contributions

Perhaps not surprisingly the respondent whose husband's account is quoted above felt that she wanted more control over how her household finances were organized. She also said that she thought she would only stay with her husband for another couple of years.

When their children were six months old roughly equal numbers of married women (excluding cohabiting women) in the Thomas

Coram study felt that their husbands (nine), themselves (eight) or both partners (seven) were in control of household finances. Only five married women reported any feelings of unhappiness about the way control of their finances was exercised. Nonetheless some men's perceived irresponsibility with money could be a real bone of contention. In one case a married woman had already separated from her husband by the time their child was six months old. His failure to pay the rent from the family's supplementary benefit was an important factor in her decision to end the marriage.

As we have seen early motherhood mainly occurs among couples who are poor. When their children were nearly two years old more than two-thirds of the women in the study (68%, 46) said that they found it difficult to make ends meet. It is not therefore surprising that some women expressed dissatisfaction with male partners whom they felt were not making sufficient effort to augment the household income by keeping jobs or by working hard.

> Cos I told him if he's lost his job there's no way he's moving back here. Cos that was a good job he had. There was no need to lose it. There was no need to stay off. (Temporarily separated woman; 19 years old at birth)

> He's one of those people that you know if he don't wanna work he don't go you know. He hasn't got much will power at all. . . He sort of lays in bed and says 'oh I don't wanna go. I don't wanna go' you know. I suppose it ain't very nice working out in the cold weather but he does it in the hot weather as well. It's just laziness. I don't know. . . [This causes a lot of arguments] (18 year old cohabitee)

Other women were resigned to accepting what they felt to be a meagre financial contribution from their male partners.

> Sometimes it's [cohabitee's earnings] around £30 and you know. . . It's not really worth it.
> Q–Do you ever talk about the fact that it's not worth it?
> A–Yeah sometimes, but it might end up into an argument so I don't really bother, just let him – let him. It's something for him to do really. I suppose he'd just be a misery around the house.
> (19 year old at birth; cohabiting)

Parental and other support

In late pregnancy when most women who had been employed no longer were, many parents helped to improve their daughters' standard of living in a number of ways. Firstly, women who lived with their parents lived more cheaply than they would have done in their own households.

> I decided to tell my mum that I wanted to give her money for food. . . So she said to me that I don't have to pay. And I don't really have to give money for food. But because I'm staying here I'm going to want to eat more and she can't really afford it. . . so I said to her that I would give her a certain amount of money and she said to me that she didn't want that much. . . So just started giving her £10. And now and again I give her £15 because I'm not paying rent, so I'm actually living here for nothing. (19 year old single woman)

> Q–How much do you give to your parents?
> A–Eighty to £100 a month. Because now I've stopped working I don't know what things will be like at the end of the month, so we'll have to see.
> Q–How do you feel about the amount you give?
> A–I don't think anything is enough, but we try and give her as much as we can.
> (18 year old living with her husband in her mother's house)

Secondly, parents whose daughters no longer lived with them would frequently feed their children several times a week when they visited, give them foodstuff and/or buy them clothes or baby items. Without actually giving money, they made material contributions to their daughters' households.

> Our mums sometimes invite us over to dinner. That's their way of helping us without giving us money. They buy us little bits and pieces. . . for the baby or they bring something up for the home. So they don't actually give us money. They just do it in their own sort of little way. (17 year old married woman)

On the whole, parents' material resources were stretched, and few were able to give their daughters substantial material assistance. Many, however, helped as much as they could and a few parents could afford to give more than meals.

> Like I mean my family's helped us with the house. Getting the settees. . . the cabinet, the wardrobe and everything. They've helped us a lot to pay it all off. But apart from that I don't really get any money. (19 year old married woman)

Now and again. . . my dad treats him for a tenner more. (19 year old married woman living in a house her dad is buying whose husband is employed in her father's factory)

When we got married we got some money for our wedding present. Then there was spare furniture which the family didn't want, like the bookshelves and the table. Carpets came out of our wedding present money. Pots and pans and cutlery were given by our relatives, so we've done really well. . . So it's all been gradual and due to relatives. Otherwise we'd still be sitting on the floor cushions. I was nine months pregnant and very uncomfortable sitting on a floor cushion. (17 year old woman who married in pregnancy)

One woman (the one whose mother was buying her a house) and her husband were entirely dependent on her mother for all the income she received.

She gives me a weekly £35. Thirty five pounds a week I use up for housekeeping. I know it sounds a lot, but it just flies out of your hands! And I've got about £500 in the bank saved. (19 year old with unemployed spouse)

However much material support women got from their own parents few felt that they were materially comfortable. The woman quoted above, for example, reported that her mother always made sure she had 'enough money', but that she was rather tired of having to ask her mother for money to buy specific, named items rather than being given a weekly lump sum to budget on. She also said 'I would like more'.

Families were invaluable in helping women to get the baby clothes and small items they needed in preparation for a new baby.

Q–What have you got ready for the baby?
A–Practically everything except for a sterilizer and things like a cot and a pram. [Did you buy them?] No my mum bought them and my sister bought them and his parents have bought things.
(16 year old single woman)

A–I've got Pampers, lotions, cot blankets, a teddy bear. I haven't got the cot and pram yet. Most of the things have been given to me by me nan, me mum's friends, me sister.
(17 year old single woman)

Parents did not only assist single daughters (of whom very few received money, even occasionally, from male partners). They also bought items for married daughters whose husbands were employed. Their contributions were partly because they were excited about having a new grandchild, and partly because they recognized the hardships their daughters would face in buying baby things.

> I bought everything. . . I need like my nightdresses and my stuff and that I've got to take in. . . I bought a lot of the baby's clothes as well from me and Graham. But the main accessories I need, like pram and that was bought by parents. (17 year old married woman)

Two sets of parents and one pair of parents-in-law stand out as not having offered material assistance, although it seemed they could have afforded to do so. The parents-in-law were disappointed that, having paid for a private education for their son, he had married (and had twins with) a working class woman with no educational qualifications. Similar motives inspired one set of parents who had disapproved of their daughter's early marriage, and felt that married couples should be self sufficient. The woman concerned felt strongly that she would never tell her parents how difficult she found it to make ends meet.

> They don't know we're sort of in debt. I mean cos if I say to them 'Oh I can't afford such and such this week' they'll start going on about 'oh well you let yourself in for it and you're always hard up, and you're always this. . . Cos they're always going on about how hard up I am. . . and by this. . . stage in life he said you should be a little well off. . . We've only been married three and a half years. We've got our own place which is a lot more than some people have got. . . I think they're trying to rate us up too high quite honestly. . . (Married woman, 18 years old at birth)

The other woman came from a middle class background. In late pregnancy she reported that her mother was preventing her father from giving her money on the grounds that she would never apply to get supplementary benefit if they paid for everything she needed. This particular respondent did take a long time to apply for supplementary benefit but was able to pay for things she needed by using her Barclaycard. She was unusual in the study in having a credit card.

Parents, therefore, denied their children material help either if they disapproved of some aspect of their behaviour, or if they thought that taking a hard line would be beneficial to their daughter in the long run.

Once infants were born many parents continued to give their daughters any material assistance they could. Six months after birth over three-quarters of the sample were receiving some material help (other than cash) from their families (compared with just under half who were getting similar help from their child's father's families). When children were 21 months old just under one-sixth of the sample (11) were receiving regular sums of money from their parents. Notably none of those who reported that their parents regularly gave them cash had been 16 or 17 when they gave birth. The explanation for this may be that the youngest women in the study were those most likely to be still living with their parents and hence getting board and lodging either free, or at a nominal cost. They may also have been getting money from their parents that they took for granted, and hence did not report.

If women were desperate for either money or food, their parents were likely to be the first people women turned to for help. In general women reported themselves to be reluctant to ask anybody for food (although many sometimes got food from their parents). When their children were nearly two, women were asked who they would ask for food if necessary. Two-thirds (63%, 40) said that they would ask their relatives for food. Seventeen per cent regularly got food from their relatives anyway.

Social security benefits

Just as long waits for council housing increased some women's feelings of competitiveness with other council tenants, so some women in straitened financial circumstances clearly resented some other welfare claimants. Mothers perceived to be in similar economic circumstances, but considered to be getting more welfare benefits or doing better materially, were the targets of such resentment.

Divisive resentments between people who are essentially in similar economic circumstances are fuelled by, and make sense in, a context in which the social construction of mothers under 20 (particularly single ones) serves to give widespread currency to views that the irresponsibility and fecklessness of mothers under 20 make them undeserving welfare claimants. The statements some women made about other welfare claimants directly fitted into discourse which stigmatizes teenage mothers. Statements such as the following served to indicate to interviewers that those making the statements were different from, and more deserving than, other mothers under 20. In other words some women did not question the validity of commonly held stereotypes about young women becoming pregnant for lucrative reasons, but distanced themselves from the associated stigma.

> A lot of mothers get pregnant *because* [my emphasis] they find that when they have kids they can cope better because they seem to get more money when they've got a child, than when they're on their own. (19 year old single woman)

In the last section the ways in which women attempted to accelerate their housing allocation were discussed. There were no equivalent ways in which the supplementary benefit system could be manipulated. One woman did, however, report that she was cohabiting without the DHSS's knowledge so that she and her partner could both continue to get supplementary benefit. This is because claiming supplementary benefit as a couple rather than as individuals reduces household income somewhat (Wilson, 1987). Two male partners also occasionally earned money from casual employment while relying on supplementary benefit as their main source of income.

There was enormous variation in women's knowledge of their benefit entitlement, and there was similar variation in the number and quantity of grants women received. Thus, while women were given fairly similar amounts of supplementary benefit, there was no clear pattern for discretionary payments. Six months after birth, for example, (the time by which most women who were going to, had received grants) 34 women (40%) had received grants for clothes, furniture, baby items, etc. These grants were reported to range in value from £35 to £620.

In a study such as this it was impossible to assess the basis on which grants had been allocated, particularly since supplementary benefit officers visited many women to assess their 'need', and interviewers made no such assessments. Discrepancies in the value of discretionary grants awarded, and some women's awareness or suspicion of them, were responsible for the hostility which some women expressed to the DHSS as well as to other claimants. Hostility was not only expressed by those who were dependent on the DHSS, but also by women who felt they were 'doing things the right way' in being self supporting when they had a child. Yet, while they struggled, they felt that other people were comfortably supported by the DHSS and did not have to make any effort to provide for themselves.

> She's um unmarried with a baby. She has her flat paid for. She has money in her pocket each week off SS [social security]. If she can't pay her electric she's only gotta go to SS and say 'I'm a bit hard up.

I can't pay it.' And she gets half of it paid for her. This, that and the other. I mean you think, well, I should have had [baby], not got married, lived in a council house and taken everything off the State and I'd have been better off. They get their house done up. She's had everything. Absolutely everything bought in her house down to carpets, central heating, absolutely everything furnished inside and you think to yourself well you know, you go doing it the decent way. . . you don't get anything out of it. (18 year old married woman)

Ironically the removal of special-needs payments in 1986 and its replacement with a system of loans seems likely to remove some of the above respondent's reasons for complaint about welfare claimants by worsening many women's material circumstances.

From women's accounts it appeared that supplementary benefit officers did not draw women's attention to any grants or benefits they had not claimed. Presumably, therefore, women who knew most about the benefits they could claim stood a better chance of getting everything they were entitled to than those who did not.

Women's knowledge about entitlements came from a variety of sources. Some women had read DHSS leaflets on benefit entitlement. Others had been told by medical staff or social workers (usually hospital social workers) what they could apply for, or had asked friends and relatives. By the end of the study a few women had also come to regard citizens' advice bureaux as an extremely useful source of information about benefits. In practice, most women did not wait for DHSS officials to tell them what they were entitled to, but made efforts to find out for themselves. Most had read something on benefit entitlement, and nearly a quarter (24%, 16) said that they had received some advice on which benefits they were entitled to from sources other than the DHSS. Seven had received advice from their own relatives, four from friends, four from health and welfare workers, and five from other sources (such as citizens' advice bureaux). No one reported getting help or advice from husbands or cohabitees.

Q–Do you get milk tokens?
A–No the midwife says I wasn't entitled to it [milk tokens] so I didn't apply. I looked at the leaflets – it doesn't look like I'm liable for it but the milkman reckons I am. My friend says it's very hard to get the tokens off them – she says you have to really push them.
(17 year old in late pregnancy)

Q–Did anyone help you find out what you were entitled to?
A–The citizens advice bureau. They helped last time about the request

for clothes. They wrote to the social security for me but we were refused. But they [the CAB] told me I was owed £200 by the social security because I was on supplementary benefit and I hadn't claimed something else [respondent didn't know what]. And I got this back pay.
(16 year old single woman; third contact)

Women thus made active efforts to find out which grants and benefits they were entitled to by reading, asking people and going to information centres like the citizens' advice bureaux. Many also made a lot of effort to manage on their income.

We did get budget schemes for the electric, then if you use those they bill you once a year – which last year added up to about £88 because of the winter, which was an unbelievable sum, but luckily we had it saved somehow. With the gas, we only use the cooker and it's a meter, so the man just comes and collects the money. . . So if you put about five pounds a week away, it comes out all right [for the phone]. . .
(Married woman, second interview)

Some women were assisted in their attempts at managing money by their mothers.

Q–What did you do when you were worried about not having enough money?
A–Talked to me mum. Tried saying what do you do with your money? And all things like that. She just said to me, well you should be able to cope. Put this away for that, this away for that – so that's what we've done, and it's. . . [better].
(18 year old married woman; second interview)

A few women, however, were using strategies for coping with low income which seemed likely to lead them into problems later. In particular, some had borrowed money from credit clubs at staggeringly high annual percentage rates, while others had bought items from catalogues, and had to worry about making regular weekly repayments.

Summary and conclusions

Men provided very little consistent childcare help. More involved male partners played with their children a fair amount, but not all male partners did so. Men who lived with their partners were more likely to help with childcare than non-resident male partners, but men did not provide extensive childcare help. The context in which men make little contribution to childcare is also one in which they do little else to help with other household tasks. For example less than a third (30%) of cohabiting and married men were reported to have done any household shopping in the 12 months previous to the interview. Men's non-involvement in childcare is simply one aspect of their non-participation in 'women's work'. Young men who father children with women who are under 20 years of age are not particularly different from men who father children with older women in this respect.

Most women in this study were dependent on local authorities for housing. Many expressed dissatisfaction with how they were treated by housing departments. Some women made determined efforts to improve their chances of being rehoused by making repeated visits to housing departments and by being prepared to go into bed and breakfast accommodation if necessary. Parents frequently assisted women in these attempts.

Relatives, particularly mothers, were of prime importance in providing both childcare and material support for many women. Even where women were married, and male partners were making financial contributions to their households, some parents supplemented their daughter's standard of living. A substantial number of women were reliant on supplementary benefit for income and provision of furniture, baby equipment, etc. Most found out what they were entitled to from a variety of sources, then applied for it. But even women who were not dependent on supplementary benefit reported difficulty in making ends meet. Women were, however, resourceful in using budgetting methods like saving schemes which ensured that they were able to pay their bills. A few women's friends did provide occasional childcare help and advice about supplementary benefit entitlement, etc. However women's own relatives were more likely than anyone else to provide them with practical and material support. Women were mostly dissatisfied with their experience of the DHSS (now the DSS) but, on the whole, were pleased with the help they received from their relatives.

On the whole most male partners of 16–19 year old first time mothers in the Thomas Coram study made little economic contributions to the households in which their children lived. Most male partners were either unemployed or in jobs which did not pay enough for them to give much financial support to anyone else. This profile of men who father the children of women in their teenage years has been found in other studies. Yet much literature on early motherhood assumes that most teenage mothers would fare better if they married instead of remaining single.

Women's accounts in the Thomas Coram study suggest that this is not the case. Teenage women who have followed the conventionally accepted trajectory of marriage then conception do seem to fare better economically than teenage women who conceive while they are single. This is not, however, because women have benefitted from the institution of marriage *per se*. It seems instead that the young women who are likely to follow this path are those whose male partners are relatively high earners (compared with other men who impregnate teenage women). High levels of unemployment and poor wages for young men are probably partly responsible for the decreasing proportion of young mothers who marry their children's fathers.

7

The Children

A major concern expressed in research literature on teenage mothers and by health and welfare professionals about the consequences of early motherhood centres on the welfare of the children born to mothers who are under 20 years of age. Children whose mothers gave birth before they were 20 are reported to experience a variety of disadvantages. The first half of this chapter will consider the available evidence on what happens to children whose mothers have them before they are 20 years old. The second half will use data from the Thomas Coram Research Unit study to examine, in depth, how a group of mothers who gave birth before they were 20 thought and felt about their children, as well as how those children were faring in their first two years.

The effects of early motherhood on children

From the time they are born, the infants of women who give birth in their teenage years are reported to be worse off than infants born to older mothers. They are reported to have a higher likelihood of being of low birthweight and of dying in infancy than the children of older mothers (Butler et al., 1981; Wells, 1983; Bury, 1984).

Later on in childhood, children born when their mothers were in their teenage years are apparently more likely than children born to older mothers to be educationally disadvantaged; to be subject to child abuse; and to have accidents which result in injuries serious enough to require hospitalization (Butler et al., 1981).

Popular accounts of teenage childbearing rarely fail to mention its devastating consequences for children, who are presumed likely to encounter parental neglect, child abuse, abandonment, family instability, and other forms of parental miscare. (Furstenberg et al., 1987).

The few studies (all done in the USA) which have followed children born to women under 20 into adulthood and reported their findings suggest that the gap between individuals born to younger mothers and those born to older mothers continues later in life. By early adulthood children born to mothers under 20 years of age are reported to have fewer educational qualifications and less desirable jobs than children born to older women. In addition they are reported to be more likely to start having children early in their life course, and to have more children than their peers (Furstenberg et al., 1987; Card, 1981).

This dismal prognosis for children born to young women has been linked with a variety of suggested causes. Young women's immaturity, inadequate knowledge of child development and how to bring up a child, as well as economic disadvantage have all been blamed (Lamb and Elster, 1986; Card, 1981; Newson and Lilley, 1988).

> Many are victims of child abuse at the hands of parents too immature to understand why their baby is crying or how their doll-like plaything has suddenly developed a will of its own. (*Time Magazine*, December 9 1985)

Studies which attempt to establish whether having a mother who is 19 years old or less at birth is, in itself, bad for children's development, have typically found that poor socio-economic conditions (such as household income level, level of education, occupation, type of housing, whether housing is overcrowded or not, number of household moves in the last year, marital status of mother, etc.) are important influences on children's development, even if age is reported to have an independent effect (Card, 1981; Furstenberg, 1987; Bolton and Belsky, 1986).

If early motherhood has deleterious consequences for children, it may be because women with particularly poor socio-economic characteristics form a greater proportion of mothers under, than over, 20 years of age. In other words such differences may not be due to differences in parenting styles or attitudes towards children, and may not distinguish all younger mothers from all older ones. Instead they may be a feature of particular socio-economic circumstances.

Support for this view is provided by those studies which attempt to control for differences in socio-economic status between younger mothers and older ones (Butler et al., 1981; Card, 1981; Newson and Lilley, 1988; Furstenberg et al., 1987). Such studies generally find that differences between the children of younger mothers and those of older mothers are greatly reduced (or disappear altogether) if socio-economic variables are taken into account.

Card (1981) found that differences in educational and occupational attainment between the children of younger parents and the children of older parents virtually disappeared when she controlled certain socio-economic variables. In particular the matching of firstborn children brought up in single parent households whose mothers were under 20 with those whose mothers were over 20 when they gave birth, had most effect in reducing differences between the children of younger and of older mothers.

> With head of household controlled, very little of the variance in cognitive or personality profile while in high school was attributable to adolescent parentage... With respect to the outcome measures studied 11 years after high school, adolescent parentage had greater impact on marital and fertility history than on educational or occupational attainment. (Card, 1981, p. 151)

Even where researchers conclude that poor child outcomes are related to low maternal age rather than the socio-economic variables they have controlled for, differences between children born to different age groups of mothers tend to be small (Card, 1981; Butler et al., 1981). It is not generally possible to rule out completely the influence of variables other than age.

> The children's decreased birthweight, increased death rate, decreased likelihood of immunization, increased likelihood of gastroenteritis and accidents and poorer performance at five years were related to low maternal age irrespective of attempts to 'control out' the effects by allowing for associated influences such as low parity, low social class, increased number of younger siblings and suchlike. The fact that the differences between teenage and other mothers were in general reduced by such attempts to control possibly confounding co-variables supports the view that there is little specific biological effect of maternal age that could not be explained by other intervening variables; we just haven't allowed for all the right ones. (Butler et al., 1981, p. 63)

It is therefore difficult to be certain that ill effects which are reported to result from teenage motherhood, are, in reality, attributable to youthfulness rather than to other factors.

So far early motherhood has been discussed as if mothers under 20 form a homogeneous age group. Yet in the six years from 13 to 19, individuals undergo a range of social, biological and developmental changes. Butler and his colleagues found that younger teenage women's children were more likely to do poorly than older teenage women's children. When given developmental tests, children born to mothers who were 17 years old or less did worse than all other mothers (including 18 and 19 year olds). The largest differences found were between the youngest mothers (17 or less at birth) and the oldest ones (35 years or more at birth).

Similarly, poor obstetric results (complications of pregnancy and delivery, low birthweight and perinatal mortality) are a feature of motherhood in the earliest possible years. Teenage mothers of 16 years or older are biologically better equipped to bear healthy children than are 'elderly primigravidae' (Phipps-Yonas, 1980; Morris, 1981; Carlson et al., 1986).

Teenage mothers are thus not an undifferentiated group even with respect to their age. Those whose children do poorly are likely to be the very youngest mothers. Yet motherhood under 18 years is relatively uncommon in most countries. The Child Health and Education Study found that most teenage mothers' children do as well as the children of women who give birth in their 20s (the average age for childbearing) on many tests.

The circumstances in which early motherhood occurs have undergone rapid change this decade. Studies which have attempted to determine the long term consequences of early motherhood on children may not be relevant to subsequent generations of children born to mothers in their teenage years.

> The situation for teenage mothers today may be very different from what it was two decades ago when the study began. In the first place, most women in this study did not have an adequate opportunity to terminate their pregnancy by abortion... Two decades ago, early childbearing was generally not regarded as a social problem so long as it was accompanied by marriage. Most teenagers who became pregnant hastily married to avoid social stigma. Today, relatively few are prepared to wed merely because of a pregnancy... special services for unmarried teens were less readily available... At the same time, employment opportunities for both young men and young women were somewhat better than today. (Furstenberg et al., 1987, p. 18)

Although it is not possible to generalize between generations, long term follow ups of children born to mothers under 20 provide useful information. Our understanding of the factors which contribute to some children faring well, while others fare badly, is particularly enhanced by longitudinal studies.

The fact that fewer mothers under 20 now marry, and that many have close links with their own parents, may have positive effects on how children fare. Furstenberg (1976) found that those women under 20 who did not marry after having a child were more likely to continue with their education than women who married. Seventeen years after birth women with 'educational credentials' were more likely than those without to have children who did relatively well in school (Furstenberg et al., 1987).

Furstenberg and his colleagues found that 'marital status of the mother seems to have only weak effects on the preschool child's outcomes. . . But marital status is clearly associated with academic performance and behaviour problems in adolescence' (Furstenberg et al., 1987). They suggest that this is for two reasons:

(1) Women received a lot of help from their families in the early years of childrearing, but most had moved away from their families 16 years after birth.
(2) Most early marriages ended in divorce, but those marriages which were still in existence 16 years after birth were 'much more stable'.

Such findings suggest that for most mothers under 20 the increasing trend towards single motherhood seems unlikely, at least in the early years, to be disadvantageous to children.

Another way in which the profile of mothers under 20 has undergone change is in regard to their later fecundity. It used to be accepted almost as axiomatic that the earlier a woman had a child, the more children she was likely to have, and the more closely spaced her children were likely to be (Phipps-Yonas, 1980). Some North American research has, however, found that this is no longer the case.

> The strong inverse relationship between age at first birth and lifetime fertility of women, long taken for granted, has come under closer scrutiny in recent years. In US data, the relationship, while still significant, has weakened among the younger women. . . There seems to be a new trend for those who had a first birth early to have fewer children in their later reproductive years, and therefore to complete their fertility at a level not much higher than those who start their childbearing later in life. (Balakrishnan et al., 1988, p. 167)

In his longitudinal study of women who gave birth when they were under 18 years of age, Furstenberg et al., (1987) found that many women had second children within five years of first giving birth. Over half had already reached their desired number of children when seen at the five year follow up. Given that they had many childbearing years left at that stage, it seemed likely that they would reproduce families as large as the ones in which they grew up (half had four or more siblings). This expectation was not, however, borne out.

> We were wrong. . . Overall, about a fifth of the women never had a second birth, two-fifths had only one more child, 26% had two additional births, and the remainder (12%) had three or more children. *Of all additional births, 61% occurred in the first segment of the study* [their emphasis]. (Furstenberg et al., 1987, p. 35)

It seems that women who are currently giving birth in their teenage years are less likely than those who did so in previous decades to have a higher than average number of children. This may make a difference to their children's educational attainment since children from large families are less likely to do well on tests of intellectual development (Osborn and Milbank, 1987).

The mothers of women who give birth in their teenage years are consistently reported to have been under 20 themselves when they had their first child (Simms and Smith, 1986; Furstenberg, 1987). One of the consequences, for children, of early motherhood is thus reputed to be a repetition of early mothering. It is, however, also true that rates of early motherhood have diminished over the last two decades. It is less common for women under 20 to become mothers now than it was in their parents' generation. The significance of this is that many women whose mothers started bearing children early do not start having children in their teenage years. The corollary is that at least half of those who become mothers early in their life course had mothers who had not done so.

While adverse biological and social effects have been reported for the children of mothers who are under 20 years of age, it is not clear that it is the youthfulness of these mothers which is responsible for any differences found between younger and older mothers. Those studies which have indicated the existence of long term negative consequences for the children of mothers under 20 are not necessarily relevant to children currently being born to teenage women since the social context in which early motherhood occurs has under-gone rapid change.

Parenting style

Relatively little is known about the kind of parenting that children born to teenage mothers experience (Lamb and Elster, 1986). Several USA observational studies have, however, suggested that mothers under 20 years of age are less responsive to their infants than are older mothers (Landy et al., 1984; Crnick et al., 1981). By the time they are a year old Landy (1981) suggests that this lack of responsive-ness results in children being insecurely attached to their mothers.

Teenage mothers have also been reported to engage more in physical interaction (including punishment) and less in verbal inter-action with their infants than do older mothers (Field et al., 1980). Differences in parenting style between mothers who are under 20 years of age, and those older have been considered to indicate:

> That adolescents are less effective caregivers than adults in terms of providing a nurturant environment for their infants. . . environmental stimulation input to infants of adolescents is deficient in terms of frequency and stability of maternal contact, amount of verbal stimu-lation, need gratification, emotional climate, avoidance of restriction on motor and exploratory behaviour, provision of audiovisual and learning toys, and home characteristics indicative of parental concern with achievement. These findings strongly suggest that infants of adolescents may be at some developmental risk as a function of the postnatal environment typically available to them, insofar as that environment does not facilitate cognitive growth. (Carlson et al., 1986, pp. 10–11)

This profile of inadequate parenting in the teenage years has been attributed to several factors, including inadequate knowledge of child development (Fry, 1985) and hence unrealistic expectations of their children (Wise and Grossman, 1980). Additionally mothers under 20 are reported to be less tolerant of their children once they pass early infancy (Lamb and Elster, 1986). In their review of the 'parental behaviour of adolescent mothers and fathers' Lamb and Elster conclude that:

> There are several reasons for concern that the psychosocial circum-stances of teenage parents may adversely affect the quality of their parental behaviour. Psychological immaturity, lack of parenting skills,

economic stress, and stresses implicit in premature role transitions. . .
(Lamb and Elseter, 1986)

But the picture of inadequate parenting from young parents is far from clear. Lamb and Elster found that many of the studies they reviewed used inadequate comparison groups. For example:

Whereas the teens were all unmarried and living at home, most adult mothers were married. In addition, the mean parity was greater for the adult group. Thus we do not know whether maternal age, parity, or marital status accounted for the reported group differences. (Lamb and Elster, 1986, p. 97)

Concerns have also been voiced that the under 20s are likely to abuse their children, but the available evidence suggests that this is a rare occurrence. Bolton and Belsky (1986) report a study done for the Child Welfare League of America, which examined both officially reported cases of child maltreatment and ones dealt with by community agencies, but not necessarily reported. Miller found that 'adolescent parents' who abused their children in their teenage years were overrepresented by only 3 per cent. Those who give birth in their teenage years, but abused their children in their 20s were overrepresented by about 7 per cent. 'The expected "epidemic" of maltreatment perpetration by adolescent parents simply failed to materialize' (Bolton and Belsky, 1986, p. 125).

Newson and Lilley (1988) suggest that single mothers under 20 years of age are no more likely to report that they smack their one year old children than are older women. This phenomenon is, however, mediated by class. Far fewer middle class women than working class women admit to smacking their children. But there are no significant differences between younger, single women and their married older counterparts from social classes IV and V.

Most mothers who are under 20 years of age are reported to be affectionate towards their children and not to neglect them.

Yet we found little evidence that most mothers neglected their children. On the contrary, the energy put into providing adequate care while they were in school or at work, the pride they take in their teens' accomplishments, and the strong feelings of love are evident from the interviews. Most mothers feel they have done a good job, in less than ideal circumstances. . . (Furstenberg et al., 1987, p. 104)

There were no group differences in feelings of love for the infant.
(Lamb and Elster, 1986, p. 97 [reporting Mercer, Hackley and Bostrom, 1984])

> The general picture that emerges is that of some nine out of ten teenage mothers being pleased with having their babies so young... when their babies have reached the toddler stage. (Simms and Smith, 1986, from a nationally representative sample of British mothers under 20)

In summary, the evidence on the effects of early motherhood on children born to mothers who are under 20 is far from clear cut. Many published studies suggest that such children fare badly in a number of ways. Poor outcomes are said to result partly from parental characteristics, and partly from the parenting styles of women under 20. Yet the evidence available does not strongly support the belief that early motherhood is, in itself, detrimental to children's development.

The Thomas Coram study

Given the many questions which remain unanswered about the effects of early motherhood on children, it would be surprising if any one study could provide definitive answers. Information from the Thomas Coram study is limited for two reasons. Firstly, the study ended when the children being studied were nearly two years of age, and hence relate to a very small proportion of the children's childhoods. Secondly, most information was collected from interviews with mothers rather than by direct observation. Although this is a common method of investigating maternal feelings about and care of their children, accounts do not, of course, necessarily adequately reflect feelings about or behaviour with children. The data presented here, however, does give some insight into how this group of mothers thought about their children and felt themselves to be relating to them. Some data are also presented on the children's development.

The welcome the children received

By the time they were born, the majority of children in the Thomas Coram study were anticipated with pleasure. When they first realized that they were pregnant, 60% of the women had some negative feelings about being pregnant. But only 6% remained generally unhappy about the prospect of having a child in late pregnancy.

Although th moment when mother and baby actually meet is romanticized as a magical moment, women do not necessarily fall in love with their babies the moment they see them. Ann Oakley (1979) found that 70% of the women she studied reported that initially they felt nothing for their children. When interviewed six months after birth, one woman in five (20%) in the Thomas Coram study reported that she had had no feelings for her child immediately following birth. Lack of feeling usually lasted no more than a couple of days, and gave way to feelings of love and wonder. Very few women (4%) reported themselves to have been disappointed with their children, or said that they had felt any anger (6%) with their children at first. The fact that a smaller proportion of women reported having no initial feelings for their children in this study rather than in Oakley's study may be because women were asked to give retrospective accounts (six months after birth) and their recollections may have become romanticized. No one said that they had continued feeling either disappointment about, or nothing for their children beyond the immediate postnatal period. Nearly a fifth of the women (19%) reported that they occasionally felt very angry with their child at six months, but nearly three-quarters (73%) said that they had never felt such anger.

Most women (65%) said that they had never experienced much anxiety about their children either. Of those who reported that initially they had felt very anxious, most (24%) said they no longer did so six months after birth. Feelings of anxiety were almost exclusively about the possibility of cot death. Many women had seen television programmes on the topic, which had made them worry in case their child died. A few women were worried about handling their newborn infant. This general lack of anxiety probably reflects the confidence (based on their earlier experience with younger relatives or their friends' children) that many women felt about looking after small children.

As in Oakley's (1979) study, most women (84%) reported that they had had a clear sex preference for their children and more wanted a boy (46%) than a girl (37%). Boys were, however, not as popular as they were in Oakley's study (where 54% of women reported wanting a boy, compared with 25% who wanted a girl). Once children were actually born, most women (73%) reported themselves to be immediately happy with their children's sex. Only 8% claimed they had initially been entirely unhappy with the sex of the child they got, and all of them had stopped feeling negative about it in the first few months after birth. In this they were no different from older mothers (Oakley, 1979).

Although the majority of the children's fathers were reported to have a preference for either a girl or a boy, fewer of them than of the women were reported to have such a preference. More than a third (36%) apparently did not mind whether they had a boy or a girl. However those who were reported to have a preference that women knew about were more than twice as likely to want a boy as a girl: 42% wanted a boy, compared with 18% who wanted a girl.

Relatively few members of either women's or male partner's families expressed preferences for the sex of their grandchild (39% and 30% respectively). Yet male partners' relatives were more than three times as likely to express preferences for boys as for girls (21% cf. 6%). Women's relatives were more equally balanced with regard to sex preference: 18% preferred a boy, while 13% preferred a girl.

Although boys were more desired than girls, slightly more girls than boys were born (53%). Expressed preferences were rarely reported to have had any effect on how male partners and relatives reacted to the child's sex once it was born. Over 90% of fathers, 94% of women's relatives, and 97% of the child's father's relatives were said to be satisfied with the child's sex at birth. For those few who were disappointed, the child's sex reportedly made no difference to the help given.

According to women's accounts, therefore, nearly all the children in the study were welcomed warmly when they first arrived. If mothers had no feelings initially or felt disappointment with or anger towards their babies, those feelings did not last long. Similarly most of the babies' fathers, other relatives and friends seem to have been unequivocally positive about them at birth.

Breastfeeding

In their 1980 survey of infant feeding Martin and Monk (1982) found that roughly two-thirds of mothers initially breastfed their infants, but only about a quarter of mothers continued to breastfeed for the four months recommended by health professionals. In the Thomas Coram study a greater percentage of women (82%) started breastfeeding than did in the Martin and Monk survey, but a similar proportion continued breastfeeding for four months. Half of those who breastfed did so for longer than a month, with a quarter (24%) breastfeeding for at least four months.

This compares well with breastfeeding rates in Oakley's (1979) study where 88% of women initially breastfed. It also compares well with breastfeeding rates in the Thomas Coram study of first time mothers (predominantly over 20 years of age) in dual-earner households. In the dual-earner household study 89% of women anticipating that they would return to work, and 92% of those not returning, breastfed their children at some time. By five months, half the returners had given up breastfeeding, as had 43% of the non-returners. The percentages of those who breastfed for less than two weeks (i.e. while in hospital) was similar across the two studies: 24% of the mothers in the under 20s study, compared with 27% of the 'returners', and 26% of the 'non-returners' in the dual-earner household study (Brannen, personal communication). Recent studies of women's experience of breastfeeding suggest that it is not surprising that many women give up breastfeeding within four months after birth because many are unprepared for difficulties they encounter (Woollett, 1987; Romito, 1988). In this respect mothers who are under 20 do not differ from those over 20.

In both the Thomas Coram studies mentioned above children were firstborn, and firstborn children are more likely to be breastfed than subsequent children (Woollett, 1987). High rates of breastfeeding probably reflect changes in attitudes to breastfeeding over the last two decades. Butler and his colleagues, for example, found that more than 60% of the women who gave birth in one week in 1970 never breastfed and that teenage women were slightly less likely to have breastfed than older women (Butler et al., 1981).

Nearly three women in every ten (29%) said that they had breastfed because someone had encouraged them to do so. Only two women reported, however, that they had not felt free to make up their own mind. Nine per cent reported that in retrospect they regretted the way they had chosen to feed their infants when newborn.

The children's health

Only 5% of the children had to stay in hospital for longer than ten days. None of these stayed in because of poor health. It was either because their mothers had been given Cesarean sections and were not feeling well, or because they had to wait to be rehoused, or to get heating in their accommodation.

> The only bad bit was when I could have gone home within three days, but then... they took my stitches out, and it burst open and all my insides started coming out... so I had to wait; I couldn't go home for another eleven days, so I was in there all that time. I just wanted to go home. I hated being in there all that time. (17 year old single woman)

By six months of age only one child had been confirmed to have a condition which was going to be longstanding (asthma). Two more were suspected to have such conditions, but these were as yet unconfirmed. The majority were free from such conditions.

At six months over a quarter of the children (26%) had not yet had any illnesses. Half the children (49%) had had six or fewer illnesses, but the remaining quarter had had up to 19. Most of these were minor coughs and colds, and in general the children's health seemed good. The children who had had over six conditions were distributed among the four ages of mothers in the study.

At the time that these women gave birth it was medically recommended that, at about three months of age, children should start being immunized against polio, diphtheria, pertussis (whooping cough) and tetanus. Butler and his colleagues (1981) found that mothers under 20 were as likely as older mothers to have taken their children to have at least one vaccination. By the time their children were five years of age, however, younger mothers were less likely to have taken them for as many immunizations as had older mothers. According to Butler and his colleagues, this difference was not related to age but to differences in socio-economic circumstances between the under and over 20s.

At the six month interview most women (96%) in the Thomas Coram study reported that they had taken their children to be immunized. The majority of infants (70%) had had all the immunizations they could have done, but over a quarter had had some immunizations, but not all that they could have. Immunizations were usually missed either because children had been unwell when they were due, or because parents were anxious about possible side effects from whooping cough vaccines and had, therefore, refused it on their children's behalf.

Children were most likely to be taken to child welfare clinics in their first six months. Most children (87%) had been taken to a clinic at least once between three and six months. Half (52%) had been at least once a month, and health visitors had visited half the children at least once between three and six months of age. Only one in ten, however, had been visited three or more times in that period.

As children got older more chronic health conditions became evident. At 21 months, eight children were reported to have longstanding health conditions. None of these was life threatening; they consisted mainly of asthma, bronchitis, eczema and strabismus.

Most 21 month olds in the study (87%) had had some bouts of

illness in the six months before their mothers were interviewed. The maximum number of illnesses mentioned was 20 (one child). Unlike the situation at the six month interview, there was a discernible trend for the number of illnesses children had to be related to the age of their mothers. None of the children whose mothers had been 19 years old at birth had had more than ten illnesses in the last six months; none whose mothers had been 18 years old at birth had had more than 14. A quarter of the children of women who had been 16 or 17 years of age when they gave birth had been ill more than 14 times in the previous six months, but they were the only age group of mothers whose children had been ill so many times. A similar finding was reported by Butler et al. (1981).

The illnesses reported were mainly coughs, colds, raised temperatures, asthma, eczema, loss of appetite, diarrhoea and vomiting as well as 'childhood ailments' such as mumps and measles. Accidents were mainly falls (which in one case resulted in a broken arm) or fingers and toes being caught in doors. Two children suffered minor burns from irons. The most serious illness reported (by an 18 year old who lived with her mother) was meningitis.

Most mothers considered that their child's health was the same as, or better than, other children's of the same age. The mothers who had been 16 and 17 years old at birth were more likely than those who had been 18 and 19 to say that they thought their child's health was worse than other children's. This is, of course, an accurate assessment if mothers were classifying bouts of illness in similar ways. Younger mothers were also more likely than older ones to report themselves to be worried about their child's health, behaviour or development. Two-thirds of those who had been 16 at birth reported such a worry, compared with just over half of the other mothers.

It is unfortunately not possible to disentangle whether children with the youngest mothers in this study were the most ill, or whether differences in reporting illnesses were mainly due to differences in maternal perception.

Feelings for children in the first two years

The children in the Thomas Coram study seem to have got off to a good start in life. The majority of their births were welcomed. They were fit when born, and were as likely as a group of contemporary older mothers to have been breastfed. But greatest difficulties have been said to occur when the children of mothers who were under 20 at birth become toddlers (Lamb and Elster, 1986), who want their own way and are not easily dissuaded. In that context it is important to establish whether mothers had experienced any diminution in positive feelings for their children by the time they were nearly two years old. The data presented here is based on maternal reports rather than observations of women's behaviour with their children.

More than half of the sample (56%) said that their 21 month olds were easy to look after. Only 14% felt their child to be difficult. The rest (30%) said that their child was sometimes difficult, and sometimes easy. Most women also thought their child was generally contented: 78% said their child was contented, while only 6% said their child was mainly unsettled. Relatively few children were considered always to be shy with unfamiliar people: 9% said their child was shy, while just over half the women (55%) said their child was friendly, and just over a third (36%) said it depended on the circumstances.

Women were, therefore, positive about their children, and most perceived their children to be easy to look after. Asked what they enjoyed about their child, only one woman could not think of anything she liked about her child. Half the women (51%) mentioned two or more things they enjoyed. Most women also mentioned something that irritated them about their child. But in contrast to answers about what they enjoyed about their child, 17% said nothing irritated them. Most (58%) mentioned only one thing as irritating.

When asked to assess whether there had been any change in their relationship with their child over the previous year, most women (61%) portrayed their relationship as having improved. Mother–child relationships were felt to have been continually good, but improvement was felt to have resulted from the child's developmental advances (in communicative skills, mobility and dexterity).

Q–Do you think your relationship with [child] has changed over the last 12 months?
A–Oh he's company. I really enjoy his company and I'm gonna miss that when I actually start to go to work, but I really do enjoy that. [?] It's just being with him really. I find that really sort of – absorbing I should say [laughs]. [?] I enjoy him more at this age because. . . he's got more to offer than what he was when he was younger. [?] Well he responds more, as I said, to when you actually tell him to do something, and it's really nice to see him, and he doesn't like to be helped. He likes to do things for himself. So he's turned into an

independent little boy.
(16 year old at birth; did cohabit, but moved back to her parent's home when her child was two years old)

Enjoyment of young children as company may well be class specific Boulton (1983) studied 50 married woman aged between 22 and 34 years old who had at least two young children, one of whom was under five years old. Boulton found that working class, but not middle class, mothers reported that they enjoyed their children's company.

> In their accounts of their daily lives, working class women built up very clear pictures of their children as important and valued companions. They chatted to their children on their own level, shared their interests with them, and spent much of their time with them (Boulton, 1983, p. 72).

Nearly all the women in the study therefore had strong, positive feelings about their children. Those feelings had reportedly increased, rather than diminished, as children became toddlers.

How were the children cared for?

Although women were generally happy with their children, it is, of course, possible that the circumstances in which they lived may have caused them to neglect their children. They may, for example, have left their children (as in popular stereotypes of mothers in this age group), with a succession of caregivers. They may have been ignorant of their children's health or developmental needs, or been so depressed by the poverty in which most lived, that they took relatively little notice of their children. This section explores these issues.

WHO WERE THE CHILDREN'S CAREGIVERS? Given their youth, women in this study held what may be considered surprisingly traditional views about who should have the main responsibility for looking after children. In late pregnancy most women said that mothers, or mothers and fathers, should have primary responsibility for bringing up their children.

In late pregnancy 98% said they felt that fathers should contribute to the upbringing of their children. (87% felt this contribution should be of both physical care and money, while 11% thought it should just be a financial contribution.) By comparison 94% said they thought that their own parents should not contribute to children's upbringing. At the same time nearly three-fifths (58%) did expect their own parents to be involved in their child's upbringing, and only two-thirds (66%) expected the child's father to be involved. (Only 12% expected the child's father's parents to be so involved.) Women appeared to be espousing views which fit normative expectations that a nuclear grouping will take full responsibility for its children, while simultaneously recognizing that many of their own situations did not conform with it.

Only 5% of the sample were positive about the idea of women with small children being employed outside the home. Nearly half of the women (49%) were not critical of mothers who were employed, and felt that there were circumstances in which it was understandable that mothers should be employed outside the home. But many women (41%) were antagonistic to the idea of women having young children *and* being employed. Such traditional attitudes to maternal employment are not apparently unusual in this age group. The British Attitudes Survey found that the young people interviewed similarly felt that mothers should ideally stay at home with their young children (Jowell, Witherspoon and Brook, 1987).

When their children were 21 months old three-quarters of the sample (74%) were unemployed. Almost equal numbers were employed part time (9%) as were employed full time (10%). A further 7% were in colleges of education. Over half of those who were unemployed at home (52%) considered their situation to be ideal. For those who would ideally have chosen not to be at home all the time, the most attractive option was part time work. Of those who were full time caregivers, 23% would ideally have chosen to be employed part time. Only 14% felt they wanted to be employed full time, and just 8% felt they wanted to pursue any course of study.

Although some women felt they wanted adult company, stimulation, and to do something other than childcare, the major attraction for those women who wanted employment was, not surprisingly, financial. Only one of the seven women who were employed full time said that she would ideally have chosen to continue in full time employment. One wanted to enter full time education, two wished to be at home with their child full time, and three would have preferred to cut down their employment hours and work part time.

Nearly three-fifths of women interviewed (59%) were satisfied with their current situation with regard to paid employment, or being at home with children full time. A substantial minority (40%) were, however, dissatisfied with their current situation. Yet only nine women (13%) would ideally have chosen to be employed full time. The majority of women wanted to be with their children full time. Those who wanted employment mainly wanted part time jobs. A lot of women believed that they should look after their children themselves, and in addition wanted to do so.

Most mothers were therefore available to look after their children full time, but did they do so? At 21 months three-quarters of the sample (78%) were not in any form of day care. Only two children (3%) were in local authority day nurseries full time while their mothers were employed. An additional child was attending a private nursery because her mother hoped to find employment. Six children (9%) were looked after by relatives, and three (5%) by minders or friends. An additional four women (6%) had more than one childcare arrangement.

Eighteen women (26%) had attempted to get a nursery place for their child at some time over the two years since birth. Only four had, however, been successful. The others had mostly been told that they were not in sufficiently dire circumstances because they were not in danger of abusing their children. Some women who wanted to be employed were therefore unable to look for employment, because they had no prospect of finding childcare. Others had to rely on relatives to provide childcare.

Women were asked whether in the previous week anyone had looked after their child while they were not there. For a third of the sample (32%) the answer was no. For a further 39% someone had looked after their child three times or less in the previous week. Only 11% of the children in the study had experienced between 7 and 11 episodes of childcare by someone other than their own mother in the previous week. These children's mothers were either employed, or studying, and in some instances care was for an hour or two, so that women could go shopping. The majority of women (66%) said that the previous week's pattern of childcare was typical.

Most women had primary responsibility for caring for their toddlers themselves. Some women recognized that young women are stereotyped as frequently leaving their children with other people and, as a consequence, took particular pride in providing childcare entirely by themselves. Their answers to questions about how they were coping with childcare sometimes seemed designed to pre-empt possible criticisms that they did not look after their children themselves.

> I think I cope quite well. I don't leave him wi' anybody. (16 years old at birth; cohabiting woman; second interview)

Yet some women's mothers were crucially important in looking after children when, for one reason or another, it was difficult for women to manage. For example two women's mothers kept the children while their daughters were depressed. In both cases this allowed the women to move to their own flats and settle in before resuming responsibility for their children.

> My mum looked after her for a little while [about two months] when I was feeling depressed. (Married woman living with her husband; second contact)

> My mum had him for one-and-a-half-months when I first moved into my flat. I was round there every day, but she had him at night, and she did most of the looking after. (Single woman living alone)

In addition six relatives (mostly mothers) who were unemployed provided primary daycare for their grandchildren while their daughters were employed or studying. One mother had actually left work so that she could care for her grandchild. Another mother took her grandson out of London with her while her daughter looked for employment. When they were available many mothers were prepared to provide childcare, and some routinely cared for their daughter's child while their daughters went out or did shopping. As is evident from chapter 5, male partners provided little childcare help. Married women in Boulton's study were also dependent on female relatives' (often mothers') provision of childcare help. 'When female relatives were available, childcare remained a female activity and men were once again excused' (Boulton, 1983, p. 157).

In summary, children did not experience a stream of caregivers. Most women looked after their own children most of the time, and where they did not, it was usually one of the woman's relatives who provided care. Relatives were also perceived to be the first alternative source of childcare.

It is not necessarily praiseworthy that the women in the Thomas Coram study shouldered the major burden of childcare themselves. All women with young children would arguably profit from some time away from their children. The social construction of mothers under 20 years of age as not being sufficiently responsible for their children may make some women reluctant to ask for childcare support when they most need it.

PROVIDING FOR THE CHILDREN Just as recognition of the ways in which
young mothers are stigmatized led some women in the Thomas
Coram study to feel they should not ask other people to look after
their child, so it influenced the way in which they dressed their
children. There was a marked reluctance to accept secondhand
clothes for children, even when couples were very poor.

Many women felt (probably correctly) that the adequacy of the
care they provided for their children would be assessed on the basis
of children's appearance. It was therefore important to keep children
clean and neatly dressed.

So although six months after birth half the sample (52%) said that
they did get some baby clothes handed down from other people,
they were either very choosy about what they dressed their child
in, or regretful that they were obliged to accept things other children
had worn. There was a strong feeling that, particularly for a first
child, new clothes were preferable.

> No I don't. . . really like passed on things. . . Especially as it's my first
> baby I like everything new. (19 year old single woman; first contact)

> Q–Would you be prepared to accept hand downs?
> A–I don't really think so. I don't want people to think we can't afford
> things for him.
> (Married woman; second contact)

The desire to dress children in the best available clothing did not
simply indicate women's desire to project themselves as good
mothers. They definitely wanted to provide well for their children
in every possible way. Despite the straitened financial circumstances
in which they lived, only just over a quarter of the sample (27%)
had tried to economize on heating costs when their children were
six months old. Those who had done so had invariably tried to
make economies in ways that did not involve the baby being cold,
by for instance only heating one room, and keeping the baby in
that room all the time.

> Like. . . I used to put him with me and we used to stay in my room
> all day. It used to be a little warm for him. I used to take drink in there,
> biscuits in there, sandwiches in there and everything. . . I hardly used
> to go out as well. . . Like when we stayed up at my dad's in December
> it was so nice and warm I didn't want to come home. I says 'Dad, I'm
> not going yet.' Cos it's central heating. When you go in there the heat
> just hits you. (17 year old single woman)

More than two-fifths of women (42%) expressed concern that their accommodation was sometimes not warm enough for their children. This was always for reasons beyond women's control. In the above example, for instance, the women's council flat was not centrally heated, and there was a two inch gap between the glazing and the window frame throughout the flat. The gap was designed to ventilate the flat, but it let the cold in. When her child was 21 months old, she was still in the same flat, and the windows were still not sealed. Although she had an electric heater on throughout the interview, the room was too cold for comfort.

Most women perceived their children to have first priority in having things bought for them from household resources. Half the women in the study reported that since having their child, they no longer wanted to spend money on themselves. Twenty nine per cent claimed that birth had not changed the way they felt about spending money on themselves. Yet when asked who or what they would spend any spare money on, the reply was almost universally 'the baby' first, then usually (for those who were cohabiting or married) male partners next.

> I think I should spend it on her more [Why?] I think I have an obligation to buy her things first. She comes first anyway whatever happens. That's what I think. (17 year old at bith; married woman; third contact)

It was probably because women were more likely to spend their limited money on their children than on themselves, that fewer felt that there were things they would like to buy for the baby rather than themselves. Two-fifths (39%) felt that their children had everything they needed, compared with 17% who felt they had everything they needed for themselves.

> No, he's got everything. (Married woman; second contact)

> No, it's enough. (Cohabiting woman; third contact)

> If I need anything for Tommy then I'll go short myself. (Single woman living alone at third contact)

> I've went without plenty. I go without things, but Angela never. I always buy her things. Even if sometimes that leaves me with no money, but I always get her it because I wouldn't have her having any less than any other kid. (Married woman; third contact)

> No, I mostly go short. . . Once a week I try and buy him something – If I try – I buy him like sleeping clothes and vests and like track

suits and that – jeans, and like sometimes I'm in the same clothes. (Single woman; third contact)

But given the poverty in which many women lived, it is not surprising that some were concerned that they could not provide things they felt their children needed. Others felt they would have liked to be able to afford to buy more toys or more clothes for their children.

Um clothes. I'd like to get *her* some more things which I can't do. (Owner-occupier married woman; third contact)

You know there's food and you know she's got adequate clothing. Um. . . I suppose just wants really. Not what we need 'cos we do have what we need. It's just a matter of what we want or what we see in the shop and what we would like. (Single woman who wanted more toys for her child; third contact)

Many women perceived child benefit payments to be children's own money rather than part of general household income. It was, therefore, either used to buy things for children or saved for them.

When I get her money, that is *her* money, so it's spent on her. (Single woman; third contact)

Assisting children's development

The things women reported wanting for their children indicated that they had clear ideas about what would help their children make good developmental progress. They may not have had formal knowledge of child development (although 'child development' had been on the curriculum at some of their schools), but they did use currently circulating ideas (about the importance of healthy diets, and of stimulating children's cognitive development) to guide their assessments of what their children needed, or what they would ideally like to provide for them.

She does need some more toys, some more learning toys, and we'll probably get her some later on as well. (18 year old at birth, married woman)

She needs more toys. She's a lot active. . . As soon as I can afford it – I'll get her some. (Single woman; second contact)

Um I like him to have all like learning toys you know. Nothing just to play with you know. I like him to have a reason – like his bricks. He can count 'em and they've got colours and things with numbers on and colours or shapes. I like him to have learning toys rather than things that just sit and look at you, and I can't afford that. (Cohabiting woman; third contact)

Yeah, we don't sort of starve. We manage. As long as he gets a decent meal every night that's all I'm worried about. That's why Ian [boyfriend] tends to buy stuff for me because I'll go out and spend money and make sure *he* gets the proper vegetables and the proper dinner, and I'll have a sandwich or something like that 'cos his health is more important to me. (Single woman; third contact)

Well for Kelly not to be able to eat the right foods, you know we can only sort of live on egg and chips some nights you know, whereas it's bad for her – well it's bad for us as well you know. I mean they're saying on the telly you gotta eat the right sorts of foods, but you just can't afford it on their money [supplementary benefit] can you? That's the only thing I'm worried about. (Married woman; third contact)

Although women were interviewed for the last time when their children were nearly two years old, they were clearly intending to influence their children's developmental progress. Six months after birth women were asked what they thought were the most important influences on children's health and happiness. The majority considered it most important to provide children with a settled home environment. Four-fifths (81%) said the most important influence was the way the child was brought up, while only 16% thought that the child's own character was most important.

Most women were, therefore, concerned to provide an environment that would facilitate their child's development. Love, adequate nutrition and stimulation were the elements most frequently singled out as components that would ensure children's health and well being. Such beliefs are, of course, similar to those held by older women. Failure to provide nutritious food or the toys women considered necessary to children's stimulation was more likely to result from lack of economic resources than inadequate knowledge of child development.

Q–What do you think affects the way that children grow up?
A–I think it's the atmosphere they're brought up in really. I suppose it could be in their genes, but I think it's the atmosphere they're brought up. That's what does it really.
Q–What about so that the child grows up happy?
A–Just to make him happy. Like if you've got family arguments try

and keep it away from the child. Don't argue in front him and fight
– don't do it at all, but if you have to don't do it in front of the kids.
Q–What about so he grows up to be healthy?
A–Give him all the fresh food, vitamins that he needs.
(Cohabiting woman, 19 years old at birth; second contact)

From informal observations made during interviews it did seem
that some mothers had reason to be concerned that they were not
providing 'healthy food' for their children. Several women simply
did not seem to have the wherewithal to provide three nutritious
meals a day for their children, and children were sometimes not fed
during interviews which lasted from late morning to late afternoon.
In some cases relatively cheap and filling, but not nutritious, foods
were provided at lunchtime. In 1988 Lyn Durward of the Maternity
Alliance costed the kind of diet recommended for pregnant women
by hospital dietitians. She reported that such a diet cost more than
half of the income support women under 25 receive. It is thus not
surprising that once they have their children many young women
find it difficult to feed them as they would ideally like to. Some
children may, therefore, be malnourished (even if not hungry), not
because their mothers are ignorant of their nutritional needs, but
because they are too poor to provide for those needs.

In the past mothers who were under 20 years of age have been
found to go on to have more children than average, more closely
spaced than usual. Some writers suggest that the more children
there are in a household, the less likely children are to do well
intellectually because they have diminished access to resources such
as parental time and attention. Recent literature suggests that women
who start childbearing before they are 20 are now not very likely to
go on to have more children than average. But Furstenberg (1987)
suggests that births to this age group of mothers may be closely
spaced.

The data from the Thomas Coram study is too short term to
establish whether women ended up having more children than
average. But it can indicate whether second children were conceived
or born within two years of the first.

A third of those interviewed (31%, 21) had been pregnant again
in the 21 months following their first child's birth. All had been
pregnant only once more. Eight (12% of the sample) were still
pregnant, ten (15%) already had a second child, and three had
miscarried. Of the ten who had a second child, three had given
birth when their first child was 12 months old, five had given birth

at 14 or 15 months, and the remaining two had been born at 16 and 18 months.

More than seven in every ten (73%) of the children were therefore going to be their mother's only children until they were at least two-and-a-half years old. Most women were not, therefore, having closely spaced children. Nor were they particularly different from older women in their spacing of second births.

Coping with childcare

The issue of how women were coping with looking after their children, particularly as they neared the 'terrible twos' has so far not been addressed. Yet this has been suggested to be a period when young mothers undergo particular stress with their children. Did the women in the Thomas Coram study seem to be at the end of their tethers with their children?

Six months after birth women were asked how other people felt they were coping with motherhood. Nearly three-quarters (72%) reported that they had been praised by someone for coping well. Only 15% reported that somebody they knew thought that they were not coping well. Asked how they felt that they themselves were coping, 91% said they felt satisfied with how they were.

At 21 months women were asked whether they had found the previous six months as a mother easy or hard. Just over a quarter (27%) said they had found it only difficult. This compares with nearly two-fifths (38%) who said they had found everything easy, and just over a third (35%) who found some things easy, and others difficult. More than half the women (56%) said that motherhood had become easier over the previous six months, and less than a fifth (19%) thought it had become harder.

> I think it's getting easier and easier as she's getting older 'cos she's. . . very independent. (Cohabiting woman; third contact)

> Easier. It seems to have got easier as he's grown older. I won't say that too soon, but I mean so far. (16 year old at birth; living with parents; third contact)

> Well when I had Jane you know everything was so hard. I didn't know what to do if there was anything wrong, but with Jackie I got into a routine so quick. . . It's been easier bringing them both up than it was with Jane. (Married woman; third contact)

Table 7.1 shows that when their children were nearly two, none

Table 7.1 How women considered they were coping with childcare

Very well	19 (30%)	
Quite well	40 (62%)	
Well in some ways, badly in others	5 (8%)	
Badly	0 (0%)	(N=64)

of the women considered that overall she was coping badly with her child, and few considered that they were coping badly with any aspects of childcare. Nearly two-thirds said they felt they were coping 'quite well' with their children, and just under a third said they were coping 'very well'. More than four-fifths considered themselves to be coping as well with motherhood as they felt they wanted to.

Everybody felt they got some satisfaction with motherhood. While most women (83%) felt they also got some dissatisfactions from motherhood, most reported themselves to be more satisfied than dissatisfied. Women at each age point between 16 and 19 reported themselves to be satisfied with motherhood, and with the childcare they provided for their children.

It may be argued that interview data is likely to produce halo effects because most women are unlikely to report themselves to be 'bad mothers', particularly when they know they are in a stigmatized age group of mothers. Yet, as will be seen later, some women did express dissatisfaction with motherhood, and with the mothering they provided. Perhaps more convincingly women's love for, and pleasure in, their children shines out from many accounts when women are asked to describe their children.

> She's good company. She's always good to me, and I'm very happy when I'm with her too. (Cohabiting woman; third contact)

> [She's] picking up words and coming out with funny things and dancing and putting my shoes on, and putting my hat on and things like that.
> Q–What do you enjoy about her?
> A–Well everything about her really.
> (Married woman; third contact)

> I really enjoy playing with him, because some of the things he does, it makes me die laughing. You get a sense of proudness sometimes you know. You feel so proud of him sometimes. I enjoy him more now – he's more company. . .

Q–What do you enjoy about him?
A–He's very boisterous. Mischief! On the whole he's a really good boy. He is. A great little imitator. He loves to imitate as you know!
. . .
Q–Would you say that it's easy or difficult looking after him?
A–Easy. No way is he difficult.
(Single woman living alone; third contact)

The minority of women who were dissatisfied with elements of motherhood or felt that things were more difficult for them than they had been, were either dissatisfied with the particular conditions in which they lived, or with particular, short term childcare tasks which were exacerbating the difficulties they were experiencing.

I think its getting harder rather than easier really. . . He's getting into more things. He's doing more things, and I don't know really. He's just getting a little sod. Potty training, getting off the bottle, and it all seems to be getting harder now, whereas if I done it before, it might have been a lot easier. (Cohabiting woman; third contact)

I just enjoy being a mum really. But I don't enjoy my circumstances like being a single parent. But I enjoy being his mum.
Q–What don't you enjoy about your circumstances?
A–If I didn't have so much of the work load on my own. I know I get all the good bits as well, but I get all the work that goes with it. . .
Q–Would anything help you enjoy it more?
A–I think if I just found someone to share it with.
(Single woman; third contact)

There was no statistical relationship between women's feelings for their children, their enjoyment of motherhood, and how they felt they were coping as mothers. It was, for example, possible for women to report that they loved their children, did not enjoy motherhood, but felt that they were coping well with motherhood. A couple of the youngest women, who had been 16 or 17 years at birth, did, however, seem to be having particular problems, or feeling particularly dissatisfied with their children.

One (16 years old at birth) reported that she regretted having had her child when she did. Twenty one months after birth she was living in very difficult circumstances. She had moved house four times since she became pregnant, and during the interview her gas supply was cut off because the cooker was unsafe. She had no money to buy another one, and had discovered many things wrong with the housing association flat she had just transferred into. She felt low and depressed much of the time.

Although she loved her daughter she felt that she would never advise anyone to have a child as early as she had (16 years) and wished she hadn't done so.

I mean when you're pregnant you think that it's gonna be a fairytale, but the worst thing is that you gotta face up to reality. . . You know it's nothing what you expect it to be. I mean people always told me 'don't expect. . . for it to be good'. But you say 'no, no, no' you know. You never expect the worst. . . That is the worst thing about it.[?] The easiest part is having the baby – the hardest part is looking after them and even harder is to have a flat. I mean. . . you say 'oh I want a flat. I want this. I want that.' But when you've got it you wish you never got. You wish that you were back home. You wish that you never had a kid or whatever because you spend most of your money buying. . . paint, wallpaper, and that lot. . . I mean if I could've turned the clock back and had *some* experience of what I was thinking now. . . I would have waited until I was about 28, I had a good job, money that I know that when I get a flat I'm not gonna have to wait on Social for carpet and all them sorts of thing. . . (16 years old at birth; living with a woman friend at third interview)

To a large extent, lack of material resources was responsible for this woman's depression. Although she said that it was difficult being on her own with her child (her relationship with her child's father having ended) she felt that it would be 'harder when you're with the father. . . they always wanna go out, and you're the one that is left there with the baby. . . '

Despite her depression, and her feeling that her daughter is difficult to manage, she did not ignore, or neglect her child.

If Samantha's awake I sort of like teach her little things, like how to count. 'Cos she can count up to ten now, and say a *little* bit of her ABC, except when you say 'A', she jumps to 'D', and um play with her little games like ring a ring o' roses and all that lot. . . (16 years old at birth)

In addition Samantha stayed with her grandmother most weekends so that her mother got a break from her, and Samantha got attention from her aunt and grandmother who loved her, and were not depressed. (When Samantha's development was assessed on a developmental test she scored normally for a child of her age.) After the interview the respondent was going to stay at her mother's at least until her gas supply was reconnected. Ironically she had left home in the first place only because she wanted to assert her independence with her own child. Her mother's support was, however, crucial to her.

Another woman who had been 16 when she conceived, but 17 when she gave birth, felt that she was coping all right with motherhood, but was very unhappy with her child.

> God! He's a terrible child. He's always crying. A real cry baby. Got a bottle. A bottle hanging all day. He don't concentrate on nothing. Hassle all day. He's only sleeping now because of Phenergan.
> Q–Do you think that he's more difficult to look after than other children?
> A–More difficult because of the crying.
> Q–Is that the only way in which he's more difficult?
> A–He don't play for long. He don't concentrate. Like that one [child the interviewee was childminding] will play for half an hour. [He] will just throw them at you.
> (Cohabiting woman; third contact)

What had led to this rather worrying state of affairs? Was it simply that the woman had been too young to have a child, and as a consequence couldn't cope?

This woman had lived with her child's father from before she became pregnant. Twenty one months after birth, she was rather depressed. One reason for this was that she wanted the child's father to leave their maisonette, but he had refused to. She was also worried about her son's language development, and would have liked to get out of the house more. She was also very tired, because her son got up a lot at night and she was getting very little sleep. In the day she childminded a six month old, and so could not sleep when her son did.

She had a lot of experience of childcare. She had helped look after her six year old niece from birth. Her niece had actually lived with her for six months after her brother had separated from his wife. She seemed particularly to dislike her son's characteristics, seeing him as too active, too fretful and lacking concentration. At the same time she felt that 'except for the speech', he was developing well. She had taken him to see a health visitor about his language at 20 months, and been told that he was 'alright for his age'. A few weeks later she took him to the health centre, and was told by the speech therapist that because her son was very active he couldn't concentrate. She was told she would be asked to bring him again later.

When given a developmental test (in the Thomas Coram study)

her son gave a performance which was average for a child of his age. So she could be misjudging her child, either because she dislikes him, is depressed or does not know what to expect from a young child. But the speech therapist did seem to agree with the woman that her child was unusually active. She could, therefore, have been sensitive enough to pick up the early stages of a speech problem before it became evident to anyone else. It is difficult to sort out the causative factors, but although the prognosis for this particular child did not seem good, his mother's problems were unlikely to be age related.

It was, however, a pity that this mother had been unable to get a nursery place for her child, because there was none available. She had, unusually for the sample, received a visit from a health visitor at 21 months (the week before the interview) perhaps because her child had suffered three accidents in the last six months (a burn from an iron, a needle broken in his foot and a broken tooth), two of which required hospital treatment.

While the woman described in the penultimate example was in miserable circumstances, her relationship with her child did not seem worrying in the way that it did for the woman in the last example. The second woman was, however, distinguished from most of the other women who had given birth at 16 or 17 in that she did not regularly stay with any relatives, (or in one case, child's father's relatives). She was, however, in regular touch with most of her relatives and her sisters did provide some childcare. She was the only one of those who had been 16 when they conceived to be cohabiting when interviewed 21 months after birth. That relationship did not help, however, but added to her problems particularly since her child's father was a heavy drinker.

These two cases were discussed at length because they were unusual. They hint that a tiny minority of the children conceived by 16 year old mothers may eventually not fare as well as most children born to teenage women. Most women did not regret having had their children in their teens. Nor were most either struggling to manage childcare, or on the brink of abusing their children.

Children's cognitive development

A major reason for concern about children born to adolescent mothers is the fear that their educational attainment will be poorer than that of children born to older mothers. The discussion at the start of this chapter indicated that various studies have found that

USA children born to mothers who are under 20 do not do as well at the end of their school careers as their peers who were born to older mothers. While studies on older children born when their mothers were less than 20 years old rely on children's scholastic achievement, studies of preschool children generally use standardized tests. Several studies have found that children born to teenage women do less well on standardized cognitive tests than those born to older women.

Data from two parts of the life course thus appear consistent. Children born to mothers who are under 20 years of age are cognitively impaired in comparison with children born to older mothers. Yet it is highly questionable whether infant developmental tests give a useful indication of how children are going to do later (Messick, 1983).

> The assessment of children is also rendered problematic by the occurrence of rapid changes, especially during the early years. It is difficult to assess a child's characteristics adequately at a given point in time. . . if those characteristics are in effect moving targets. . . there may be instability of scores even over the short run. (Messick, 1983, p. 479)

If a child does poorly on an infant developmental test, and poorly later at school, the later poor performance may not be related to the earlier poor one. This is particularly so since language has not yet developed in young children and many later developmental tests (and certainly school performance) are heavily dependent on linguistic skill. In addition young children are difficult to test.

> In the assessment of young children, many problems that are ordinarily handled by the standardization of instructions and procedures and by reliance on the past testing experience and expectations of the respondents become highly magnified by virtue of the limited experience and understanding of many youngsters in coping with novel task demands. These include problems of establishing rapport and motivation; of ensuring that instructions are well understood; of maintaining attention; and, of coping with boredom, distraction, and fatigue. (Messick, 1983, p. 479)

For young children, standardized tests may tell us little about a child's future developmental progress; and may not truly represent a child's capabilities, if that child is shy, or not in a co-operative frame of mind. Yet standardized tests continue to be used on young children because they offer an apparently objective and relatively simple means of assessing children's developmental standing in comparison with what other children of the same age are supposed to be able to do, and with other studies that have used the same methods.

In order to have information about the children's development from a source other than the children's mothers in the Thomas Coram study, it was eventually decided to use the Mental scale of the Bayley Scales of Infant Development (Bayley, 1969). This was one of the more difficult decisions to reach agreement on in the project team for three reasons. Firstly, because of the limitations of infant developmental tests (discussed above). Secondly, because tests with standardized norms involve implicit comparisons with the 'normal population', and the focus of the project was on intragroup rather than intergroup comparisons. Finally, it was impracticable to bring women and children into a uniform testing environment. Yet it was evident from the first two interview contacts that many women lived in crowded or cramped homes that would not constitute ideal testing situations.

The project advisory group of black women sociologists and psychologists gave many hours of their time, and held two special meetings to discuss these issues with the research team. Their objections were finally overruled, however, because a standardized test provided a relatively easy method of collecting data on the children independently of maternal report.

The Thomas Coram data cannot shed light on the school achievements of children born to women under 20 years of age. It can, however, provide some insights into the use of developmental tests on young children living with mothers who were under 20 when they were born, as well as data on how the children actually performed on the Bayley Scales.

At 21 months many of the women and children in the study were living in impoverished circumstances. Space was sometimes overcrowded, and furniture was sometimes sparse. As a result the circumstances in which the Bayley test was conducted were often far from ideal.

In nearly two-fifths of the testing situations (39%) the physical environment was judged to be distracting for the child. Often the distraction was from televisions, stereos and radios, two of which were sometimes on simultaneously, and being watched or listened to by someone who could not retreat into another room. The volume would sometimes be turned down low, but there was still a lot of auditory distraction. Sometimes the distraction came from a variety of items which had to be within the child's view because there was nowhere else to put them. It also came from the sparseness of furniture sometimes, because it was difficult to find anywhere on which to balance the case containing the test items.

Distractions sometimes lengthened the testing time considerably. Tests ranged in length from 20 minutes to 95 minutes, with 80% of the tests lasting 40 minutes or more. Ideally children would have been tested on another occasion in those instances where it took a long time to present the test items. It was, however, very difficult to find women and their children at home, and many interviews took several visits to arrange. Since it was important to try to see children as close to 21 months as possible, it was often felt undesirable to leave the assessment procedure for a further occasion. This may, unfortunately, have prevented some children from doing as well as they might have, either because they became tired or bored.

Nearly two-fifths of the children (39%) had two or more adults present during the test. A quarter (26%) had another child present. In 26% of the testing situations, the tester rated people as a distraction to the child. Other people could not simply be sent to another room, since even when there was another room available, it was often not warm enough, cramped or uncomfortable.

The majority of children (82%) heard only English spoken in their home, but for a minority, the Bayley instructions must have been rather bemusing, and in some cases it was necessary to rely heavily on mother's translations of instructions to children. In addition to this many children were rated as being unco-operative during the test. Three-fifths (58%) were rated as unco-operative, although only 28% were rated as being tired, ill or upset, and the majority (71%) were friendly to the tester.

All of these factors contributed to making the circumstances in which children were tested non-standard, and different from those recommended by Bayley (1969). Somewhat surprisingly, however, testers felt that relatively few children seemed to be prevented by these distractions from doing the test adequately. Testers were asked to note when they considered that distractions had interfered with test presentation and/or children's ability to perform on tests. Other people were considered to have distracted children in such a way that it interfered with the test in only 10% of tests. The physical environment was thought to disrupt the test in only 7% of cases. However more than a quarter of the children (26%) were felt to be so unco-operative that although tests were completed, test scores did not necessarily reflect children's abilities.

It is obviously not possible to be certain quite how much the environment or distractions from other people did affect test scores. Testers were probably influenced in their judgements that distractions made little difference by the fact that most children scored well. The normal range of scores on standardized tests is between 85 and 115, with 100 being the norm. The average score (and the most frequently occurring one) for children in this study was 116, ranging from one child who scored 61 to five children who scored 150 (the highest possible score). Four-fifths of the sample (79%) scored over 100. Good performances may, therefore, have encouraged testers to believe that circumstances made no difference to most test scores, when they may well have done. The high scores (relevant to the standardized norm) obtained by the sample are not unusual since average Bayley scores in reported studies have increased since Bayley standardized her test. Such an increase perhaps reflects the common nature, and hence familiarity, of items such as clocks which are part of the recognition tasks on the Bayley test.

Mothers under 20 are found to be predominantly poor, and living in impoverished accommodation in most research studies. It is, therefore, likely that testers in some other studies have also encountered these non-standard testing circumstances. Reported differences between the test scores of children born to younger women and those born to older women may, in some cases, reflect differences in test environments.

In the Thomas Coram study whether women were cohabiting or single, living alone or with other people, made no difference to children's test scores. Furstenberg and his colleagues (1987) also found this for children's test scores at five years. Nor were there any significant effects for mother's age. The children of 16 year olds were likely to score as well as the children of 19 year olds (although the children of 18 year olds did slightly better than those of 16 and 19 year olds).

This is at variance with the findings from the Child Health and Education Study. Butler and his colleagues (1981) found that children with mothers who were under 17 years at birth scored less well on developmental tests than children born to 18 and 19 year olds. In this study, however, the children's scores were not significantly related to whether their mothers were younger or older teenage women at birth.

Three variables were significantly related to children's Bayley scores. These were:

- whether or not children were felt by testers to be co-operative in the test situation;
- whether children were girls or boys;
- whether or not mothers were satisfied with motherhood.

Those children who were rated as unco-operative in the Bayley test did less well than children who were rated as co-operative. Boys did less well than girls, and children whose mothers (on the basis of a range of interview answers) were rated as not being satisfied with motherhood (which is not necessarily the same as not being satisfied with their child) did less well than those whose mothers were rated as satisfied with motherhood.

While the above mentioned differences were significant, it must be emphasized that for all these variables, children's average scores in each category were over 100 (the average score). The biggest average difference was between children felt by testers to be unco-operative, and those rated as co-operative. Average scores were 102 and 125 respectively; a difference of 23 points.

Boys scored an average of 106, while girls scored an average of 122 (an average of 16 points more than boys). Children with mothers rated as being dissatisfied with motherhood had an average score of 104, while those whose mothers were rated as satisfied with motherhood had an average score 22 points higher, at 126.

The interpretation of these differences is not straightforward. If, for example, children are felt to have been unco-operative in the testing situation it could be either that they did not do themselves justice on the test because they were interested in other things, or simply did not wish to perform. Alternatively it could be that they were unco-operative because they could not do the test, and were bored. If testers could not get children to respond in the test situation, they may well have rated children as unco-operative either because they could not do the tasks instructed, or had not understood what was required of them.

Boys (who did not score as well as girls) were more likely to be rated unco-operative than girls. The difference in boys' and girls' scores cannot all be accounted for by differences in co-operation. It is, in fact, difficult to account for this difference. Some studies find no gender differences while others find some. Many studies do, however, find gender differences in children's verbal abilities and infant developmental tests have language components from about 18 months.

It could be that, for whatever reason, boys and girls are already behaving differently from each other at 21 months. Behavioural differences may have been responsible for differences in children's test scores. Yet maternal descriptions of their children were, with one exception, not significantly related to the children's test scores, the exception being whether children were reported to be shy or friendly. The average score of children who were said to be shy was 88, in comparison with 115 for children who were said to be friendly (either all the time or sometimes). Relatively few children were, however, reported to be shy, and shyness was not the explanation for the gender difference in test scores. There was no correlation between children's gender, and the likelihood of them being reported to be shy.

Mothers were asked to say whether they thought their children's health, behaviour and development were better than, worse than, or the same as other children of the same age. Whatever children's sex, mothers were equally likely to give the same answers. It is, of course, highly likely that mothers were implicitly comparing their children with others of the same sex. Nonetheless hardly any mothers, of either sex (17%) perceived their children's behaviour to be worse than other children's behaviour.

With regard to 'satisfaction with motherhood', could it be that those mothers who were not satisfied with motherhood did not enjoy being with their children? This explanation seems unlikely given that only one mother had nothing she enjoyed about her child, and most found few things about their children irritating. Children's Bayley scores were not correlated with the number of things their mothers enjoyed, or found irritating about them. Nor were they correlated with whether their mothers were pregnant or had another child, whether their mothers were employed, or from where the household income came (all things that Furstenberg and his co-workers found to be correlated with children's later school achievement).

Butler at al. (1981) found that overcrowding and frequent household moves were correlated with children's test scores at five years of age and explained some of the differences between children born to teenagers and those born to older women. When children in this study were tested, however, they were more likely than not to have experienced at least one household move. Household composition was not correlated with test score.

The three factors found to be correlated with children's test scores (child co-operativeness, gender and satisfaction with motherhood) do not necessarily operate in isolation. A mother who is dissatisfied with the conditions in which she has to mother her child may also have a son who is rated as unco-operative in the test situation. For example one woman, Janine, whose son scored 104 (above the norm, but relatively low for the sample) on the Bayley test was rated as very satisfied with motherhood, but said:

> I just enjoy being a mum anyway really. But I don't enjoy my circum-
> stances – like being a single parent. But I enjoy being his mum.
> Q–Would anything help you to enjoy motherhood more?
> A–If I didn't have so much of the workload on my own. I know I get
> all the good bits as well, but I get all the work that goes with it. . . I
> think if I just found someone to share it with.

Janine felt that she was doing a good job of caring for her child and encouraging his development, although she felt she should be more patient with him. She said:

> I think I cope really well with him. Like I'm always talking to him
> and trying to involve him in what I do. I think I'm good in that way.
> But sometimes I get so sick of him. . . I just want him to go away and
> leave me alone.

Janine was very positive about her son. Asked to describe him, she said:

> Oh you get a very biassed opinion don't you?. . . I don't know. I don't
> think you could wish for a better son. I mean I can't be the only one
> who thinks that because everybody says how good he is and that.
> He's a very loving child. If I'm crying he sits there, and he goes 'Oh
> mummy crying!' And he gets all upset. I wouldn't be without
> him. . . If anything happened to him, I'd kill myself. I couldn't live
> without him. (Single woman living alone; third contact)

This response indicates that the mother thinks her child is 'good'. By way of contrast, the psychologist who tested the child commented:

> I did not enjoy this Bayley. During the [preceding] interview C spat
> upon me, hit me, threw coffee and milk over me; all to the accompani-
> ment of his mother's laughter.

It could, therefore, be that respondents and interviewers had different views of what constitutes acceptable (boy) child behaviour. The
child's relatively low score could simply reflect the fact that he was
accustomed to behaving in a manner which is not conducive to co-
operating with a developmental tester. It must also be said that this

child was not only mischievous. He was, on occasion, affectionate to the tester, and did show her his toys. The test was done immediately following the interview, and the interview situation was difficult for him because he was used to having his mother's undivided attention, but she spent two hours talking to someone else.

The quote from this mother gives another possible reason for the child's possibly poor performance. His mother was depressed following her own mother's death ten months previously. She still cried 'quite a lot' about it, and her son was often with her when she was upset. Her depression may well have affected how she treated her son sometimes, and his awareness of it may well have affected his behaviour.

Yet there were points of similarity between the above respondent and women whose children were scoring highly. For example Ann was 18 and had been married for two years when she gave birth. She had not got on very well with her husband after the birth, and had been very depressed. She had left her husband for a day when her daughter was a year old, but had gone back to him because she felt she could not bear to live with her parents again. The couple were having a struggle to make ends meet, partly because they had just bought their second house. At 21 months the woman was heavily pregnant, but was feeling happier with their new house than she had been with the old one. Her child scored 150 on the Bayley test (the highest possible score). Yet, fundamentally, her account of how she experiences motherhood is similar to Janine's:

> Q–Would anything help you enjoy motherhood more?
> A–No, because she's fulfilling. I mean I stimulate her as much as I can, and I play with her – although sometimes I'd like to play with her more, but I mean you've still got to run the household as such but er I mean you can't drop everything for them. . . but I mean I think I'm doing quite well at it. I'm getting – you can see what she's like. She is quite good so I don't think I could get more out of it. Perhaps I'd enjoy it more if I didn't feel so tired, but I'll have to see what I'm like after I have the other baby. See whether this tiredness will go away, and then perhaps I'll enjoy it more.
> (18 years old at birth; married woman; third contact)

In another instance where a child (a boy) scored way below the norm (71) his mother had some reservations about her relationship with her child's father (with whom she was cohabiting). She was generally content with her situation, however. She liked her flat and the 'O' level package she was pursuing at a local college, and was content with motherhood generally. The only clue to her son's poor test performance came from her expressed worries about his behaviour and his development:

> Like um how can I put it. He's very touchy and troublesome... So I wonder whether he's going to grow up to be a bad boy you know, like them little kids and that. But my mum goes well he'll change and quiet down, so I can't really judge him for what he's doing now. Well he's my first one really. So I don't really know [laughs][?] The way he talks as well that makes me... wonder as well he's gonna be a bit slow at sch- you know slow at doing things. [Why?] Cos some things he doesn't do. Like the way he's talking. My mum goes he's talking all right for his age and that, but I think he could be doing better things for his age you know, talking plainer than that. (19 years old at birth; cohabiting; third contact)

The picture that emerges is thus a hazy one. Most children are, as assessed on a standardized test, developing well. There are indications that child co-operativeness with the tester, gender and maternal feelings about motherhood are all related to children's test performance. The fact that variables are statistically correlated does not, of course, indicate that one variable explains another. While it might be expected that children's co-operativeness would influence test performance, it is more difficult to establish whether, and if so how, gender and mothers' feelings about motherhood affect children's performance on developmental tests.

The accounts given by women whose children did not score as well as the majority of children in the Thomas Coram study suggest that there is a diversity of factors related to (but not necessarily causative of) such relatively poor performances. Some of these factors (such as temperament and developmental progress) can be said to relate to the child. Some (such as depression and style of interaction) can be said to relate to the mothers. Some are due to factors extrinsic to the couple (relations with male partners, financial stringencies, etc.). In reality, however, these factors are not discrete. They intersect in complex ways that are beginning to be recognized (see for example Furstenberg et al., 1987) but are, as yet, not fully understood.

Summary

A major concern about the consequences of early motherhood centres on the welfare of children born to mothers who are under

20 years of age when they give birth. Evidence from the Thomas Coram Research Unit study of mothers who were in their teenage years when they gave birth suggests that up to 21 months after birth (when the study ended) there was no reason to be concerned about most children's welfare.

When they were born most children were welcomed enthusiastically. Over their first 21 months most women were consistently positive about their child, although they disliked some aspects of childcare, like getting up at night and hearing their child crying. A high percentage (82%) of the children were breastfed, and by six months the vast majority (96%) had had some immunizations. Most had also attended child welfare clinics.

The majority of women cared for their children full time. At 21 months three quarters of the sample were at home full time with their children. Most women (two-thirds) had someone (usually a female relative) who would look after their child for a couple of hours each week. But the majority of childcare was done by women themselves.

Many women reported that they would have liked to be able to afford more educational toys, clothes and, in a few instances, more nutritious food for their children. Women gave priority to their children's material needs in preference to their own. Many reported that they 'went short' in order to buy things for their children.

Women were familiar with popular medical and psychological thinking about children's needs. They reported that children needed emotional nurturance, nutritious food and stimulating play in order to develop into happy, healthy, aware children. On the whole women were satisfied with motherhood. Only one woman reported that she regretted having had a child when she did, while a second woman was exceptional in being very critical of her child.

Twenty one months after birth children's developmental status was assessed using the Bayley Scales of Infant Development. The circumstances in which many children were tested were not optimal because of the number of distracting factors in the children's homes (where tests were conducted). Most children, however, scored above the standardized norm. Three variables were found to correlate with children's test scores. These were the children's co-operativeness in the test situation, gender and maternal satisfaction with motherhood. Children who were rated by testers as unco-operative in the test situation, boys and those whose mothers were less satisfied with motherhood did less well than those who were rated as co-operative, girls and those whose mothers were more satisfied with motherhood. These factors are, however, not necessarily causative of better or worse test performance. Further research needs to be done to clarify these issues.

8

Young Women as Mothers: Employment, Education and Satisfaction with Motherhood

Women who become mothers while they are under 20 years of age have been widely reported to fare badly in comparison with women who become mothers later in life. They are reported to rear children who do less well than the children of older mothers. They are expected to gain fewer educational qualifications than their peers and to be more likely to be unemployed or to be employed in poorly paid jobs. In addition they are reported to become disillusioned with motherhood once their children become toddlers.

This chapter considers whether motherhood appears to have limited the educational and employment opportunities open to women who give birth before they are 20.

The effects of motherhood on women's lives

Pregnancy and the early months

Before they became pregnant many women in the Thomas Coram study had experienced unemployment at some time. When they conceived two-fifths (39%) were unemployed. If job training schemes and part time employment are included in the 'employed' category, the same percentage of women were unemployed as were in employment. The jobs women tended to get were frequently temporary, so that many had experienced redundancy despite being under 20, having only been in the employment market for short periods. Six per cent were employed on Manpower Service Commission training schemes, which were necessarily temporary, and 4% were employed part time. A further 17% were in full time education.

By the end of pregnancy seven in every ten women were unemployed. For those on MSC schemes, this was largely because the scheme itself had ended. Those in full time education had given up school or college attendance. One 16 year old, however, did, as she intended, return to school for a term after the birth. The proportion unemployed had therefore nearly doubled during pregnancy (from 4 in 10 to 7 in 10) although three-quarters of those who were employed at conception remained in their jobs until late pregnancy.

Women sometimes left work, school or college before colleagues and employers could find out that they were pregnant because they feared adverse reactions. Some women who did tell employers and teachers that they were pregnant were subjected to such displays of disapproval that they left education or employment anyway. A few women left employment because their jobs were too physically taxing to be continued late into pregnancy.

Only 8% of women in the study were eligible for maternity leave. Some women, particularly those under 18, had not been in the employment market sufficiently long to qualify for maternity leave. However the difficulties many women had experienced in finding jobs and the transient nature of many of the jobs they had managed to find were mainly responsible for women's ineligibility for maternity leave.

Pregnancy was more disruptive of school and college attendance than it was of employment. The majority of those who had been employed at conception remained in employment until late in pregnancy whereas women left school and college early in pregnancy. Birth, however, did make a difference to women's employment status. The majority (88%) of women interviewed six months after birth were unemployed. Eight per cent of the sample were employed (5% part time and 2% full time). One per cent was attending college part time, and 4% were on MSC programmes.

Most women reported that they had not 'planned' to become pregnant when they did. Yet by late pregnancy all were (with one exception) excited by the prospect of having a baby. This was partly because women who had not 'planned' their pregnancies had mostly expected motherhood to be an important part of their lives at some time in the near future. It was also because by late pregnancy the people who were important in women's lives were positive about the forthcoming children.

In late pregnancy it seemed unlikely that more than a handful of the mothers in the Thomas Coram study would be employed outside their homes while they had young children. Four factors militated against this.

1. 'CHILDREN NEED THEIR MOTHERS' Most women in the Thomas Coram study held conventional beliefs about the roles of mothers. Many subscribed to the discourse of children 'needing' their mothers to be at home full time. In a complementary way they perceived motherhood to be an important part of their lives and did not want to 'miss out' on seeing children's development by leaving them with other people. Many of those who expected to return to work at some time favoured part time, rather than full time, work.

> I would like to be with it until it's about four but I'd like a part time job, but I wouldn't leave it until it's about seven months old because I think it needs you then. (17 year old married woman)

In late pregnancy most women were not in favour of maternal employment. Only 1 in 20 (5%) were wholeheartedly positive about mothers with young children being employed, while 2 in 5 (41%) were unequivocally hostile to the idea.

It was not, therefore, surprising that less than two-fifths of the sample (38%) considered that they would seek paid employment during infancy (up to 18 months. See table 8.1). Most women reported that they either could not foresee a time when they would return to paid employment or that they would seek employment only when their child was over 18 months or that they had no idea when they would get jobs.

2. UNREWARDING EMPLOYMENT Paid employment was not perceived to be in competition with, or to be as attractive an option as motherhood. This was because few women were in jobs which either had inbuilt career progression or were intrinsically rewarding.

Table 8.1 Attitudes to returning to paid employment

Will never return	8%	
Will return in child's first year	28%	
Will return when child is 12 to 18 months	10%	
Will return when child is over 18 months	33%	
Doesn't know when will return	21%	(N=79)

> I don't think you can have a career and kids as well. (18 year old married woman)

> I think. . . I'm more for being a mother. . . than I am to working. (18 year old married woman)

3. COST OF CHILDCARE Women who had investigated the childcare options available realized that the cost of a childminder or of a private nursery place would take a substantial proportion of their earnings. They were also aware that council day nursery places (which were cheap) were scarce. If relatives (usually mothers) could not provide free childcare, employment was frequently not a viable option. In the Thomas Coram study of dual-earner households, women (who were mostly over 20 and all married or cohabiting) did not consider it worth their while to be employed unless they earned enough to pay for childcare and have what they considered a fair proportion of their wages left over (Brannen and Moss, 1988)

> For one thing I don't think I could put her with a childminder plus they're too expensive. They're £30 a week and that's over half my wages, so it's not worth it to me. (18 year old married clerical assistant taking home £56 per week and on maternity leave at first interview)

4. INADEQUATE PAY At the time that women in this study gave birth unemployed women who held tenancies for council flats and lived alone or with unemployed male partners received supplementary benefit and had their rents paid by the DSS. Once they became employed, they lost both these benefits, and if their income was low they had to rely on family income supplement. If women were to be employed, therefore, it was essential that they earned enough to pay their rents as well as (if necessary) to pay for childcare. Since most women in this study could only hope to obtain poorly paid employment they were caught in unemployment and poverty 'traps' because they could not afford to be employed. The 1988 changes in social security legislation are likely to make such women's situation more desperate because many will not be able to afford to pay their rents and fully provide for their own and their children's needs, whether employed or not.

Given the combination of the four factors discussed above it is not surprising that only one woman who was eligible for maternity leave eventually took it, fully intending to return to her job.

It would seem, therefore, that motherhood had significantly worsened some young women's employment prospects. Those who would have to pay for childcare were unlikely to be able to earn enough to make it worth their while to be employed. In any case the majority considered that it was women's duty to give up their 'commitment' to employment in favour of a commitment to motherhood at least for a few years. It would be surprising if the near impossibility of obtaining sufficiently well paid employment did not strengthen women's commitment to providing full time childcare for their children.

Neither low pay nor disapproval of maternal employment are exclusive to the youngest age groups of mothers. Many older working class women employed in poorly paid occupations cannot afford to pay for childcare. In addition the current social construction of motherhood in Britain still proscribes maternal employment, although increasing numbers of mothers with young children are employed outside their homes.

Had they stayed in the labour market, many young women would have continued to experience periods of unemployment and/or poorly paid jobs. It is not early motherhood which can, therefore, be said to have damaged most women's employment prospects and earning potential. Many women are not able to obtain employment with good prospects and much money. Motherhood itself, at any age, damages women's career prospects and lifetime earning potential (Martin and Roberts, 1985; Joshi, 1987). Remaining childless throughout the life course (rather than deferring motherhood) would probably enhance some women's employment prospects, but it would do little for the majority of those interviewed in the Thomas Coram study.

Educational prospects were more likely to be damaged by early motherhood than were employment prospects. Women who were in full time education, whether at school or at college, usually did not complete their courses. Nine women (11%) had been at school when they became pregnant; all except one (a 17 year old) were 16 year olds. Five (6%) were at colleges of further education; none of these was 16 years old. Only one woman (a 16 year old) returned to school full time and took her Certificate of Secondary Education (CSE) examinations (examinations for less academic students). Other women left school or college before they would otherwise have done. They did not necessarily mind this, however. The majority of women in the study did not consider themselves to be academic, and most had left school as early as possible. Some of those who would have stayed on at school but for pregnancy did not regret having left.

> I didn't enjoy school. I dunno. There was too much fighting going on.[?] I left because I was pregnant. I thought I was happy at leaving, but it's boring at home, especially when mum's not here. (16 year old engaged woman)

Another 16 year old who left school when she was pregnant, but not because she was pregnant (she reached the end of the school year very early in pregnancy), expressed animosity to examinations.

> I didn't wanna do it [exams]. I thought it was a waste of time. I didn't wanna do no examinations or nothing. [Why not?] Cos I thought it would be too hard and I couldn't take all them hours sitting down writing boring things on the paper. [?] I knew I needed them but I wouldn't bother. I didn't study or nothing to get them. (16 year old single woman)

In three cases women were in danger of not being allowed to take the examinations they had anticipated they would. Two of these women did eventually take 'O' levels, although in one case it was necessary to argue with the school about this.

> Well they [school] wanted me to leave 'cos I could have some kind of accident or something like that. I said I wasn't going to 'cos if a teacher could walk round the school and nothing could happen to her, why should anything happen to me? So I stayed on. I took my mock exams and after that I left. (16 year old single woman)

In this instance the woman was insistent on taking her mock examinations because passing those guaranteed that she would be allowed to sit the State examinations a few months later. Her persistence paid off, because she did get some 'O' levels soon after birth.

> I passed the English, but not the language. The literature, but not the language. My Maths I got a B, which is equivalent to a pass but I mean I wanna do like work for the metropolitan police [secretarial work] or whatever, but you have to have a grade A at 'O' level so I decided to take that one again. I got my Art and Chemistry and Biology. (16 year old single woman)

Another 16 year old who left school during pregnancy also returned to sit examinations and gained three 'O' levels. Another two 16 year olds were provided with home tutors so that they could sit their CSE examinations.

In the four instances just described, each woman made attempts to continue with her education after birth. Two of them did so within the first six months of their child's birth. One woman who had a home tutor took a City and Guilds Physical Education teacher's course. The other woman who had a home tutor went back to school after birth and sat her CSEs. The woman who got some 'O' levels at school and was studying three more 'O' level subjects at evening classes soon dropped out of the course, reportedly because she was missing her son. Nonetheless, she did not rule out the possibility of studying for more examinations at a later time.

One student did not attempt to resist her tutor's recommendation that she should leave college. As a result she did not take her nursery nursing examinations although she had nearly completed the course when she became pregnant.

> Because my tutor said to me that there was no way I would have been able to carry on up until the end of July so there wasn't much point in me staying until however long. (18 year old single woman)

It was unfortunately not possible to re-interview this woman, so it is not known how she fared after childbirth.

The tiny minority of women who were close to sitting examinations when they became pregnant seem to have had their life chances most limited by motherhood. Although some were determined enough to ensure that they did get some qualifications, their chances of further study and employment may well have been curtailed. It was possible to see whether these limitations continued when children were nearly two.

Nearly two years after birth

EMPLOYMENT Women in the Thomas Coram study were subject to contradictory pressures with regard to employment and education. On the one hand they subscribed to the social construction of children's development being optimal in conditions where mothers are not employed outside the home. On the other hand, the majority of women were poor. Paid employment might have been expected to play an important part in easing some of their financial burdens. Yet, two years after birth, the pressures of paying for childcare, rent, etc., made employment impracticable for most women.

> Not at the moment no. I wanna like see him at school first, then try and go after something. See at the moment – I'd have to have a really good job. See at the moment anyway I'm better off on the dole, because my rent's paid and that. So I'm better off as I am really. I

mean I'm poor, but I'm better off than I would be if I'm working. (18 year old single woman)

Well cos my husband's unemployed I feel that well why don't I get a job you know? [?] Well I would, but I can't bring enough money home. I can't bring as much as he could... [?] Oh I'd only be able to get part time anyway wouldn't I? So it wouldn't be a lot. It'd only be about 40, 50 pound – not even that really. (18 year old married woman)

This woman was worried that she would not be able to rely on her husband either to be there consistently or to keep their children properly clean and fed while she was out at work. She had in fact done a job in a fish and chip shop for four hours two weeks prior to the interview, but had given it up after the first evening because it was both poorly paid and hard work. She was still considering the possibility of doing early morning or late night cleaning.

Some women managed to earn a little extra money without having to leave their children with other people. One way was to look after someone else's child as well as their own. By the time the children were 21 months old, three women (two single and one cohabiting) had done this, two still were, and another (a married woman) was expecting to start doing so. None of them had actually sought childminding work. All had been asked if they would look after a friend's child. They provided childcare for much less money than childminders would usually charge and, therefore, hardly earned anything in this way.

Another way to earn money at home was to sell cosmetic products at parties in other women's homes. A married woman with an employed husband was able to earn occasional small amounts of money by this means in the evenings when her husband was available to look after their daughter. A third way was to provide a childcare service outside the home. Another married woman whose husband was also employed had managed to supplement their income and get out of the house without being parted from her own child by becoming a part time creche leader in a community centre. The final way in which women in this study considered earning money without leaving their children was to engage in paid employment in the home. Nobody in the study had actually done this after birth, but two married women with employed husbands were considering taking on machining as homework when their children were nearly two.

Twenty one months after birth many women (and often their male partners and parents) still felt that their children were too young to be left regularly in someone else's care while mothers were out at work. Most women in the study were at this stage unemployed, and more than half of them (52%) said that even if they found the idea of being employed attractive, they would ideally choose to be at home with their children.

> Well I ought to be [at home with daughter] because you know she's young you know. You can't leave her somewhere else or with other people, but um I don't like to be at home full time, but I have to. So – there's not much I can do about that is there?
> Q–You feel that you can't leave her?
> A–Yeah because I mean she's not even two yet.
> (Married woman who was selling cosmetics in her spare time)

> Yeah I wouldn't leave her with anyone else. Like um I was gonna get a job full time in a little chip shop, and I said to my mum would she look after her. But I wouldn't give her to a stranger. (This woman did not take the job she was offered because her mother said that she should not leave her child.) (18 year old married woman)

> I don't want to get anyone to look after her, though I would like to work part time. (19 year old married woman)

> Yeah and so does Alan [husband] till they [current child and the one about to be born] start school. [?] Well sometimes I feel that I would like. . . to go out to work to earn extra money and that but I also feel that I should be at home with her. So she's more important. When she starts school I can start working. I chose to have her. It's my place to stay with her. (17 year old married woman)

Nearly half the sample (48%) did, however, feel that they could separate from their children in order to be employed or to study. By 21 months after birth some women were beginning to feel that their children needed to mix with their own age peers.

> Since before we went away [on holiday] I was determined that when we come back I'd get a job and go a work full time. But then Paul don't really like me to work. He thinks I should stay at home with him until it's time for him to go a school, but I think. . . he does need other children, and I'm not prepared to give him any more at the moment [laughs]. (Cohabiting woman whose son had already had a council nursery place for two months)

Twenty-one months after having given birth fewer women were employed (19%, 13 women) than had been prior to conception.

Table 8.2 Employment and education from conception to 21 months after birth

	Conception	6 months	21 months	
In education	17%	1%	7%	
Job training schemes	6%	4%	0%	
Part time jobs	4%	5%	9%	
Full time jobs	29%	2%	10%	
Unemployed	44%	88%	74%	(N=68)

There was an increase in the proportion of women who were employed part time rather than full time. Nearly half of those who were employed were only working part time at 21 months (six part time and seven full time). In these respects the women interviewed did not differ from most British mothers because breaks in women's employment careers after childbirth are extremely common. When they do return to paid work women are more likely to work part time than full time, and hence to experience downward career mobility (Brannen and Moss, 1988).

Although the numbers of employed women were small, there was a definite increase in the percentage of women employed in the two years following birth. Throughout the study employed women remained largely in the same occupational groupings. This is hardly surprising since most women were employed in occupations where there was little career progression and hence no corresponding possibility of downward occupational mobility. Re-entry to such jobs was therefore likely to be at the same point as original entry had been.

More women may have sought employment if they had been able to arrange childcare, and to find sufficiently well paid part time work. It is true that more than half (52%) of those who were at home with their children claimed that this is what they would ideally have chosen. But nearly half (48%) wanted either to find employment or to take an educational or training course. Half of those who did not want to be full time caregivers would ideally have chosen to work part time. A third wanted to find full time work. Only a sixth wanted to pursue further education.

Childcare was difficult to arrange for those mothers who wanted to work. Because they could not afford to pay much for alternative childcare, women had few choices open to them. Council day nurseries were an obvious option since they are cheap to the consumer and often have a sliding scale of charges, so that poorer women pay less. Twenty six per cent of the sample (18 women) had tried to get a council day nursery place for their child. Most (14) had not been successful in doing so because they were not considered to have enough 'social problems' to be given priority. The demand for council day nursery places so outstrips supply that most places are now reserved for those considered by health visitors, social workers or nursery workers to have pressing social problems. Having mothers who were young and single used to be considered sufficient criteria for children to be given nursery places, but this is no longer the case.

> Well I did [put daughter's name down on council nursery waiting list] when I was working but um they told me she didn't fit into the criteria list so they told me they'd have to turn down my application. They advised me to get a childminder. [?] But as I said to them it's not worth it to get a childminder because I'll just be working to pay a childminder so might as well stay home and look after her myself. (18 year old semi-cohabiting woman whose mother had provided childcare for the six months she was employed)

> Her name was down but they have taken it off because there are too many kids waiting. Only left those with special needs. (18 year old single woman)

> I put it down when he was born and then they refused him then and then I tried again, say that he moved up back to my mum and they still say well he's not a priority case. (19 year old woman who started cohabiting after birth)

Just as women's perceptions that other people were getting more benefits than they were fuelled discontent and resentment (see chapter 6), so the perception that some children got council day nursery places more easily than others was considered to be unfair.

> When Camilla was about nine months [put her name down on council nursery list]. . . What really hurts me is that um the woman that lives downstairs, her child is six months right and she's not working. She's not doing nothing. She's in the same position as me, and it's going to a nursery and Camilla's what – two next week and she's just being stuck indoors. She's not mixing with other kids and there's no other kids round here for her to sort of like play with her or anything. (16 year old single woman living alone)

At 21 months only two children were in council nurseries while their mothers were in employment (a further two children were in council nurseries while their mothers looked for employment). There were no obvious differences in the circumstances of women who got a nursery place compared with those who did not.

The majority of children whose mothers were employed or pursuing further education courses were cared for by relatives (six) or by minders and friends (three). Four children had more than one childcare arrangement. These were a combination of relatives and friends when the main alternative caregiver was employed part time.

Women's reluctance to leave their children, coupled with the general unavailability of childcare and the unattractive jobs available to them, makes it unlikely that the majority of women in this study will be employed outside the home before their children start school.

While a minority of women who remained unemployed 21 months after birth would ideally have chosen to be employed, most women who were employed full time did not want to be. They found it stressful and difficult to combine employment and motherhood. Nine women (13%) said they wanted to be employed full time. Only one of these was already employed full time (seven women were employed full time). She had been 16 at birth, had returned to school and obtained five CSEs and been employed continuously since leaving school (although she had twice changed jobs). She lived with her parents, and her mother had given up work in order to look after her child. Both parents believed she should be encouraged to experience employment, to save money and to go out in the evenings sometimes.

> Q–Does that mean you think you should be at home with him?
> A–No, no I think I should be at work. [?] Well me mind tells me I prefer work, but me heart when he's crying on the doorstep here waving goodbye to me tells me I should be at home. [?] Um well I'm just happy with a full time one [job]
> (16 year old single woman living with her parents)

Although this woman's parents had pressed her to have an abortion

Table 8.3 Childcare arrangements at 21 months

Not in day care	78%	
Nursery	3%	
Minder/friend	5%	
Relative	9%	
Combination	6%	(N=68)

(and indeed she would have had one had she not been too advanced in pregnancy) they were now delighted with their grandson. The woman's mother expressed this after the last interview by saying, 'He's really one of the family now.' This woman clearly got a lot of support from her parents and felt that she shared responsibility for her child with them. Asked whether she had considered using a day nursery for her son she replied, 'No, *we* haven't done that and *we* won't' (my italics). Yet even she found it tiring to work by day and tend her son in the evenings and nights, and difficult to part from him in the morning. She admitted that she would feel more like a mother if she did not live with her parents.

> *Q*–Would anything make it easier for you?
> *A*–Um if I had my own house. [?] I think me and William would be happier. [?] Well I'd think myself more of a mother cos I wouldn't have mum here you know all the time. [?]. . . I don't mind it. I think William would be happy having more room. . . for him.
> (16 year old single woman)

Judging from other full time employed women's reports of their dissatisfactions with combining employment and motherhood, the support this woman received was probably crucial to her well being as an employed mother. Yet that very support was in part experienced as oppressive.

Other women who were employed full time complained of overwhelming tiredness. One woman's case (Debbie's) is presented at length because she was unusual in this study in having been continuously employed since before conception. Debbie returned to her apprenticeship after maternity leave, completed it and was working as a fully fledged member of her manual trade 21 months after birth. She earned more than any other woman in the study (£120 to £140 a week) and had a childminder who often kept her daughter overnight on week nights so that she did not have to worry about taking the child out early in the morning (since she started work at 7.30 a.m.). This childminder, a friend of Debbie's stepmother, charged £20 per week if the child did not stay overnight, and £30 if she did. Debbie mostly liked her job. But she was exhausted by employment and childcare responsibilities.

> When I wake up in the morning I'm really knackered. . . my body always feels tired. It feels like it's on its limit and it's gonna drop down. But you know I just go ahead and keep pushing myself you know. I just go up the road and pass out [this happened to Debbie

at work two months before the interview when she had flu. She also has sickle cell trait which may increase her tiredness and vulnerability when ill] or I just drop out of exhaustion or something you know. . .
(18 year old single woman)

Although she was well paid by comparison with other people in the sample, Debbie's disposable income (after paying for childcare) was not sufficient to cushion her from worrying about money. Part of her tiredness resulted from sometimes lying awake worrying about money.

Even if Shelley's over there [at her minder's] I still can't sleep because I'm wondering. Probably I got money matters on my brain or something like that and I'm worried about that all through the night.

Money was not the only matter that prevented her from sleeping, however. She was the only woman in an otherwise male trade and was fed up with the sexual harassment she continually experienced. In addition her relationship with her child's father was not currently very happy. She had anticipated that he would be more supportive than he had been.

[Ideally] I would stay at home until she goes to school. . . and then get a part time job so it fits in with her – like when she leaves for school I leave to go to work and when she comes home I come home.
Q–Why didn't you do that?
A–Well. . . me and the boyfriend's relationship wasn't really that steady for me to say that I would do that. . .
Q–Does that mean you wouldn't have finished your apprenticeship?
A–No, what I would have done is wait till I qualified then stop.

Some of Debbie's desire to stay at home with Shelley seemed to come from her perception of what her role should be with regard to her child. Asked whether she would like any help with childcare, she replied:

I mean I'd rather do it myself cos that's what I'm there for. I wouldn't like to know anybody does it you know. Well the childminder does because she's there with her, but otherwise I just like *me* to do it.

Given her circumstances, however, she was happy with the amount the childminder did for Shelley.

I'm happy because at least it. . . you know eases some of the pressure off me. Cos with me working I don't really find that much time to say I'm gonna be with her. So if the childminder's making her feel you know relaxed you know giving her everything she needs at least I know she's happy. I mean cos she knows who her mother is. . . So you know no matter how the childminder spoils her or treats her, Shelley will always know who her mummy is. (18 year old single woman)

Debbie provides a good example of the various and contradictory pressures operating on young, single women who attempt to combine employment and motherhood. She was only able to continue in employment because her earnings (although not enormously high) and her childcare arrangement were better than most other women's in the study. Despite her remarkable achievement (in finishing her apprenticeship in a sexist, male enclave, after birth and continuing to practise her trade there) she would have preferred to be at home with her daughter.'. . . I mean I'm always depressed. . . When I started to go back to work, the depression started to come in.'

Debbie's vision of herself and her future did not include existing on supplementary benefit, however. She would have been prepared to give up her job only if her male partner could support her. The way in which this degree of stress affected Debbie's view of whether she should have become a mother when she did, will be discussed later in this chapter.

Another woman, Sarah, did stop working. She was employed as a hairdressing apprentice for six months from when her child was eight months old. Although she had her own flat her mother looked after her daughter for free, and Sarah was happy with that arrangement. It was, however, very tiring work and very long working hours (nine or ten hours a day, including Saturdays) for hardly any pay (£54 per week if the shop was busy and £40 if not) so she gave up. Sarah said 'I'd like to go back to work actually. I don't think staying at home is me.' Yet she also felt that she would not go back to work until her child was older. She did not argue that her child needed to be with her all the time, but that as a mother she would miss seeing her daughter's development if she worked full time.

Um I think – yeah until she goes to school – starts nursery, cos there's so many things you miss first two, three years of their lives you know and I' like to spend that time with her at home and then go back out to work. (18 year old semi-cohabiting woman)

Sarah had been looking after her sister's eight month old child for the last three months. '. . . I couldn't really charge her, because he's my nephew you know. I mean if I was going out to work and she wasn't, she would look after Evey.'

EDUCATION: 21 MONTHS AFTER BIRTH　Twenty one months after birth five women (8%) were pursuing educational courses. These courses were office and business skills, sports management, 'O' levels and manual trades. One single woman who had been 17 years old when she gave birth had started a job with a national charity and been seconded to do office skills and business studies. Her child had a nursery place. A single woman (19 years old at birth) had been advised by a college that she could do a course for women returning to employment. Her child was looked after by her mother while she did computer studies. Her mother was, however, paid £45 per week as a sponsored childminder.

The other women had decided what they wanted to do, and pursued their chosen courses themselves. One woman's child went to a private nursery, one to a childminder and one went to his grandmother in the mornings and his father in the afternoons. Two women had been engaged in study before they became pregnant (one at college and the other at school). Three had not been attracted to study before conception.

For most women attending further education 21 months after birth it seemed that having a child had acted as a spur to getting formal qualifications. Women felt that they needed qualifications in order to get jobs which paid well enough to allow them to support their children. They therefore felt a determination to succeed which had not been evident before.

> I went on the course so that I would be able to get a job to support Sophie. . . It's important to train now because without qualifications I wouldn't be able to get a decent job. (16 year old single woman)

> Cos I couldn't get the kind of job I really want.
> Q–What kind of job did you really want?
> A–Mainly computer work and word processing and you need 'O', 'A' levels. . . so I decided to go back and do my 'O' levels.
> (19 year old cohabiting woman doing three year package of five 'O' levels)

The few women who were engaged in further education were not concentrated in any particular part of the 16 to 19 age range when they gave birth. One woman was cohabiting (although she did not consider her relationship to be a permanent one) but none was married. This is not an unusual finding. Furstenberg (1976) found that those teenage mothers who were most likely to gain academic credentials were single, rather than married women.

One woman was unfortunately prevented from studying because she could not afford to pay for childcare. She had not been successful in getting a nursery place, and her mother was employed full time.

> Well I went to college for a little while [three-and-a-half months when her child was one year old] but I gave it up because I mean I didn't have no one to look after Lucy so that meant I had to give this girl money out of my benefit money to sort of look after her and I was losing out because I didn't have enough money to sort of buy things I needed. [?] Well I just used to pay her like £10 a week and all that lot and just provide food for Lucy and I thought that the social services would help me out but you know I mean they kept on saying they would but they never got round to it. So I just didn't bother, but I decided I'm gonna go to evening classes instead this year so I'll be better off. [?] Well I'll leave her with my mum then. You see my mum finishes work at half four. . . (16 year old single woman whose friend had recently moved in with her)

It is a measure of this woman's determination to get qualifications that she continued to study for a whole term in such unsatisfactory circumstances. She may well manage to pursue a course of evening study later. She had already managed to pass four 'O' levels at school after her child was born. But childcare responsibilities had clearly prevented her from achieving as much academically as she otherwise might have done. She herself perceived her child to have been a limitation (see chapter 7) and felt that she had held a romantic view of motherhood which was unrealistic for her age group.

The second woman who gained 'O' levels when she was pregnant was also 16 years old when she gave birth. She had attended evening classes for three months when her child was seven months old. Her child's father (with whom she was then cohabiting) looked after their child. She gave up because she said she missed her son, and found it difficult to do the necessary studying. Twenty one months after birth she had moved back to her parents' home and was about to start a one year MSC job.

> I mean there were so many things I could have done and I just didn't want to. I used him [child] as a nasty excuse and now that things have sort of changed I feel that it's time I got off my big ass and sort of get out and actually do something for myself instead of sort of waiting for it to come to me. And if I did I think I'd still be sitting here. I mean it's only working for a year, but it's a start. [?] My ideal

is to be working full time and to be actually getting some qualifications at the same time.
Q–What prevents you from doing that?
A–Myself. As I said I use him as an excuse. It's just me.
Q–So you think you could do it?
A–Oh yeah. And I think I will do it.
(16 year old at birth)

This woman did not perceive her child to have limited her prospects at all. She felt that she had used him as an excuse not to do more in the first two years, but that she would eventually do the things she wanted to. Although this woman did attempt to do some studying when she was cohabiting, it is perhaps significant that it is when she moved back in with her parents that she found a job, and felt that she would also be able to study. Living with supportive parents did seem to give women more opportunities (or at least the perception that more opportunities were open to them) to study or to be employed if they wanted to be than either living alone or living with male partners.

This woman's male partner had not actively attempted to prevent her from taking up employment but he had refused to assist by providing childcare, although he had looked after their child for the three months she had attended evening classes.

I asked his father [who is unemployed] if he could look after him, and his father turned round and said 'no'.
Q–Do you know why. . . ?
A–He hasn't given me no reason and I'm not asking for no reason really. I'm not really bothered. But I mean he said – before I had a job I asked him and he goes 'oh yeah' he'll look after him, but now he's turned round and said 'no'. So I've just left it at that. Cos I mean as far as I'm concerned it's just either spite or what – so what I can do is sort of get him into – sort of if I can get him into nursery or childminder. But I mean I sort of want to pursue the job.
(16 year old whose aunt is going to look after her son initially while she is on sick leave)

The fact that employment decisions were sometimes influenced by the composition of women's households is illustrated by Sharon, who was 18 years old when she had her son and lived with her parents until he was 18 months old.

When I started going back with Tony [child's father and now cohabitee] we talked about it [applying for a council flat] and I weren't too sure because of my mum. I weren't working because of the baby. My dad weren't working and my mum was the only one working and she had to pay all the money out and everything. So I went back to work and said 'no' [to applying for a flat] because me mum wants the money. So I was giving my mum the money. (18 year old cohabiting woman)

Sharon then got herself re-engaged as an apprentice in an almost exclusively male part of the food trade (the same apprenticeship she had worked in until three days before she gave birth) and worked there from when her son was eight months until he was 14 months old.

Pay was disgusting. I was doing the same things [as qualified people] and I was getting sort of like £50 and it was no good you know – from 9 until 6 o'clock at night and 7 until 6 o'clock on Saturdays and I was getting £50. And I went down the road – it was in an underwear shop, and it was four days a week about six hours a day and I was taking home £60, maybe £70.

Sharon's mother was working part time, and was able to look after Sharon's son. Eighteen months after the birth Sharon decided she would like her own flat. Her father had never liked her boyfriend 'because he thinks that all black people are the same you know'. It was therefore uncomfortable for him to visit Sharon while she lived with her parents. In addition, although they shared a house, Sharon's father had completely ignored her son for at least three months 'because he was half caste' (although by 21 months he was very fond of him). Sharon was offered a council flat as soon as she applied for one.

I stopped working there when I got the flat because I thought I ain't gonna come home from work and have to cook and clean up and look after David. I thought well I'll stay at home and look after David, look after the house. (18 year old at birth, cohabiting at third contact)

In this case Sharon had worked when living with her parents only to help them out financially. She was not attempting to further her career, nor had she been keen either to return to her apprenticeship or to any other employment. She did not like the trade she had been apprenticed to, and felt that she did not want to be employed again until her son was at school. Her decisions, firstly to seek employment and later to stop being employed, had both been made to suit her living circumstances.

Life chances beyond the early years

The Thomas Coram data is limited to a very small proportion (two years) of the lives of women who become mothers in their teenage years. There are few studies which go beyond children's preschool years and attempt to determine how early motherhood affects women later in life. It is, in fact, difficult to make such predictions for young women who are currently becoming mothers on the basis of information gained from long term follow ups of previous generations of women (see chapter 7).

Nonetheless the study done by Furstenberg and his colleagues (1987) is a welcome addition to the literature on early motherhood. Furstenberg has followed a sample of predominantly black women who gave birth when they were 17 years old from pregnancy until their children have reached adulthood (currently being done). Their 17 year follow up of children showed that the picture of the effects of early motherhood that emerges in the first years is not only limited, but can also be misleading. When, for example, mothers were interviewed five years after birth, it appeared that they were set to have more children than they wanted to, and more than average. Seventeen years later, this was patently not true. Women had completed their families quickly, but most had gone on to have less children than they originally intended to. Family sizes were comparable to those of women who started childbearing in their 20s or 30s.

What of women's education and employment 17 years after birth?

> By the 5-year follow-up, just under half of the mothers had completed high school. A majority of the dropouts continued to report that they would like to complete high school, but in 1972 only 8% of the women who had not graduated were currently enrolled. . . The prospects of further education. . . seemed poor. . . (Furstenberg et al., 1987, p. 25)

Yet a third of the women who had not graduated by the time their children were five did eventually do so. Many graduated when they were well into their 20s, after their children had started school. They were still, however, significantly less likely to complete high school than later childbearers, and on average had about a year of education less. Furstenberg and his colleagues suggest that this difference may be less than 'some observers' might anticipate.

> And it would be inaccurate to attribute all of the difference. . . to the effect of early childbearing because women who become mothers early in life are generally less able and motivated students than those who

avoid premature parenthood. . . This result could be taken as evidence that young mothers probably narrow the gap in educational attainment in later life. (Furstenberg et al., 1987, p. 30)

These findings support the suggestion that early motherhood may provide an incentive for some women, who might otherwise not do so, to take educational courses later in life. Women who obtain qualifications are likely to improve their employment chances and prospects. With regard to employment, the findings also run counter to popular beliefs that early motherhood causes long term unemployment.

As we discovered in examining the educational careers of the adolescent parents, the prognosis at the 5-year follow-up was somewhat worse than the actual outcome a dozen years later. Unlike the popular stereotype, most teenage mothers did not become chronic welfare recipients. . . welfare use is more prevalent among women with young children. Many teenage mothers no longer have young children. . . the finding that the great majority of adolescent mothers in the Baltimore and national samples are not reliant on public assistance is unexpected, as is the rather small difference between early and later childbearers. (Furstenberg et al., 1987, pp. 40, 42, 43)

Income level differentiated between early and late childbearers rather more than other factors.

The comparison of these women with older childbearers reveals a substantial difference in the level of family income. Later childbearers are much more likely than teenage mothers to have incomes of $25,000 or more. Conversely, many fewer are poor. Compared to other indicators of well-being, family income is quite sensitive to the timing of childbearing. (Furstenberg et al., 1987, p. 46)

There was wide variation in how the Baltimore sample fared. Furstenberg and his colleagues suggest that parental education and income level, race, differences in women's competence and motivation, the pace of any subsequent births, whether women married or not and decisions to stay at school and take welfare all influenced whether the women in their study did well economically. As in the Thomas Coram study, therefore, the effects of early motherhood could not be related to age in any simple fashion.

Furstenberg's sample differed in six important ways from the Thomas Coram sample. The two samples became mothers nearly 20 years apart. The Baltimore sample gave birth in 1967, and the Thomas

Coram sample gave birth in the mid 1980s. The Baltimore sample was a USA one whereas the Thomas Coram sample was London based. The Baltimore sample were relatively unusual because they had enrolled in the pre-natal programme from which they were recruited, whereas it is usual for pregnant women in Britain to attend antenatal clinics like those from which the London sample was recruited. No women in the Furstenberg sample were over 17 when they gave birth, whereas most of the Thomas Coram sample were 18 and 19 year olds (the most frequently occurring 'teenage mothers'). All in the Baltimore study were single, whereas a minority of the Thomas Coram sample were married. Nearly all the Furstenberg sample were black whereas the Thomas Coram sample was of different colours.

It is probably wise, therefore, to be cautious in making assumptions that outcomes for the women interviewed in London will be similar to those reported by Furstenberg et al. (1987). Nonetheless two general conclusions seem warranted. Firstly, that early motherhood is not as detrimental to women's lives as it is widely believed to be. Secondly, that women who become mothers early in their life courses are heterogeneous in a number of respects before they become mothers, and heterogeneity is maintained after birth. The impact of early motherhood cannot therefore be said to be uniform. Concern expressed about young mothers in general is therefore misplaced.

Furstenberg and his colleagues draw a further conclusion from the Baltimore study.

> Even if the stereotype of the adolescent mother in later life is much exaggerated, it is not wholly wrong. Many teenage mothers manage to break out of the seemingly inevitable cycle of poverty, but the majority did not make out as well as they probably would have had they been able to postpone motherhood. (Furstenberg et al., 1987, p. 47)

The evidence from the Thomas Coram study did not support this conclusion. This may be because the study is of too short a period of the life course for it to be apparent that women would have done better if they had postponed childbearing. It may be because the Thomas Coram sample gave birth in a different time and place, and chose (given the option of abortion which was not available to most of the Baltimore sample) to have their children. But it is necessary to ask whether comparisons with women who did not have children in their teenage years (who may differ in unrecorded ways from women who do give birth before they are 20) provide a wholly satisfactory basis on which to draw that conclusion.

It seems that some women may have done better if they had postponed childbearing, but early childbearing may equally have spurred some women on to get qualifications and be consistently employed. The personal and wider social contexts in which women give birth early in their life course therefore need to be taken into account in assessments of the impact of early motherhood. It is unlikely that women who give birth early in their life course, and those who give birth later, will live in identical social contexts.

Women's feelings about motherhood

Chapter 7 discussed how women in the Thomas Coram study felt about their children in the first two years after birth and how they managed childcare. This section considers how women felt about motherhood itself rather than about their children. While feelings about motherhood and about the children being mothered are generally the same, they are not necessarily identical.

All women reported that they found some aspects of motherhood satisfying, with more than four-fifths of the women being rated as gaining quite a lot of satisfaction (84%). Most women (83%) also reported feeling some dissatisfaction with motherhood.

The tenor of what women said was that the greatest pleasure they got from motherhood came from caring for their children and having them around because they loved them so much. They reported that they got a lot of pleasure from seeing the developmental advances children made and enjoyed aspects of their children's behaviour. Many women had long anticipated that motherhood would be a crucial aspect of their lives and actually having a child gave them a sense of meaning and purpose also reported in other studies of older women (Boulton, 1983) as well as those who gave birth in their teenage years (Simms and Smith, 1986; Sharpe, 1987).

The things many women disliked about motherhood were mainly getting up to attend to children at night, not being free to do things like going out at will, having to deal with tantrums and prolonged crying and having to be continually alert to the possibility that their toddlers could get into mischief very quickly.

> Q–What are the best things about being a mother?
> A–I like playing with her. . . I like having her around.
> Q–What would you say are the worst things about being a mother?
> A–I don't find nothing worst.

Q–Some mothers say that they don't like changing nappies or getting up at night. . . ?
A–No I like changing her nappies. I don't get up at night. She sleeps right through the night. She always did when she was little didn't she? [to her mother].
Q.–Would you say that you've always enjoyed being a mother?
A.–I enjoyed her even when she was a baby. I enjoyed her all the time.
(Married woman)

Q.–What are the best things about being a mother?
A–Bringing up Leah and taking care of her and cooking meals for her. I think it's lovely, and dressing her. Looking after her. . . some of the things that she does makes you feel so proud. . .
Q–And the worst things. . . ?
A–It's when they get up to mischief and you're trying to do the housework and everything. You have to have eyes in the back of your head to look after them. . .
Q–Does that affect how you feel about Leah?
A–No I like everything she does really.
(19 year old single woman)

Q.–What are the best things about being a mother?
A–They make you laugh and pleased you had them. They are company.
Q–And the worst things?
A–Not being able to do things you want when you want.
(Cohabiting woman with two children at 21 months)

Contrary to the popular stereotype of mothers under 20 being unable to cope with their children as toddlers, more than half the women in the Thomas Coram study (56%) reported that they found mothering easier when their children were toddlers than they had during infancy. Less than a fifth (19%) thought mothering had become harder, although over a quarter (27%) said they found motherhood difficult at 21 months.

Mm. I find it easier now he's getting bigger. [?] It's not so demanding as when. . . he was a baby you know. I mean I can – he gets on with what he wants to do and things like that. . . (Single woman)

I think it's been easy and exciting really because she's talking now and she makes sentences and she asks to go places and that. Which is quite good. [?] Yes as she grows it gets easier. [?] Well the nappies for one. She's out of nappies, so she asks to go to the toilet. I don't have to um constantly change and clean and that and her eating habits. . . have more or less stabilized, so it's been easier that way.
(18 year old single woman)

> Well like this age is the best age I suppose so far. I mean all the little things she can do. She's always making me laugh. (Cohabiting woman who was pregnant again at 21 months)

In the last chapter two women (a 16 year old and a 17 year old) who felt negative about motherhood were discussed. It was argued that their feelings could only be understood by considering the conditions in which they lived. Difficulties they were facing in other areas of their lives made motherhood extremely stressful for them. Yet, in the case of the 16 year old, feelings about motherhood were not synonymous with feelings about her child.

Women in the Thomas Coram study were not directly asked to assess whether, in retrospect, motherhood had been a good idea for them. But when women were spontaneously contemplative about the effects of motherhood, they discussed their perceptions of how motherhood had affected other significant life careers. As Boulton (1983) found, these assessments were independent of their feelings for their children.

> Sometimes I wish I'd never had her. Not in the sense that I wish she wasn't here, but in the sense I wish that I'd waited perhaps a bit longer. . . I sometimes get that feeling you know cos we never really had much of a life when I was single, being Italian – the way I was brought up. So I miss the fact that I've never been to a disco. [Never at all?]. No. No. I've hardly ever been to the pictures and that sort of thing. Doing what other teenagers would have done. I sometimes get the feeling that you know if only I hadn't got married maybe things would have turned out differently, but I don't think they would have done with my parents because I would have been going to work, and then going home. That would have been it. I would never have been allowed out at night so – that's the only thing about it. I sometimes wish it's never happened. Then when I think about it deeply I think well I probably would have been worse off cos all I would have had would have been work. I wouldn't have had any social life. I don't have much of a social life now but at least I am my own person here in the sense that I can do practically what I want. . . so I'm pleased with that – that bit of it. (18 year old married woman)

When asked in pregnancy if she would like to change anything in her life, this woman had replied that she would have liked to have been born to different parents, parents who were less strict. Marriage had been the only route she perceived out of her parental home, and she had married at 16 years. She had been having fertility investigations after a year of trying to become pregnant before eventually conceiving, and was clear that her daughter had been wanted and was much loved. Her regrets were to do with aspects of her life she perceived as immutable.

Another women (discussed earlier in this chapter) who was continuously employed throughout the study in a manual trade, and who said that she found things very difficult, had also 'tried' to become pregnant. She had feared that she was infertile because she had had an infection which had affected her Fallopian tubes. Her assessment of whether having her daughter when she did had been a good idea centred around her relationship with her child's father.

> I mean sometimes I say to myself I wish I never had her you know. Maybe I would probably have had a boyfriend and we been going out regular and you know a decent one who's here round me, maybe then I would have decided to have a child because I thought that maybe he was the right one, and have a kid now you know. Things just didn't turn out that way. Maybe I was a bit – well 19 – I wouldn't say I was young but I didn't know much about him anyway to say I should've had a child with him. When I sit down and think about it now I say no, I shouldn't have had [child]. He wasn't really the right one to have her for. Cos I mean he's changed drastically from the time I was pregnant. Before we used to have a bit of a laugh and fun and I used to see him all the time, but since I've had [her] things have just gone downhill and there's gonna be a time when it's gonna reach rock bottom where I ain't gonna take no more and I'm just gonna tell him to get out and that's it. . . You know from there on I've just got to build myself back up again.
> Q–So do you regret having had [her]?
> A–Um I do and I don't. I mean sometimes I wish I didn't have her. Sometimes when I've got money problems I say to myself if I didn't have her I'd probably be well off now. I'd probably be in mummy's house saving and I could buy myself a car and everything but then when I think of her I say no. She's mine, and I'm happy she's here. You know I can sit down and play with her and give her the love I never had from my father when I was small. . . and I'm two parents in one really.
> (19 year old single woman)

To record these women as being only regretful of their decisions to have a child would be an oversimplification and a distortion of their accounts. Both women were sometimes regretful of aspects of their lives which they saw as being limited by having a child, but neither could seriously imagine themselves without their daughters. The first woman was aware that her regret was idealized because she was unlikely to have had as much freedom as she would ideally have liked, even if she had deferred marriage. She had also had two childless years after marriage when she was free of her parents' restrictions but still did not go to a disco. The second woman was dissatisfied with many more areas of her life than the first woman and felt that she would have been both economically better off and likely to have a more reliable male partner if she had deferred childbearing. Even so she was still happy with her daughter.

Other women were less self consciously contemplative of the effects of motherhood on their lives. Yet their satisfactions and dissatisfactions with motherhood were also clearly related to its effects of various aspects of their lives like their financial or employment situations, relationships with kin, or staving off loneliness later in life. Their ages when they gave birth did not feature in their consideration of their feelings about motherhood.

> There's less money to spend but um I wouldn't say it was that hard and I wouldn't say it was easy neither. [?]. . . I'm not bringing her up on my own you know. I've got her dad and my parents and his parents so I just have to phone one of them and say d'you want to keep her for a couple of hours? And it's like putting gold in their laps. . . (Semi-cohabiting woman)

> Well when you get older you know. . . you still have someone to look after – you know you still have someone to care about. I don't know you know. You'll never be lonely. He'll probably get married and have children so I can always go round there. You got someone to care for. Of your own to look after [laugh]. [?] I don't have to go out to work [laugh]. Maybe when he gets older I will go out [to work], because you don't get enough money but. . . I enjoy looking after him even though he's a handful, but he's all right. (18 year old single woman)

Both these women were well supported, having excellent relationships with supportive mothers who lived nearby and visited frequently. Both children's fathers were also supportive. In the second case, the couple no longer had a sexual relationship, but were very good friends. Her child's father paid £10 per week towards caring for his child. While this did not benefit the woman materially because it was deducted from her supplementary benefit, it did clearly demonstrate his commitment to their son. Like most women in the study, money was scarce for these two women, but both were managing. The relative absence of other problems made motherhood a positive experience for them both.

The 16 year old discussed earlier in this chapter as having started college but stopped because she missed her child did not express any regrets about motherhood. She reported that her son had not prevented her from doing anything she wanted to do. Similarly the woman who had been 16 years old at birth and reported that she was studying in order to be able to get a well paid job so that she could support her child, felt that motherhood had been beneficial to her.

> It's made me more responsible. It's changed the sort of person I am. I used to be a trouble maker and get into fights all the time. People have been amazed at the change in my personality.
> Q–How do you feel about that?
> A–I'm happy with that.
> Q–Has being a mother made any other difference in your life?
> A–I feel less lonely. I feel more love being a mother.
> (16 year old single woman, six months after birth)

Summary

Most women who became mothers before they were 20 years of age in the Thomas Coram study did not appear to have their employment or educational prospects damaged by early childbearing. This was largely because most had neither been academically inclined nor in jobs which offered training or career prospects. Many women felt that they should not leave their children in the first years after birth. For all the women motherhood was at least as important a career as (and for many women, more important than) employment.

Women's attitudes to motherhood in combination with social conditions in which childcare is scarce and takes a large proportion of many working class women's income, made it unlikely that many women would return to employment or education (even part time) before their children started school.

The stresses involved in combining motherhood and employment or education led a few women to discontinue their educational courses or employment. In none of these instances was motherhood perceived as permanently limiting. The only woman who was continuously employed throughout her pregnancy and child's life found the effort of combining motherhood and employment so draining that she would have preferred (had her child's father been prepared to support her) to give up employment.

In all the cases discussed above, it is evident that the context in which the women were living was an important influence on how they fared. All the women live in a society in which childcare provision is not available for most under fives and women are expected to rear their children without State intervention. Many women were influenced by that social expectation to feel that ideally they should be with their children rather than at work. Poor childcare provision reinforced the belief that it was their job to care for their own children.

The high costs of the childcare available in relation to the poor earnings they could attain made it impracticable for women who were dependent on supplementary benefit to pay for childcare. In practice, therefore, only certain groups of women could afford to be unemployed. These were married/cohabiting women whose male partners earned a reasonable wage and single women who either managed to get a cheap nursery place, or a childminder paid for by social services, or whose relatives were able to look after their children.

In the Thomas Coram study no married women worked or studied full time outside the home (although one was a full time childminder at home). Most women who were either employed or in education were single (two were cohabiting). It may be that single women are most likely to feel that they should attempt to improve their children's financial position by being employed, while married or cohabiting women may feel that their children's fathers have major responsibility for making such economic provision. Despite the scarcity of nursery places, social services are also more likely to treat single women more favourably than married women when it comes to the provision of nursery places and sponsored childminders. In addition, women who lived with their parents were sometimes supported and encouraged in employment by mothers who provided childcare. By 21 months all married and cohabiting women had moved away from their parental homes.

The numbers of those employed and in education are too small for any conclusions to be reached about why married women are less likely to seek employment or training. It is also not possible to say whether such small differences are sustained over time, particularly as two married women reported that they intended to return to education at some time in the future.

Early motherhood is generally portrayed as being detrimental to young women's career prospects. Yet while motherhood seemed to have worsened a few women's positions with regard to employment and education, it had also acted as a spur to getting qualifications and employment for a few other women.

This discussion indicates that it would be overly simplistic to conclude that early motherhood had clear, unitary effects on young women's prospects. Early motherhood did not seem to be detrimental to the educational and employment prospects of the majority of women interviewed in the Thomas Coram study. Where it did seem to have negative effects there were always particular factors, other than age, which were adversely affecting young women's lives. An understanding of the social contexts in which particular women live is therefore crucial to an understanding of how (and why) early motherhood affects their lives as it does.

Most women's experiences of motherhood were positive ones. But a few women expressed regrets that motherhood had adversely affected their lives. While many young women are affected in similar ways by the wider social context (such as welfare regulations) there are aspects of women's lives (such as the fit between their expectations of male partners and male partners' actual behaviour) which are unique to each one. There was no one-to-one correspondence between women's feelings about motherhood and their feelings for their child. Some women expressed negative views about motherhood and yet almost all were positive about their own children.

Endnote

A major theme throughout this book has concerned the effects of early motherhood on young women and their children. In addressing that issue many aspects of women's lives have been considered. Relationships with parents and male partners; the social support available to them; socio-economic circumstances including education, employment, housing and welfare benefits; feelings for children and satisfaction with motherhood have all come under scrutiny. In other words the most significant 'careers' in women's lives have been explored.

Contrary to popular belief and the ways in which 'teenage motherhood' has been socially constructed, early motherhood does not constitute cause for general concern. The majority of mothers investigated in this study (as in many other studies) were coping with motherhood well. Their children, according to maternal reports and assessed on a standardized developmental test, were also faring well. This is consistent with the findings of other studies. For even studies which report that children born to teenage women score less well on developmental assessments than those born to older women find that they generally score above the standardized means.

Concerns about the effects of early motherhood on women and children often seem to be based on the assumption that they would necessarily fare better if they deferred motherhood beyond the teenage years. Yet it is not pregnancy and motherhood that prevent most women who give birth while still teenagers from obtaining educational qualifications. Most have already failed national examinations or left school without taking them. Prior to conception most young mothers have experienced difficulty in finding permanent jobs. Their male partners come from similar backgrounds and, having equally poor experiences of the employment market, are mostly unable to make much financial contribution to women and children. For most women early motherhood cannot be said to be causative of poverty. Indeed it seems that early motherhood is most likely to occur if young women have experienced unemployment. Deferring motherhood, therefore, will not necessarily improve women's socio-economic circumstances. The ways in which poverty and early motherhood are interrelated merits further research.

Since most women who become mothers in their teenage years are inexperienced and unqualified when they enter the labour market, the employment opportunities available to them are limited, particularly in periods when youth unemployment is high. The jobs they are generally able to get provide little possibility of career progression and are usually poorly paid. As a result the intersection of the motherhood career with employment and educational careers is often not as disruptive for those who give birth early in their life course as it is for women whose educational or career trajectories are such that career breaks are likely to result in downward mobility and to be costly in terms of loss of potential earnings.

Young women's accounts indicated that they had become pregnant and chosen to give birth for a variety of reasons. These reasons ranged from having 'planned' their pregnancies to not having considered that they were likely to become pregnant. Young women are often presumed to have become pregnant because they have insufficient knowledge about sex and contraception. Yet none of the women interviewed had become pregnant through ignorance of contraception. All knew that different kinds of contraceptives were available. Many contraceptives were, however, unpopular with young women and/or their male partners. With greater awareness of the existence of AIDS and appeals for 'safe sex' young couples may in future be more inclined to choose the sheath as their favoured contraceptive method, and the general dislike of it reported by women interviewed in this study may diminish among young people.

Despite recent suggestions that young women become pregnant in order to get council housing or social security benefits, we found no evidence of this. Similarly Clark (1989) found that the single teenage women she studied were astonished to be asked whether they had become pregnant in order to obtain council housing. It may be argued that women are unlikely to admit to such nakedly instrumental reasons for having children. But corroboration for the suggestion that women do not become pregnant for those reasons comes from studies in the USA which relate trends in single parenthood to changes in welfare provision. Such studies find that rates of single parenthood increase when benefits do not and that reproductive trends are not related to welfare provision. The scarcity of adequately paid permanent jobs was, however, the context in which young women in this study decided that early motherhood would not be damaging to their lives.

By late pregnancy women were looking forward to having their children although one woman was not enthusiastic about being pregnant. Once children were born women got on with the tasks of mothering. In the two years of the study most found childcare relatively easy and unproblematic and, with one exception, all reported that they loved their children. Children's needs were reported to be the most important in the hierarchy of household needs and several women reported that they sometimes went without food and clothing in order to ensure that they could provide food, clothing, and some toys for their children. Most women who were dependent on supplementary benefit in this study were adamant that they would prefer to be able to make independent provision for their children.

Given the weight of negative opinion against 'teenage mothers', women's accounts of their feelings for their children, their provision of childcare and their children's health were strikingly unremarkable. They loved their children and were determined to provide for them. Women were familiar with current thinking on what children's needs comprise. Adequate provision was generally reported to include love and stimulation (often from educational toys) as well as provision for physical needs. Women thus accepted dominant ideologies in Western societies which suggest that childhood should ideally be a commercialized period with educational toys and smart clothing being lavished on children. Poverty, however, made the acceptance of such ideologies oppressive in that many women could afford to buy their children manufactured toys only by going short of things they themselves needed. Women did not, however, experience such ideologies as oppressive but simply accepted them as taken for granted knowledge.

Why were women who, by virtue of their age, might be expected to be engaging in youth cultural practices and developing 'style' rather than taking on the responsibilities of childcare reportedly so content with motherhood? One reason is that most women interviewed had long anticipated that motherhood would be the most fulfilling aspect of their lives. The majority had expected that they would become mothers earlier rather than later in their lives. Most who said that ideally they would have deferred motherhood said that their preferred aged to have children was only a couple of years older than their current age. Furthermore, early motherhood was common in most women's social networks. Most had friends and relatives who were having or had had children at similar ages. Many of their own mothers had also had their own first children before they were 20 or soon afterwards. The age at which they became mothers was not, therefore, censured by significant people in women's networks. In addition relatives, particularly mothers, were generally very supportive in providing childcare and material resources in a way that male partners frequently were not. In many cases parental support seemed essential to the good outcomes found.

Boulton (1983) suggests another important reason why young women may be satisfied with motherhood. She found that women who have had experience of dull, unskilled and uncreative work are more likely than women who have been in skilled, prestigious occupations in which they have held responsibility to give a positive assessment of their experiences of motherhood. Boulton argues that different employment experiences prior to birth tend to develop different expectations of how rewarding daily life should be. 'It is not surprising, then, that the working class women were more satisfied than the middle class women with a less than highly rewarding experience' (Boulton, 1983, p. 196). Those women in this study who had been lucky enough ever to find a job had employment experiences akin to those of Boulton's working class women. It is not, therefore, surprising that motherhood was reported to be more satisfying than much of the paid work women had previously done. Women's commitment to motherhood mostly did not diminish their commitment to future employment. In fact having a child sometimes proved to be a 'turning point' in that it spurred some women on to further their education in order to improve their employment prospects, with the aim of being able to make better provision for their children than they otherwise could. In making provision for their children women got substantial support from their social networks (particularly their mothers). Few received help from health visitors or social workers.

Mothers who are under 20 when they first give birth are generally discussed as if they constituted a unitary group. This is not the case. They differ with regard to colour and ethnicity, marital status, employment histories, reasons for becoming pregnant and having children, as well as with respect to how they and their children fare. There are also large differences between younger (under 17s) and older (18 and 19 year old) mothers under 20. In this study, as in others, older teenage women (who constitute the majority of mothers under 20) experienced least problems with motherhood.

Despite their heterogeneity, the majority of women interviewed in the Thomas Coram study were united in their experience of poverty. Although they got a great deal of pleasure from caring for their children, women's lives were complicated by their material circumstances. Since most of their male partners, many of their parents and the women themselves had poor experiences of the labour market, many were dependent on social security payments for income. Women found it difficult to manage on the supplementary benefit (the welfare payment available at the time) they received. Lack of money was the major problem most women reported that they faced. Even women whose partners earned well in comparison with the rest of the sample reported that they had financial problems. Many women's parents were invaluable in giving any childcare and material help they could. Many, for example, provided women and their children with meals as well as clothes and equipment for the children. The help they could give was, however, limited by the fact that most had little money to spare and, if employed themselves, little time available to provide childcare.

Interviewers were often struck by the poverty evident within households. Furniture was often sparse, food cupboards obviously bare and meals apparently often skipped in the middle of the day. It was easy to see why many women considered 'money problems' to be their major worries. Their claims that supplementary benefit was insufficient to provide them with food throughout the week or fortnight it was designed to last were sometimes borne out by informal observations. Interviewers were rarely offered cups of tea in the women's homes, but when they were it was often obvious that kitchen cupboards were almost bare and there were very few tea bags left and no milk available. Most women clearly needed more household income. It is well established that the living standards of many lone parents are unsatisfactory (Millar and Bradshaw, 1987) but in this study many couples were also struggling to bring up their children.

The 1986 Social Security Act which came into force in Britain in April 1988 aimed to use income support and family credit to target help more effectively on low income families than had supplementary benefit and special-needs payments, etc. It also aimed to remove the poverty and unemployment 'traps' which made employment not an economically viable proposition for women (see chapter 8). The

Act came into force too late for its impact to be apparent in this study. However analyses done by the National Council for One Parent Families suggest that single parents (and few mothers under 20 are legally married when they give birth) who are employed part time are worse off than previously because no allowance is now made for their childcare expenses. Single parents who work full time and (like almost all the employed mothers in this study) have gross earnings of less than £110 have apparently lost at least £4 per week in the transition from family income support to family credit. Other changes in the Act, like the abolition of long term rate of benefits for single parents, the reduction in rate rebates and abolition of help with water rates, loans from the Social Fund (instead of grants for special needs) and reduction of housing benefits for single parents have also been reported to worsen the conditions in which many poor families live (NCOPF, 1989).

It has been suggested (Ball, 1989) that women who give birth before they are 18 years of age are hardest hit in these reforms because, regardless of whether they are householders or not, they are now expected to live on about £14 less benefit per week than mothers aged 18 and over. They are, furthermore, only entitled to claim income support from 11 weeks before their child is born. If they are unemployed, therefore, their only chance of getting an income is if they are on youth training schemes, most of which they would have difficulty getting on if they were already pregnant. The onus will, therefore, be on the parents of mothers under 18 to give them support. Many parents of women who were interviewed in this study provided as much material and childcare support to their daughters as they could. In future, however, resources may be even more strained for some. Under 18s who, for whatever reason, cannot rely on parental support may well find themselves even less able to make independent provision for their chidlren than are other mothers under 20.

The introduction of the community charge ('poll tax') in England and Wales in 1990 is also likely to exacerbate the poverty experienced by women in similar circumstances to those described here. The women interviewed in the Thomas Coram study lived in boroughs where community charges are among the highest in the country. Although (by virtue of being in receipt of income support) many mothers under 20 will be exempt from paying the full community charge, it is difficult to see how they will be able to afford to pay the 20% of their community charge that they are likely to be required to pay.

The issue of welfare benefits becomes increasingly important as more mothers remain single. There is an increasing trend towards lone motherhood for all age groups of mothers, but this is particularly the case for mothers under 20 who are now more likely to be single than to be married when they give birth. Women interviewed in this study gave a variety of reasons for not having married when they had children. Among these were negative attitudes towards marriage because women considered that there were few benefits and too much domestic labour for women in marriage. Some women considered that cohabitation was preferable to marriage because it was easier to dissolve a cohabiting union than marriage if relationships failed. Some women had experienced parental divorces and were determined not to marry in order to avoid such experiences. Most did not consider that marriage and childbearing had to be linked, and many of those who were single were not averse to marrying later in life. Since marriage in the teenage years is associated with later divorce, it was perhaps a sensible strategy for most young women to defer marriage beyond the teenage years.

Although women did not mention economic reasons for marrying or remaining single, it did appear that marriages were most likely to occur if men were able to augment household income through their own earnings. Since many women reported that their male partners were either unemployed or earning very little in late pregnancy, this is probably one reason that most were not married when they gave birth.

This book started by quoting Angela McRobbie suggesting that there is a 'subdued moral panic' about young women who become mothers. The findings of this study as well as of others make it clear that moral panics about motherhood in the teenage years are unjustified. Women who become mothers in their teenage years often do so under very difficult circumstances. In particular they are often very poor and lacking in other resources such as educational qualifications and employment when they conceive. But these difficulties are not really due to their age or confined to mothers in their age group. Although early motherhood is associated with poverty there is no evidence that motherhood in the teenage years causes poverty. In most cases there is no reason to believe that their situation would improve as they got older. Although teenage women who become mothers are often believed to constitute a social problem, it may be more accurate to view them as a group of mothers with problems – often not of their own making – who are struggling against the odds. Most fare well under difficult circumstances.

References

Alan Guttmacher Institute (1976) *Eleven Million Teenagers*. New York: Alan Guttmacher Institute.

Alan Guttmacher Institute (1981) *Teenage Pregnancy: The Problem That Hasn't Gone Away*. New York: Alan Guttmacher Institute.

Allen, I. (1987) *Education in Sex and Personal Relationships*. London: Policy Studies Institute.

Archer, J. and Lloyd, B. (1982) *Sex and Gender*. Harmondsworth: Penguin.

Arney, W. and Bergen, B. (1984) Power and visibility: the invention of teenage pregnancy. *Social Science and Medicine*, 18(1).

Balakrishnan, T. R., Rao, K. V., Krotki, K. J. and LaPierre-Adamcyk, E. (1988) Age at first birth and lifetime fertility. *Journal of Biosocial Science*, 20(2), 167–74.

Ball, L. (1989) Pregnant young women and YTS: no choice. *Maternity Action*, 40, 10–11.

Bayley, N. (1969) *Manual for the Bayley Scales of Infant Development*. New York: The Psychological Corporation.

Belle, D. (1982) Social ties and social support. In D. Belle (ed.) *Lives in Stress: Women and Depression*. Beverley Hills: Sage.

Benjamin, L. (1987) The new caste: toward an alternative framework for understanding adolescent pregnancy. *Practice*, 5(3), 98–109.

Birksted-Breen, D. (1986) The experience of having a baby: a developmental view. *Free Associations*, 4, 22–35.

Bolton, F. (1980) *The Pregnant Adolescent*. Beverley Hills: Sage.

Bolton, F. G. and Belsky, J. (1986) The adolescent father and child maltreatment. In A. B. Elster and M. Lamb (eds) *Adolescent Fatherhood*. Hillsdale, NJ: Erlbaum.

Boulton, M. G. (1983) *On Being a Mother: A Study of Women with Pre-school Children*. London: Tavistock.

Brannen, J. and Collard, J. (1982) *Marriages in Trouble: The Process of Seeking Help*. London: Tavistock.

Brannen, J. and Moss, P. (1988) *New Mothers at Work*. London: Unwin Paperbacks.

Brannen, J. and Wilson, G. (eds)(1987) *Give and Take in Families: Studies in Resource Distribution*. London: Unwin Hyman.

Brazzell, J. and Acock, A. (1988) Influence of attitudes, significant others, and aspirations on how adolescents intend to resolve a premarital pregnancy. *Journal of Marriage and the Family*, 50(4), 413–26.

Broman, S. (1980) Longterm development of children born to teenagers. In K. Scott, T. Field and E. Robertson (eds) *Teenage Parents and their Offspring*. New York: Grune and Stratton.

Brown, C. (1984) *Black and White in Britain: The Third PSI Survey*. London: Heinemann.

Bucholz, G. and Gol, B. (1986) More than playing house: a developmental perspective on the strengths in teenage motherhood. *American Journal of Orthopsychiatry*, 56(3), 347–9.

Bury, J. (1984) *Teenage Pregnancy in Britain*. London: Birth Control Trust.

Busfield, J. (1974) Ideologies and reproduction. In M. Richards and P. Light (eds) *The Integration of a Child into a Social World*. Cambridge: Cambridge University Press.

Butler, M., Ineichen, B., Taylor, B., and Wadsworth, J. (1981) *Teenage Mothering*. Report to DHSS, Bristol: University of Bristol.

Caldwell, B. and Bradley, R. (1980) *Home Observations for Measurement of the Environment*. Little Rock, Arkansas: University of Arkansas.

Campbell, B. (1984) *The Road to Wigan Pier Revisited*. London: Virago.

Card, J. J. (1981) Longterm consequences for children of teenage parents. *Demography*, 18(2), 137–56.

Carlson, D. B., Labarba, R. C., Sclafani, J. D., and Bowers, C. A., (1986) Cognitive and motor development in infants of adolescent mothers: a longitudinal analysis. *International Journal of Behavioral Development*, 9, 1, 1–14.

Carroll, L. (1988) Concern with AIDS and the sexual behaviour of college students. *Journal of Marriage and the Family*, 50(2), 405–12.

Central Statistical Office (1988) *Social Trends*. London: OPCS.

Chilman, C. (1980) Social research concerning adolescent childbearing: 1970–1980. *Journal of Marriage and the Family*, 42(4), 793–805.

Chilman, C. (1986) Some psychosocial aspects of adolescent sexual and contraceptive behaviors in a changing American society. In J. B. Lancaster and B. A. Hamburg (eds) *School Age Pregnancy and Parenthood: Biosocial Dimensions*. New York: Aldine de Gruyter.

Clark, E. (1989) *Young Single Mothers Today: A Qualitative Study of Housing and Support Needs*. London: National Council for One Parent Families.

Cohen, P. (1986) *Rethinking the Youth Question*. Working Paper 3. London: Post 16 Education Centre.

Coleman, J. (1976) *The Nature of Adolescence*. London: Methuen.

Commission for Racial Equality (1984) *Race and Council Housing in Hackney:*

Report of a Formal Investigation. London: Commission for Racial Equality.

Crabbe, P. (1983) Teenage pregnancy: an overview. Paper presented to the *Women and Children Outside Marriage Conference*. National Council for One Parent Families, 20 May 1983.

Crnick, K., Greenberg, M., Ragozin, A., Robinson, N. and Basham, R. (1983) Effects of stress and social supports on mothers in premature and full term infants. *Child Development*, 54, 209–17.

Cunningham-Burley, S. (1985) Constructing grandparenthood: anticipating appropriate action. *Sociology*, 19, 421–36.

Daly, S. (1989) Family and welfare policy in the USA: an analysis. In *A Fairer Future for Children*: Speeches from CPAG's National Conference, 15 April 1989. London: CPAG.

Davis, R. A. (1989) Teenage pregnancy: a theoretical analysis of a social problem. *Adolescence*, 24(93), 19–28.

Dowrick, S. and Grundberg, S. (1980) *Why Children?* London: Virago.

Dunnell, K. (1979) *Family Formation 1976*. London: OPCS, HMSO.

Durward, L. (1988) *Poverty in Pregnancy: The Cost of an Adequate Diet for Expectant Mothers*. London: Maternity Alliance.

Elster, A., and Lamb, M. (eds)(1986) Introduction. *Adolescent Fatherhood*. Hillsdale, NJ: Lawrence Erlbaum.

Erikson, E. (1968) *Identity, Youth and Crisis*. New York: W. W. Norton & Co.

Farrell, C. (1978) *My Mother Said*. London: Routledge and Kegan Paul.

Field, T., Widmayer, S., Stringer, S. and Ignatoff, E. (1980) Teenage, lower-class black mothers and their preterm infants: an intervention and developmental follow-up. *Child Development*, 51, 426–36.

Finkel, M. and Finkel, D. (1975) Sexual and contraceptive knowledge, attitudes and behaviour of male adolescents. *Family Planning Perspectives*, 7, 256–60.

Ford Foundation (1983) *Teenage Parents* (letter, 1 August 1983). New York: Ford Foundation.

Francome, C. (1986) *Abortion Practice in Britain and the United States*. London: Allen and Unwin.

Fry, P. S. (1985) Relations between teenagers' age, knowledge, expectations and maternal behaviour. *British Journal of Developmental Psychology*, 3(1), 47–56.

Furstenberg, F. (1976) *Unplanned parenthood: The Social Consequences of Teenage Childbearing*. New York: The Free Press.

Furstenberg, F. (1987) Race differences in teenage sexuality, pregnancy, and adolescent childbearing. *The Millbank Quarterly*, 65(2), 381–403.

Furstenberg, F., Brooks-Gunn, J. and Morgan, S. P. (1987) *Adolescent Mothers in Later Life*. Cambridge: Cambridge University Press.

Gittins, D. (1986) *The Family in Question. Changing Households and Familiar Ideologies*. London: Macmillan.

Gottlieb, B. H. (1981) Social networks and social support in communities' mental health. In B. H. Gottlieb (ed.) *Social Networks and Social Support*. Beverley Hills: Sage.

Graham, H. (1986) *Caring for the Family*. London: Health Education Council.

Griffin, C. (1985) *Typical Girls: Young Women from School to the Job Market*. London: Routledge and Kegan Paul.

Hanson, S., Myers, D. and Ginsburg, A. (1987) The role of responsibility and knowledge in reducing teenage out-of-wedlock childbearing. *Journal of Marriage and the Family*, 49, 241–56.

Henriques, J., Hollway, W., Urwin, C., Venn, C. and Walkerdine, V. (1984) *Changing the Subject: Psychology, Social Regulation and Subjectivity*. London: Methuen.

Henwood, M. (1987) The family and the home. In M. Henwood, L. Rimmer and M. Wicks (eds) *Inside the Family: Changing Roles of Men and Women*. London: Family Policy Studies Centre.

Herold, E. and Goodwin, M. (1980) Development of a scale to measure attitudes towards using birth control pills. *Journal of Social Psychology*, 110, 115–22.

Hewitt, R. (1986) *White Talk Black Talk: Inter-Racial Friendship and Communication Amongst Adolescents*. Cambridge: Cambridge University Press.

Ineichen, B. (1984/5) Teenage motherhood in Bristol: the contrasting experience of Afro-Caribbean and white girls. *New Community*, 12(1), 52–8.

Ineichen, B. (1986) Contraceptive experience and attitudes to motherhood of teenage mothers. *Journal of Biosocial Science*, 18, 387–94.

Johnson, K. (1986) *Building Health Programs for Teenagers*. Washington: Children's Defense Fund's Adolescent Pregnancy Clearing House.

Jones, E., Forrest, J., Goldman, N., Henshaw, S., Lincoln, R., Rosoff, J., Westoff, C. and Wulf, D. (1986) *Teenage Pregnancy in Industrial Countries*. London: Yale University Press.

Jones, S. (1988) *Black Culture, White Youth: The Reggae Tradition for JA to UK*. London: Macmillan.

Joshi, H. (1987) The cost of caring. In C. Glendinning and J. Millar (eds) *Women and Poverty in Britain*. Brighton: Wheatsheaf.

Joshi, H. (1990) *Mothers' Foregone Earnings*. Seminar at the Thomas Coram Research Unit, 7 February 1990.

Jowell, R., Witherspoon, S. and Brook, L. (eds)(1987) *British Social Attitudes: The 1987 Report*. Aldershot: Gower.

Kantner, J. and Zelnik, M. (1973) Contraception and pregnancy: experience of young unmarried women in the United States. *Family Planning Perspectives*, 4, 9–18.

King, T. and Fullard, W. (1982) Teenage mothers and their infants: new findings on the home environment. *Journal of Adolescence*, 5, 333–46.

Kitzinger, C. (1987) *The Social Construction of Lesbianism*. London: Sage.

Lamb, M. E. (1987) Teenage Fathers. Paper presented at the Fatherhood Research Group, Thomas Coram Research Unit.

Lamb, M. E. and Elster, A. B. (1986) Parental behaviour of adolescent mothers and fathers. In A. B. Elster and M. Lamb (eds) *Adolescent Fatherhood*. Hillsdale, NJ: Lawrence Erlbaum.

Landy, S., Cleland, J. and Schubert, J. (1984) The individuality of teenage mothers and its implication for intervention strategies. *Journal of Adolescence*, 7, 171–90.

Lees, S. (1986) *Losing Out: Sexuality and Adolescent Girls*. London: Hutchinson.

Lewis, C. and O'Brien, M. (1987) *Reassessing Fatherhood*. London: Sage.

Luker, K. (1975) *Taking Chances: Abortion and the Decision not to Contracept*. Berkeley: University of California Press.

McRobbie, A. (1978) Working class girls and the culture of feminity. In Women's Studies Group (eds) *Women Take Issue*. London: Hutchinson.

McRobbie, A. (1989) Motherhood, a teenage job? *The Guardian*, 5 September 1989.

McRobbie, A. (1990) Teenage mothers: a new social state. In A. McRobbie *From Jackie to Just Seventeen*. London: Macmillan.

Mansfield, P. and Collard, J. (1988) *The Beginning of the Rest of Your Life: A Portrait of Newly-wed Marriage*. London: Macmillan.

Martin, J. and Monk, J. (1982) *Infant Feeding 1980*. London: OPCS Social Survey Division.

Martin, J. and Roberts, C. (1984) *Women and Employment: A Lifetime Perspective*. The Report of the 1980 DE/OPCS Women and Employment Survey. London: HMSO.

Maternity Alliance (1989) Editorial: Pocket Money Parents. *Maternity Action*, 40.

Messick, S. (1983) Assessment of children. In P. Mussen (ed.) *Handbook of Child Psychology*, Vol. 1. New York: John Wiley.

Millar, J. and Bradshaw, J. (1987) The living standards of lone-parent families. *Quarterly Journal of Social Affairs*, 3, 233–52.

Monck, E. (in press) Patterns of confiding relationships in a population of adolescent girls. *Journal of Child Psychology and Psychiatry*.

Morris, N. (1981) The biological advantages and social disadvantages of teenage pregnancy. *American Journal of Public Health*, 71(8), 796.

Morrison, P. (1985) Adolescent contraceptive behaviour: a review. *Psychological Bulletin*, 98(3), 538–68.

Moss, P. and Lav, G. (1985) Mothers Without Marriages. *New Society*, 73(1180), 9 August 1985.

Murcott, A. (1980) The social construction of teenage pregnancy. *Sociology of Health and Illness*, 2(1), 1–23.

National Council for One Parent Families (1983) *Single and Pregnant: a Guide to Benefits*. London: NCOPF.

National Council for One Parent Families (1989) Press release: *The Social Security Act 1986: Impact on One Parent Families*. London: NCOPF.

Newson, J. and Lilley, J. (1988) The childrearing attitudes of young unmarried mothers. Unpublished paper.

Newson, J., Lilley, J. and Lalonde, S. (1987) Childrearing attitudes of teenage parents. Unpublished paper.

Oakley, A. (1979) *From Here to Maternity: Becoming a Mother.* Harmondsworth: Penguin.

OPCS (1985) Trends in conceptions in England and Wales during 1983. *OPCS Monitor*, Reference FM1 85/8.

OPCS (1986a) Fertility Trends in England and Wales: 1975–1985. *OPCS Monitor.* Reference FM1 86/2.

OPCS (1986b) Trends in conceptions to women resident in England and Wales: 1974–1984. *OPCS Monitor.* Reference FM1 86/3.

OPCS (1987) Trends in conceptions to women resident in England and Wales 1975–1985. *OPCS Monitor.* Reference FM1 87/2.

OPCS (1988) Live births in 1987. *Population Trends,* 53, 35–40.

Osborn, A. and Milbank, J. (1987) *The Effects of Early Education.* Oxford: Oxford University Press.

Oskamp, S. and Mindick, B. (1983) Personality and attitudinal barriers to contraception. In D. Byrne and W. Fisher (eds) *Adolescents, Sex and Contraception.* Hillsdale, NJ: Erlbaum.

Penhale, B. (1989) *Associations between Unemployment and Fertility among Young People in the Early 1980s.* Working Paper no. 60. London: Social Statistics Research Unit.

Phillips, A. (1990) Fatherhood is a lifelong responsibility. *The Independent,* 22 January 1990.

Phipps-Yonas, S. (1980) Teenage pregnancy and motherhood: a review of the literature. *American Journal of Orthopsychiatry,* 50(3), 403–31.

Phoenix, A. (1988a) The Afro Caribbean myth. *New Society* 4 March 1988, 10–13.

Phoenix, A. (1988b) Narrow definitions of culture: the case of early motherhood. In S. Westwood and P. Bhachu (eds) *Enterprising Women: Home, Work and Culture among Minorities in Britain.* London: Routledge.

Pilcher, H. and Williamson, J. (1988) *A Guide to Young People's Experience in the Labour Market.* London: Youthaid.

Pines, D. (1978) On becoming a parent. *Journal of Child Psychotherapy,* 4, 19–31.

Pittman, K. (1986) *Adolescent Pregnancy: Whose Problem is it?* Washington: Children's Defense Fund's Adolescent Pregnancy Prevention Clearinghouse.

Riley, D. and Eckenrode, J. (1986) Social ties: subgroup differences in costs and benefits. *Journal of Personality and Social Psychology,* 51, 770–8.

Rimmer, L. (1981) *Families in Focus: Marriage, Divorce and Family Patterns.* London: Study Commission on the Family.

Robbins, C., Kaplan, H. and Martin, S. (1985) Antecedents of pregnancy among unmarried adolescents. *Journal of Marriage and the Family,* 47, 567–83.

Romito, P. (1988) Mothers' experience of breastfeeding. *Journal of Reproductive and Infant Psychology*, 6, 89–100.

Scott-Jones, D. and Nelson-Le Gall, S. (1986) Defining black families: past and present. In E. Seidman and J. Rappaport (eds) *Redefining Social Problems*. New York: Plenum.

Seidman, E. and Rappaport, J. (1986) Introduction. In E. Seidman and J. Rappaport (eds) *Redefining Social Problems*. New York: Plenum.

Sharpe, S. (1987) *Falling for Love: Teenage Mothers Talk*. London: Virago.

Simms, M. and Smith, C. (1986) *Teenage Mothers and their Partners*. London: HMSO.

Skinner, C. (1986) *Elusive Mister Right: The Social and Personal Context of a Young Woman's Use of Contraception*. London: Carolina Publications.

Stanley, L. and Wise, S. (1983) *Breaking Out: Feminist Consciousness and Feminist Research*. London: Routledge and Kegan Paul.

Stone, N. (1989) The gas chamber mentality. *The Guardian*, 14 December 1989.

Taylor, B., Wadsworth, J. and Butler, N. (1983) Teenage mothering, admission to hospital, and accidents during the first five years. *Archives of Disease in Childhood*, 58, 6–11.

Wallis, C. (1985) Children Having Children. *Time Magazine*, 9 December 1985.

Wellman, B. (1981) Applying network analysis to the study of social support. In B. Gottlieb (ed.) *Social Networks and Social Support*. Beverley Hills: Sage.

Wells, N. (1983) *Teenage Mothers*. Liverpool: Children's Research Fund.

Werner, B. (1988) Fertility trends in the UK and in thirteen other developed countries, 1966–86. *Population Trends*, 51, 18–24.

Willis, P. (1984) Juventus: half way to a youth utopia. *Youth and Policy*, 10, 44–7.

Willmott, P. (1986) *Social Networks, Informal Care and Public Policy*. London: Policy Studies Institute.

Wilson, G. (1987) Money: patterns of responsibility and irresponsibility in marriage. In J. Brannen and G. Wilson (eds) *Give and Take in Families: Studies in Resource Distribution*. London: Allen and Unwin.

Wilson, W. with Neckerman, K. (1987) Poverty and family structure: the widening gap between evidence and public policy issues. In W. J. Wilson *The Truly Disadvantaged: The Inner City, the Underclass and Public Policy*. London: University of Chicago Press.

Wise, S. and Grossman, F. (1980) Adolescent mothers and their infants: psychological factors in early attachment and interaction. *American Journal of Orthopsychiatry*, 50, 454–68.

Woollett, A. (1987) Who breastfeeds? The family and cultural context. *Journal of Reproductive and Infant Psychology*, 5, 127–31.

Zelnik, M. and Shah, F. (1983) First intercourse among young Americans. *Family Planning Perspectives*, 15, 64–70.

Index

Note: page numbers in *italics* refer to figures and tables.